## No Prayer for the Dying

When Michael reached the bottom of the stairwell, he was met by Outfit soldier Nicholas "Nicky Breeze" Calabrese, who shook his hand as part of the ruse that a making ceremony was about to commence. Within seconds of the docile greeting, carnage-strewn chaos erupted. Michael was tackled by Louie Eboli. Several Outfit hit men converged on the younger Spilotro and began viciously beating and stomping him in an aggressive flurry of fists and feet. Before he could do anything to defend himself, Tony was grabbed from behind and pushed to the cold and dirty basement floor. With Tony forced to watch, Michael was finally put out of his misery, strangled to death with a strip of electrical cord by Eboli. The murderous thugs then turned their attention to Tony. Knowing his fate, he asked his killers for permission to say one last novena before he met his maker.

They refused.

# Family Affair

Treachery, Greed,
and Betrayal in
the Chicago Mafia

**SAM GIANCANA**
**and SCOTT M. BURNSTEIN**

**B**
BERKLEY BOOKS, NEW YORK

**THE BERKLEY PUBLISHING GROUP**
**Published by the Penguin Group**
**Penguin Group (USA) Inc.**
**375 Hudson Street, New York, New York 10014, USA**
Penguin Group (Canada), 90 Eglinton Avenue East, Suite 700, Toronto, Ontario M4P 2Y3, Canada
(a division of Pearson Penguin Canada Inc.)
Penguin Books Ltd., 80 Strand, London WC2R 0RL, England
Penguin Group Ireland, 25 St. Stephen's Green, Dublin 2, Ireland (a division of Penguin Books Ltd.)
Penguin Group (Australia), 250 Camberwell Road, Camberwell, Victoria 3124, Australia
(a division of Pearson Australia Group Pty. Ltd.)
Penguin Books India Pvt. Ltd., 11 Community Centre, Panchsheel Park, New Delhi—110 017, India
Penguin Group (NZ), 67 Apollo Drive, Rosedale, North Shore 0632, New Zealand
(a division of Pearson New Zealand Ltd.)
Penguin Books (South Africa) (Pty.) Ltd., 24 Sturdee Avenue, Rosebank, Johannesburg 2196,
South Africa

Penguin Books Ltd., Registered Offices: 80 Strand, London WC2R 0RL, England

The publisher does not have any control over and does not assume any responsibility for authors or
third-party websites or their content.

FAMILY AFFAIR

A Berkley Book / published by arrangement with the authors

PRINTING HISTORY
Berkley mass-market edition / March 2010

Copyright © 2010 by Sam Giancana and Scott M. Burnstein.
Cover design by David Bamford.
Interior text design by Kristin del Rosario.

ISBN: 978-0-425-22831-9

BERKLEY®
Berkley Books are published by The Berkley Publishing Group,
a division of Penguin Group (USA) Inc.,
375 Hudson Street, New York, New York 10014.
BERKLEY® is a registered trademark of Penguin Group (USA) Inc.
The "B" design is a trademark of Penguin Group (USA) Inc.

PRINTED IN THE UNITED STATES OF AMERICA

10  9  8  7  6  5  4  3  2  1

*To*
*Alex Frank, Adam Miller, and John Pink,*
*all great, kind, and talented men gone too soon*

*And to the memory of Margo Hirschfeld,*
*the "Godmother" of the North Shore*

# Acknowledgments

Thanks to Mom, Dad, Butterscotch, Mello, Grampa, Uncles Bob, David, and Jack; Aunts Sue, Arlene, Eileen, and Miriam; Jeremy, Jamie, Ian, Amy, Tyler, Ryan, Casey, Elaine; my agent, Frank Weimann; my editor at Berkley Books, the incomparable Denise Silvestro; Meredith Giordan, Jaimee Garbacik, and Elyse Tanzillo; J.R. Davis and the Chicago Crime Commission, agent Ross Rice at the Chicago FBI, Randall Sanborn at the U.S. Attorney's Office, John Scully, Chuck Goudie, Jim Wagner, Tom Bourgeois, Jack O'Rourke, Wayne Zydron, Mickey Lombardo, John Binder, Richard Stilling, Antonio Napoli, Jeremy H., Mac, Eric, Keith and Jeff at the Oakland Press, Kristy, Rob, Judd, Andy, Julie, Lauren, Jeff, Al Profit, Herm Groman, Dennis Arnoldy, Frank Cullotta, Mike Floyd and Tami, Adam Rafalski, Angelo, Alex, Anne, Jen, Ara, Morgan, Stephanie, Sara, Laddie, Robert, Tricia, Mikey, Jason, Ross, Kyle, Mike, Paul, Dave, and Matt.

*Family Affair* is the consummate epic mob saga—a lurid and compelling true story of death, deceit, and debauchery in the modern-day underworld. This complex and long-winding tale involves a group of intriguing and richly textured mob characters; spans close to forty years in the history of the mafia's Chicago crime family, known locally on the street and in the press as "The Outfit"; and covers two separate eras in the syndicate's legendary history: one being the mob's glory days of the 1970s through the 1990s, and the other being The Outfit's current landscape in the new millennium. The story has everything: an opus of sex, drugs, money, murder, lust, power, sibling betrayal, underworld politics, and government corruption.

The ever-shifting plot line of this mafia-infused soap opera culminates in a massive federal racketeering indictment, an enormous government legal effort aptly named "Operation Family Secrets," that charged fourteen defendants, several of whom were members of the current Chicago crime family administration, with eighteen previously unsolved gangland homicides. The indictment, which was announced in April 2005, went to trial in the summer of 2007. It was the FBI's biggest strike against the American mafia since the early 1980s.

**June 14, 1986**
**Chicago**

Something was amiss. Anthony "Tony the Ant" Spilotro, a forty-eight-year-old wiseguy of the most lethal variety, had a well-honed gut instinct and things just didn't feel right to him. It was a beautiful early summer afternoon in Chicago, and most residents of the sprawling Midwest metropolis were out in droves enjoying the gorgeous, sun-drenched day. Nicknamed The Ant due to his diminutive size, Tony Spilotro should have been doing the same. However, despite spending the first half of his day surrounded by family and friends at his younger brother Michael's suburban Oak Park residence, Spilotro was visibly unhappy, acting outwardly nervous, fidgety, and ill at ease. It was understandable. He had a great deal on his mind. In a few hours, he and his brother had an important meeting to attend—a top-secret mob gathering to be exact. He had attended and participated in this type of event many times, but something about this one seemed different. Something about this situation felt off. Tony began to suspect he was in grave danger and that if he went to the meeting there was a good chance that he would not be coming back alive.

On the surface, things appeared to be going great. Spilotro was one of the Windy City's most powerful mob lieutenants, tapped by the Chicago mafia—known locally as "The Outfit"—to oversee their vast and lucrative interests in the Las Vegas hotel and gaming industry. He was tremendously wealthy, lived a life of excess and self-indulgence, and was both feared and respected in underworld circles nationwide. Just a few months earlier, an article in a major Windy City newspaper named him a possible successor to then–Chicago godfather Joe Ferriola. The Ant's exploits became so notorious that in the years to come he would be immortalized on the big screen by Oscar-winning actor Joe Pesci in director Martin Scorsese's *Casino*.

Called back to Chicago from his headquarters in Nevada for what he was told was going be a formal mob initiation ceremony for his brother and protégé, Michael, as well as an official promotion for himself to the status of caporegime (capo), a much valued leadership position within any mafia crime family, Spilotro should have been sitting on top of the world. But he wasn't. In actuality, he was as far away from the top of the world as possible. And everything wasn't what it seemed.

As a result of a series of high-profile arrests in the early

1980s, Tony had been skating on thin ice with his superiors in the mob for quite a while. His increasingly insubordinate behavior and headline-garnering antics while running things in Las Vegas had earned him a great deal of enemies in Chicago, specifically several members of the recently elected crime family administration.

It was 4:00 in the afternoon, and before leaving for their meeting, Tony and Michael gave all of their jewelry and cash to their loved ones. The mood was grim. Farewells were exchanged amid a palpable aura of tension. Tony gave his wedding ring, diamond-plated Rolex wristwatch, and personal phone and contact book to his wife, Nancy. Michael told his wife that if the two of them didn't make it back to Oak Park by 9:00, she should assume the worst. A man who had personally taken part in well over three dozen gangland homicides, Tony "The Ant" Spilotro had the distinct suspicion that he and his brother were being set up for one themselves.

He was right.

**ALTHOUGH** it was already the middle of June, the wheels of the murder contract placed on the Spilotro brothers had been in motion since midwinter. In January 1986, Joseph "Joey Doves" Aiuppa, the Chicago Outfit's boss since 1972 and once an integral supporter of The Ant, was imprisoned on a racketeering conviction, and the road to Tony's violent downfall began being paved. Replacing Aiuppa atop the crime family hierarchy was Joe Ferriola, a longtime capo from the city's West Side and a man who fervently despised Tony Spilotro for the headaches and frustration he had been causing the Outfit brass. Wasting little time in planning his rival's demise, Ferriola announced during a speech made at his official inauguration dinner—held in the basement of a north suburban restaurant just days after Aiuppa's incarceration—that his first order of business as new don would be to sanction Tony Spilotro's execution. The following afternoon, FBI documents allege, he began making arrangements for the assassination, taking several underlings to start planning the specifics of the heavily anticipated mob hit.

In the minds of a lot of people in the mob, the move was a long time coming. The city of Las Vegas, once a gangster's paradise virtually free from the law-enforcement hassles encountered by wiseguys on the East Coast and Midwest, had become a magnet for police busts. A series of indictments and convictions of several mob administrations across the country, stemming from activity in Las Vegas, had put a number of powerful mafia dons behind bars. Many in the nation's underworld blamed Spilotro. At that point, even Aiuppa, once an ardent supporter of Spilotro, was fed up and signed off on the murder contract

Over the past decade, The Ant had gotten completely out of control. Sent to the mob-built desert oasis in 1971, he was given specific instructions to stay in the shadows and keep a low profile. That didn't happen. Instead, Spilotro, a cunning, brutal, and media-starved wiseguy cut from the same cloth as former Windy City crime lords Al "Scarface" Capone and Sam "Momo" Giancana, decided to plant his own flag on the glittery, cash-soaked Vegas Strip, and declared himself the desert's first mafia don. Shortly after arriving in Nevada, Spilotro recruited a band of thugs from back home in Chicago to make up a loyal power base and quickly began conducting his own street rackets—intentionally off The Outfit's radar—and hoarding the tremendous profits for himself. The Ant opened up shop on an emporium of vice, making certain his presence was felt in all bookmaking, loan sharking, and extortion operations being run in the city, headquartering his crew's activities out of his Old West–style jewelry store, The Gold Rush. He also began selling drugs—a major mafia no-no—and running a large-scale stolen jewelry ring known in the press as "The Hole in the Wall Gang." Add to all this the facts that he had been carrying on an extramarital affair with the wife of a top mob associate, had an increasingly bothersome cocaine habit, and had often spoke freely among his inner circle about killing his way to the top of The Outfit, and it was clear to his bosses in Chicago that they had no choice—The Ant had to be eliminated.

Michael Spilotro got himself included in the top-priority gangland assassination for two reasons: First, acting as Tony's emissary in Chicago, Michael's own behavior had gotten out of control. He was continually shaking down and roughing up already-connected street merchants using his brother's name as leverage and refusing to pay gambling debts based on his perceived status within the local underworld. By 1986, he had angered one too many powerful people in The Outfit and became expendable. Second, there was a fear that Michael, a well-known hothead, would eventually seek retaliation for his brother against those ordering the hit. Several years younger than his more notorious sibling, Michael was groomed by Tony The Ant; the older he got, the more he tried to emulate him in every way possible. From the way he dressed to the way he talked, Michael wanted to be exactly like his big brother. Consequently, Michael grew up to be lethal, greedy, and arrogant and sealed his own fate by appearing as a threat to many higher-ups in the Chicago mob.

**BORN** and raised on the city's notoriously rough West Side and schooled in the ways of the streets by legendary Windy City underworld figures like Salvatore "Mad Sam" DeStefano, James "Jimmy the Turk" Torrello, and Felix "Milwaukee Phil" Alderesio, Tony Spilotro was, if nothing else, old school. In terms of philosophy and attitude, he continued to live his life by a code of honor that many of his associates in the mob had abandoned long ago. So, despite his reservations and concerns for his own personal safety, when he was called and told to appear at an Outfit initiation ceremony, he went and he didn't ask questions. After being instructed to meet James "Jimmy the Man" Marcello, at that time a fellow Chicago mob soldier, in the parking lot of a Howard Johnson Inn near Schiller Park, Illinois, the Spilotro brothers kissed their wives and children good-bye on the afternoon of June 14, 1986, and were never seen by them again. Arriving at the parking lot early, they went into the hotel bar and had a drink to ease their nerves. At about 3:30 P.M., they went back into the parking lot and were met by Marcello, who was waiting for them in his silver Cadillac. Jimmy Marcello—known on the streets as "Little Jimmy," "Jimmy Lights," or "Jimmy the Driver"— knew both of the Spilotro brothers very well. He was especially close to Michael, the two of them being around the same age and known to work out together at a local health club. Leaving their car at the hotel, Tony and Michael got in the backseat, and the group of wiseguys left the parking lot. Within minutes they were on the expressway.

Driving south on Interstate 83 away from Schiller Park and toward the city, the Cadillac exited on Irving Park Road and headed for a small side street located in the town of Bensenville. A tiny suburb that sits directly on the border of Chicago proper. Stopping in the driveway of high-powered Outfit member Louis "Louie the Mooch" Eboli's house, Marcello turned off the ignition. The three men exited the vehicle, and the Spilotros were ushered into the house through a side door that had been left open for them. Still acting on the pretense that they were coming to attend a benign mob get-together, Marcello made casual conversation with Tony and Michael as they entered the residence. Met at the door by Eboli, Outfit boss Joe Ferriola, and Outfit underboss Sam "Wings" Carlisi, the men then made their way to the back of the house. Marcello opened a door leading to the basement and Carlisi escorted the Spilotro brothers, Michael and then Tony, down the stairs to their pending slaughter. A cadre of bloodthirsty hit men awaited them, murder their only agenda. Instead of an initiation ceremony, it was a death trap. They were descending into hell, and Tony Spilotro, a man who had made a reputation of being able to elude volatile situations unscathed, could do nothing but pray for a quick passing. Unfortunately for him, his prayers would not be answered.

When Michael reached the bottom of the stairwell, he was met by Outfit soldier Nicholas "Nicky Breeze" Calabrese, who shook his hand as part of the ruse that a making ceremony was about to commence. Within seconds of the docile greeting, carnage-strewn chaos erupted. Michael was tackled by Louie Eboli. Several Outfit hit men converged on the younger Spilotro and began viciously beating and stomping him in a flurry of fists and feet. Before he could do anything to defend himself, Tony was grabbed from behind and pushed to the cold and dirty basement floor. With Tony forced to watch, Michael was finally put out of his misery, strangled to death with a strip of electrical cord by Eboli. The murderous thugs then turned their attention to Tony. Knowing his fate, he asked his killers for permission to say one last novena before he met his maker. They refused.

Tony Spilotro was then beaten, stomped, and eventually strangled to death, just as his brother had been minutes before. The end result was a brutal sight, reminiscent of a Tarantino movie—two bodies on the floor, badly mutilated, massacred, and mangled.

Many believe that the extreme and gruesomely heinous nature of the double homicide indicates just how loathed Tony Spilotro had become in certain circles within The Outfit. The fact that so many powerful syndicate figures were present for the executions illustrates that belief more than anything. Furthermore, it is suspected that the pair of grisly gangland slayings were a message from The Outfit's freshly minted administration to the entire crime family that certain forms of behavior would never be tolerated, no matter how powerful the person exhibiting it. After the job was complete, the group of mob executioners filed out of the Eboli residence, each going his separate way. Another set of mob soldiers were set to arrive shortly and take care of the mess in the basement, and the crew of winded and tired hit men could finally relax. Some of them went back to enjoying the warm and sunny afternoon with their families, others went to grab a bite to eat or to a local tavern for a stiff drink—just another day in the life of some of the Midwest's most dangerous and lethal. A lot of headaches had just been cured, a great deal of future frustrations averted. The Ant had been exterminated.

Spilotro's violent demise is one of the most horrific gangland slayings in the annals of American crime, and it set off a chain reaction of events that would culminate twenty years later in the FBI's biggest strike against the American mafia since the early 1980s.

# 1.

## The Fugitive
### The Clown Goes Underground

On consecutive afternoons in mid-January 2006, two of the Windy City's most notorious wiseguys ever, both recently apprehended by federal authorities after almost a year on the run, were ushered into the courtroom of U.S. District Court Judge James B. Zagel, looking more like grandpas than gangsters. However, make no mistake about it, these two men, despite appearing meek and frail were not your average senior citizens. Although they looked as if they were supposed to be playing shuffle board in a Miami Beach retirement community, they were both, the government claimed, stone-cold killers and highly respected members of one of the most powerful and dangerous crime syndicates in the world.

These men were the then seventy-six-year-old Joseph "Joey the Clown" Lombardo, longtime Chicago mafia chieftain, and his top lieutenant, the then seventy-seven-year-old Frank "Frankie the German" Schweihs. Less than a year earlier, each had disappeared into the shadows and gone on the lamb after a massive April 2005 federal racketeering indictment fingering fourteen people and including eighteen previously unsolved gangland homicides—two of which were the brutal murders of Tony and Michael Spilotro. Both Lombardo and Schweihs ducked out of sight when they realized that, if caught, they'd be held without bail because of their previous criminal records and would probably never taste freedom again. Representing two of the final links to the crime family's glory days of the middle to late twentieth century, when the mob seemed invincible, The Clown and The German were highly-coveted government targets.

Even without initially rounding up Lombardo and Schweihs, the FBI had delivered a mighty blow to the family when it arrested eleven of their co-defendants: James "Jimmy the Man" Marcello, alleged boss of The Outfit; his half-brother and top lieutenant Michael "Big Mickey" Marcello; the Calabrese brothers, Frank "Frankie Breeze" Calabrese Sr. and Nicholas "Nicky Breeze" Calabrese, a pair of already imprisoned South Side mob heavyweights; Paul "Paulie the Indian" Schiro, The Outfit's representative in Arizona; Nicholas Ferriola, son of the late crime family Boss Joseph "Joe Nick" Ferriola; Dennis Johnson, Thomas Johnson, and Joe Venezia, three Marcello brothers' lieutenants; and Michael Ricci and Anthony "Twan" Doyle, two former Chicago police officers. Co-defendant

Frank "Goomba" Saladino, a reputed hit man and The Outfit's proxy in Rockford, was found dead of a heart attack when the Feds came to arrest him at a motel in Northeast Indiana. The list amounted to a endangered species list of Chicago wiseguys, making certain, regardless of how the case would eventually be resolved, a major shakeup among the syndicate's rank and file was imminent.

"When the indictment and the arrests finally came down, it was a real sense of relief for the Bureau," said FBI agent Ross Rice. "There is so much that goes into building this type of case, so many things that can and do pop up that you don't necessarily expect, for it to all come together is a major accomplishment. Some of these murder investigations had been lying dormant for two, three decades. To the general public that doesn't mean much, but each of those homicide victims has family members that are still alive and those people have to live with the after effects every day. That's really where the motivation for constructing Family Secrets came from on our part. The Spilotro brothers' murders may have received the most attention from the media and from Hollywood and whatnot, but to us, they're all the same and of equal importance."

As recent as just a few years earlier, however, things were looking up for the widely renowned Midwest crime family. In 2004, Jimmy Marcello, the much heralded heir apparent to the top seat in The Outfit, emerged from a ten-year federal prison sentence and assumed the post of syndicate street boss. Marcello wasted little time making his presence felt. Gone were the days when tame and less-violent tactics were the status quo in the city's underworld, replaced by an edict from Jimmy the Man to rule with an iron fist. Verbal warnings soon became vicious beatings, and everybody on the street was forced to take note of the freshly minted godfather's new regime. According to some in law enforcement, Marcello may have actually gotten a head start in his tenure as don while still incarcerated in a Milan, Michigan, federal correctional facility; it's believed Marcello possibly ordered at least two gangland hits from behind bars. With the aid and counsel of grizzled and savvy mob veterans like Joey the Clown, the crime family's consiglieri, top Outfit capo Joseph "Joe the Builder" Andriacchi, and the syndicate's overall don No Nose Di Fronzo, Marcello took aim at returning the Chicago mob to its once-held prominence.

And then, a caged bird began to sing.

That bird was Nicky Breeze Calabrese, a sixty-two-year-old imprisoned Outfit hit man and younger brother of fellow mafia assassin Frankie Breeze. In actuality, Calabrese had been singing since early 2002 and continued doing so all the way up and through the eventual indictment and trial.

Getting Nicky Breeze to play ball with the FBI was no easy task. Faced with physical evidence linking him to one of the eighteen murders named in the eventual indictment and with the threat that the government planned to ask for the death penalty at his trial, Calabrese refused to talk for a good two years. It wasn't until the FBI brought word to Calabrese in his cell at a Pekin, Illinois federal prison that his own brother had signed off on his death warrant that he chose to cooperate and testify against his mob cohorts in open court.

Nicky Breeze spilled his guts, and as a result, the U.S. Prosecutor's Office levied the biggest federal racketeering case against a mob hierarchy since the infamous Commission Case of the mid-1980s, when a young and ambitious U.S. attorney named Rudolph Giuliani took down all the leaders of New York's five crime families in one fell litigious swoop. Even more shocking, Calabrese's cooperation was precipitated by the defection of his nephew, Frank Calabrese Jr., who in 1998 had been serving time behind bars with his father. When Frank Jr. became fed up with his father's antics, he wrote a letter to the FBI offering his assistance in building a case against his uncle and dear old dad.

A mainstay on the city's streets for over three decades, Nick Calabrese had a great deal of information to offer the government. This included clearing up many unanswered questions regarding several high-profile area mob assassinations and implicating his own flesh and blood, his older brother Frank, in thirteen of the eighteen murders charged in the indictment. Gleaning what they could from their mega-turncoat, the FBI opened up shop on a sprawling underworld exposé, which came to be called Operation Family Secrets—an assault federal authorities hoped to severely cripple the foundation of the Chicago Outfit with.

"It was a major coup for us to flip Nick Calabrese," said John Scully, a retired U.S. prosecutor who was one of three government lawyers assigned to prosecute the case in the summer and early fall of 2007. "After that happend everything fit together. It was a domino effect, the information we got from him put our case over the edge. At that point, we knew we would have enough to indict. When Mr. Calabrese sent out feelers to the FBI agents, it was kept real hush-hush. When he finally turned and they started the debriefing process, only a few key people knew what was going on. I was in the dark about what happened. I didn't even know that he was cooperating. For a good two weeks, I didn't know anything. Finally getting the news was an outstanding feeling and made me feel like all of our work, put in by both our office and the FBI, had paid off."

With the mountain of information provided by Nick Calabrese, the government spent the next three years building their case, a legal blow to major organized crime with few equals. When their investigation was complete, the federal government had what amounted to a nine-count, fourteen-person racketeering indictment that charged the bulk of the leadership of the Chicago mafia, as well as others, with extortion, loan sharking, illegal gambling, eighteen allegations of murder, and one allegation of attempted murder. Following two months of grand jury testimony in January and February 2005, the indictment was announced on April 25, 2005, with arrest warrants issued that same day for all fourteen defendants. Seven of the accused in the potentially groundbreaking racketeering conspiracy case were charged with committing or agreeing to commit murder on behalf of Outfit leaders. The police officers, Mike Ricci and Anthony Doyle, were accused of passing information to and acting as liaisons for Frank Calabrese Sr., who had been imprisoned on another racketeering-related conviction since 1997.

**ON** the same April morning that fast-rising U.S. Prosecuting Attorney Patrick Fitzgerald announced the unsealing of the indictment to an anxious press corps, federal agents rounded up eleven of the fourteen men charged without incident. With Frank Saladino dead of a heart attack lying beside a bundle of cash in his motel room, the only two alleged co-conspirators of the indictment not accounted for were Joey Lombardo and Frank Schweihs. Entertaining no desire to lose their freedom and become guests of the state, Lombardo and his ace henchman, Schweihs, each vanished from sight.

A week later, in an odd twist of events, Joey the Clown sent the first of several handwritten letters to Judge Zagel, in which he outlined surrender terms, proclaimed his innocence, and—perhaps justifying his nickname—requested a laughably low bail of $50,000. In spring 2005, Lombardo was placed on the much-famed FBI's Ten Most Wanted List. However, despite the written correspondence between him and Zagel, letters sent through his attorney and conspicuously postmarked from within the city of Chicago, the trail on Lombardo and Schweihs went cold.

"I thought it was a bit out of character for Lombardo to flee," said former FBI agent Tom Bourgeois. "In a lot of ways it didn't fit his traditional way of conducting business. But then again Joey is a sharp guy, and I'm pretty certain there was a rhyme and reason to his actions. He's no dummy. He knew, at least for the sake of the media, he was the centerpiece of the case and that his capture would be a top priority for the FBI. Plus, it's not like the guy had never been behind bars before. So, whatever his thought process was, I'm pretty sure he felt that it was important for him, and maybe for The Outfit as an entity, to go on the run."

Then, in December 2005, the feds got a break. Enticed by the $25,000 reward for the capture of Lombardo or

Schweihs, an anonymous tipster—rumored to have possibly been a Schweihs family member—pointed law enforcement in the direction of Kentucky and clued the bureau in on the whereabouts of Frankie the German. On December 16, 2005, a fleet of federal agents descended on a quiet apartment complex in suburban Lexington and took Frank Schweihs into custody without a struggle. Brought in front of Judge Zagel for his arraignment, The German couldn't understand the hoard of media cramped in the corner of the courtroom watching and analyzing his every move. "What all 'dem reporters here for?" Schweihs gruffly asked his attorney as two U.S. marshals helped him, wearing leg irons and holding a cane, shuffle to the podium in front of the judge. "Slow day, I guess," replied his lawyer without missing a beat.

Still, as the new year came and went, there was no sign of Joey Lombardo, the most recognized Windy City wiseguy named in the expansive indictment and possibly the most important for ensuring the desired crippling blow to the heart of the Chicago underworld. Then, after almost ten months of chasing their elusive target, all of the FBI's diligent hard work and patience finally paid major dividends. Going on a tip via The Clown's dentist—none other than Pat Spilotro, younger brother of Tony Spilotro—the FBI zeroed in on its target in mid-January 2006. As Lombardo arrived for what he thought was going to be a top secret late-night dental appointment, agents converged on the 1994 navy blue Lincoln Mercury sedan holding Lombardo and arrested him. Although heavily bearded and sporting a mane of long straggly hair, the FBI was pleased to confirm it had found its man. Joey Lombardo, like a young child who runs away from home only to stop at the end of the block, had never left the city limits. Taken into custody with no opposition, Lombardo was finally booked, fingerprinted, and jailed on January 13, 2006.

Lombardo, with cut hair and shaved beard, was arraigned before Judge Zagel the following Tuesday afternoon; living up to his moniker, he kept everyone in the courtroom in stitches. Nicknamed The Clown by his associates and the Chicago press for his reputation for sly-witted antics—such as taking out a newspaper ad after a release from jail proclaiming his intention to abstain from future criminal activity, having a proclivity to crack jokes with officers of the law assigned to take him down, and placing a newspaper with a cut-out peephole over his face to shield himself from reporters—Lombardo had several humorous exchanges with the judge as he pled not guilty to the charges asserted against him. When asked if he was ready to tell the truth, the whole truth, and nothing but the truth, Joey the Clown responded, "Yeah, yeah, nutt'in but da truth," in a raspy tone, drawing laughter from the press gallery. Later on in the hearing, when Judge Zagel asked why he missed an appointment with his heart doctor the previous spring, Lombardo replied with a smirk, "I was, what you would say, ah, unavailable," to more laughter from the packed courtroom.

During a post-arraignment press conference, Lombardo's attorney, highly respected criminal defense lawyer Rick Halperin, said his client would seek assistance from the government to cover his legal fees and court costs, asserting that The Clown—a man long linked to the upper-echelon of a multi-million-dollar-a-year criminal empire—was unable to shoulder the financial burden himself. A month later in a court proceeding to determine Lombardo's financial solvency, Judge Zagel ruled to grant the aging mobster the benefit of government assistance in paying for what was certain to be a long list of hefty legal expenses.

Lombardo's arrest and apprehension so close to his home of the past four decades led legal experts and pundits alike to ponder why Joey the Clown, someone who most certainly would have had the ability as well as the opportunity to flee the state, if not the country, if he so wished, never even left the city limits of Chicago. Some think that Lombardo was such a neighborhood stalwart that, at the age of seventy-six, he had neither the will nor the desire to leave the area where he had spent the majority of his life. Others speculate that with the Marcello brothers in jail, The Outfit needed Lombardo around town to look after the everyday operations of the local underworld and help the crime family transition to a new power structure for the duration of the upcoming trial. In any case, one thing's for sure, the fact that The Clown's letters to the judge were postmarked in Chicago, meant that Lombardo was not trying very hard to conceal his whereabouts.

# 2.

## The Outfit
### The History of the Mafia in Chicago

At the turn of the twentieth century, vast numbers of European immigrants flooded into the United States, looking to make a new life with their families in the self-professed land of opportunity. A large chunk of these immigrants came from Italy and the tiny neighboring island of Sicily. Many of these Italian and Sicilian men and woman settled in Chicago, with their hefty ambitions in tow. Many also brought with them Old World customs and traditions that they hoped would aid them in adapting to their new surroundings.

When lofty expectations of quick success in the New World didn't come to immediate fruition, some turned to one of their home country's darkest traditions for solace—the top secret criminal societies known as the *Camorra* in southern Italy, the *Ndraghetta* in northern Italy, and the *Mafia* in Sicily. These organizations were created as early as the twelfth century to give common citizens a voice and needed protection against corrupt government forces that could not be overcome without its existence. However, when transplanted to the United States about 100 years ago, the reincarnation of such underworld societies came to exist purely for its leaders to gain financial profit and power in the community. It is sad that the core values and attributes on which the original organizations were founded were all but lost.

The first manifestation of Italian organized crime to spring up in Chicago was the extensive racket empire run by James "Big Jim" Colosimo. Getting his start in local politics, working his early years in America as a clerk for an area politician, and then eventually as a a precinct captain and "bagman" for the city's immensely influential First Ward, Colosimo used his political connections to forge a stronghold over all vice taking place in The Levee, at that time Chicago's premiere nightlife district. As his power grew, so did his organization, which by 1915 numbered in the hundreds and became a blueprint for the city's modern day crime syndicate by being multi-ethnic. By importing several key lieutenants from New York City, including his nephew John "Johnny the Fox" Torrio, to help him expand his holdings and influence to the city's surrounding suburbs, Colosimo soon became one of the wealthiest and most recognized gangsters in the country. He headquartered his activities out of a restaurant and nightclub known as Colosimo's Cafe, which became renowned for its great food and as a top spot for entertainers of all kinds to perform. As Chicago's first genuine godfather, Colosimo hobnobbed with celebrities and romanced some of the city's most beautiful women.

Colosimo's downfall began in 1918 when the United States Congress enacted the Volstead Act, outlawing the sales and consumption of all alcohol inside the country's borders. Satisfied with a criminal regime built on prostitution, gambling, and extortion, Big Jim was reluctant to dip his organization's beak into the business of bootlegging illegal liquor. This stance on America's newest and most popular growing racket was very unpopular with his men—especially his nephew Johnny Torrio, who saw the prohibition of alcohol in the country as a huge cash crop just waiting to be properly cultivated.

Big Jim's aversion to changing with the times would end up costing him his life. In May 1920, just days after returning from a European honeymoon he had taken with his 20-year-old bride, a dancer he had met at the club, Colosimo was gunned down while entering his office by assassins from New York City, who were acting under the order of none other than his nephew Johnny the Fox.

With his uncle out of the picture, Johnny Torrio took the reins of the Chicago underworld and jumped full force into the bootlegging industry, building his South Side–centered gang into one of the largest liquor cartels operating in the United States. Under Torrio's command, the organization made a number of key alliances with other syndicates around the country and created a network of area bootlegging gangs, assigning each one its own territory in an attempt to cut down on violence.

This concept worked for a while, but soon the stability

that existed among the various factions started to dissolve. The primary trouble began to fester around the later part of 1924 in suburban Chicago Heights, where each gang had most of their distilleries. Heated disputes over brewery expansion erupted, and lines were drawn in the sand; it was Torrio's South Siders against a North Side gang led by Dion O'Bannion, a violence-prone Irish gangster who owned one of the city's largest flower shops. O'Bannion's lieutenants started intercepting Torrio's product shipments and destroying his organization's liquor-cutting plants. In retaliation, a murder contract was placed on O'Bannion's head, and in the week leading up to Thanksgiving 1924, he was killed outside his flower shop by Torrio-dispatched gunmen, once again brought in from New York City.

Torrio's rule atop the Chicago underworld would come to an end soon thereafter when, in January 1925, he was shot several times and brought to the brink of death on orders from Dion O'Bannion's successor and new North Side boss, Earl "Hymie" Weiss. After his recovery, Torrio abdicated the throne to the city's kingdom of crime to Al "Scarface" Capone, a twenty-six-year-old import from the East Coast, who would go on to become the most iconic organized crime figure in the nation's history.

Born and bred in Brooklyn and mentored by notorious Coney Island mob boss, Francesco "Frankie Yale" Ioele, Capone moved to Chicago in the early 1920s and joined the Torrio gang. Getting his start as a bouncer at the legendary Four Deuces bar and brothel located in the city's red light district, the man they called Scarface eventually worked his way up the organizational ladder until he was Johnny Torrio's right-hand man and second in command.

Capone built Torrio's already burgeoning empire into a colossus of riches. He ruled with an iron fist; filled the ranks of his crew with the city's best young hoods (future Outfit leaders Anthony Accardo, Sam Giancana, and Joey Aiuppa among them), plucked from the area's toughest youth gangs (like the Circus Gang and the 42 Gang); and indulged in a life of opulence few in the American gangland landscape had ever seen or experienced. And he did it all while courting the press, a strategy never previously employed in his line of work; thus Capone became the country's first true media gangster, using newspapers and radio broadcasts to enhance and parlay his reputation to heights he could not have reached in his rule of the street alone. With the aid from a fast-growing and headline-happy mainstream media, Capone built a legacy as big as his bank account. Estimates place the Capone empire at reeling in close to $100 million a year, an astronomical feat at that time.

Even though Torrio was long gone from the Windy City—retiring to a homestead on Long Island—Capone continued to wage war with the North Side Irishmen, who steadfastly refused to get in line behind the South Sider's and acquiesce to the territory restrictions put in place by Torrio at the beginning of the decade. Maintaining a vice grip on every area of the city except the North Side, Capone became obsessed with corralling it under his gang's banner. After the murder of Hymie Weiss in October of 1926, the leadership of the Irish syndicate shifted to George "Bugs" Moran, a man who held little respect for his South Side foes and showed no deference to Capone. Moran had his lieutenants continue their assault on Capone's liquor shipments and breweries, killing anyone who got in their way.

By early 1929, Capone had reached his boiling point and decided a mass execution of Moran and his men was the only way to win the treacherous street war and conquer the last portion of the city that he needed to complete a monopoly over the entire Chicago underworld. Arranging for his allies in Detroit's infamous Purple Gang, an all-Jewish mob headed by the four Bernstein brothers, to set up a faux meeting on Valentine's Day in a North Side garage under the premise of giving Moran's gang a truckload of discounted illegal alcohol, Capone's plan was to kill everyone present.

Dressed as policemen, Capone's men stormed the garage, acting as if they were raiding the location, a well-known Moran gang headquarters. Lining up all seven of Moran's men that were there, the South Side assassins machine-gunned each of them to a bloody death, leaving behind only a barking German shepherd to alert those outside of the blood-soaked carnage within. Luckily for Moran, he was late for the meeting that morning and escaped a gruesome fate. Following the massacre, Moran gave in and surrendered control of his territory to the Capone gang. Scarface finally had all of Chicago under his thumb.

The massive publicity the ghastly event garnered, dubbed by the press The St. Valentines Day Massacre, put a huge target on Capone's back, and a law enforcement task force, named "The Untouchables," was created for the sole purpose of bringing him to justice. Unable to nail the South Side crime lord on criminal charges, they went after his financial records and eventually convicted him for not paying his income taxes. Jailed in 1931, Al Capone turned over the keys of his organization to his first cousin and the gang's unofficial business manager, Francis "Frank the Enforcer" Nitti. Capone would never rule the streets of Chicago again. Released from prison in 1939, his mind ravaged by syphilis, Capone retired to Florida before finally succumbing to the disease in 1947.

**EVEN** before Al Capone's incarceration, the nation's underworld was undergoing a major facelift. Following the conclusion of a prolonged gang war that played out in the streets of New York City, Charles "Lucky" Luciano found himself as the newly crowned king of the East Coast mob. Not wanting to assume complete and total control of the region's crime syndicate for fear of meeting the violent and untimely deaths of his two predecessors, Luciano called for a meeting of all the country's various mob bosses to lay out a proposal he created that would install a nationwide criminal combine. The conference of crime bosses was held at a hotel in Atlantic City and attended by over thirty mob heads of state. Luciano spoke of geographically designated "families," ruled over by three-man administration teams, all of which would be overseen by a national board of directors, called "The Commission," that would govern the entire entity and mediate disputes that arose between the twenty-six regional factions. He called his vision "La Cosa Nostra," Italian for "this thing of ours"; after an unanimous vote, it became the new face of American organized crime. The modern-day mafia was born.

Although the boys from Chicago went along with Luciano's vision at the conference, they tweaked the model a bit when applying it to themselves and their newly installed hierarchy. They adhered to the basic rules laid out by

Luciano, but their application of those rules was significantly less stringent. For example, in the years to come, the position of *consiglieri*, in all other families the third person in charge, actually held the most weight when it came to decision making. Where in most other families the power that could be achieved by non-Italians was capped, in The Outfit—a moniker adapted for the Chicago mafia in the late 1930s—non-Italians were able to hold very influential posts in the administration, even oversee full-fledged Italian members. This slight change from standard mob operating procedures consistently worked in favor of The Outfit, making it considerably more difficult for law enforcement to identify and take down the family's real power brokers.

**UNLIKE** Capone, who took over an organization that was thriving, when Frank Nitti assumed command of the Chicago crime syndicate in 1932 it was stagnating. Capone's legal woes and his departure from the city left a huge void and lingering questions regarding the vice conglomerate's stability. And with the repeal of the Prohibition laws in 1933, the gang was perceived to be on the decline. Though undaunted by the prospect of breathing new life into the organization, Nitti faced an uphill battle in rebuilding and reshaping the legendary unit of Windy City outlaws.

Aided by the likes of veteran Capone gang members Jake "Greasy Thumb" Guzik, Murray "The Camel" Humphreys, and his own personal protégé Paul "The Waiter" Ricca, Nitti focused his attention on expanding his new crime family's reach into labor racketeering, local politics, gambling, and loan-sharking as a means of bringing in the money lost due to the re-legalization of alcohol. Guzik, a Jew and the syndicate's point man in city hall, spearheaded the infiltration of the local labor unions, Humphreys, spawning from Welsh descent, headed the takeover of all illegal gambling being run in the area. Ricca, with the aid of Capone's former bodyguards, Tony Accardo and Phillip "Dandy Phil" D'Andrea, took the responsibility of getting in line all of the loan-sharking operations taking place within the city limits.

Nitti's strategy paid quick dividends, and by 1935, the organization was back to equaling its profits from the heyday of Prohibition. And because he went out of his way to stay out of the spotlight—a big contrast to the days of Scarface Capone—Frank the Enforcer was poised for maximum growth in the future.

His ten plus years at The Outfit's helm came to an end in March 1943, when Nitti committed suicide, after being indicted in a wide-reaching ploy by the Chicago mafia to extort money from a number of Hollywood movie studios and having been diagnosed with terminal cancer. Replacing Nitti, at least for the short term, was his underboss and protégé, Ricca. The Waiter, originally named Felix De Lucia, came to the United States in 1920 from Italy, on the run from the law on murder charges. Indicted in the same Hollywood extortion case as his former boss, Ricca was sent to prison in 1944. As he headed to prison, he tapped his best friend and the family's primary enforcer, Tony Accardo—nicknamed "Joe Batters" by Capone for his skill at using a baseball bat as an enforcement tool—to run The Outfit in his stead. It would be a role Accardo would keep one way or the other until he died almost fifty years later, having never spent a day in jail.

Under Accardo, The Outfit continued to flourish. An innovative leader, he was not one to rest on his or the syndicate's laurels and became intent on expanding the family into new and profitable horizons whenever an opportunity presented itself. The first thing he did was reemphasize the street tax—extorting tribute payments from any and all illegal businesses being conducted in the city; Frank Nitti employed this at the onset of his reign in the 1930s but extortion had not been actively enforced over the preceding years. Also known as "The Big Tuna," for his love of fishing, Accardo made certain everyone in Chicago knew that The Outfit was the only ball game in town, and that the day of independent vice merchants operating without cutting them in for a piece of their rackets were now over. Then he set his sights on staging a takeover of the local wire services, businesses that provided horse racing and professional sports' results to the area's bookmakers. Joe Batters didn't want any middlemen cutting into his organization's profit margins. The last of the independent wire operators, James Ragen—someone who scoffed at the notion of giving into Accardo's strong arm tactics—was killed in June 1946, and The Outfit's acquisition was complete.

As the end of the decade dawned, Accardo, firmly entrenched in the boss' chair and his syndicate running at its highest level ever, remained on the lookout for even more gangland avenues to exploit to his advantage. In the most daring move of his career, he decided to muscle in on the city's traditionally African American policy lottery, better known as the numbers racket. Centered in the all-black

South Side ghettos, policy was a cash cow participated in by over 80 percent of the residents in the rundown housing projects that dotted the neighborhood.

The idea to go after the lucrative numbers business was actually not Accardo's. His close confidant and childhood pal Sam Giancana, recently sprang from prison, hatched the plan while being housed with several black policy leaders. One of them was Edward "Eddie the King" Jones, who Giancana became friendly with in jail and who explained to him how the racket worked. Within days of gaining his freedom, he met with The Big Tuna and laid out his idea. Accardo fell in love with Giancana's scheme and tapped him to oversee its application, knowing it would not be an easy task to accomplish. It wasn't.

A percentage of the South Side crime lords refused to give in to the mafia without a fight. The flames of war raged between The Outfit and the black numbers czars well into the early portion of the 1950s, with both sides suffering casualties.

The mob's most ardent adversary was Theodore "Tough Teddy" Roe, a vicious crime lord who would not budge at The Outfit's demands and was unafraid of using violence against the Italians to protect what he saw as his rightful turf. When Giancana sent his brother, Chuck, and his bodyguard, Leonard "Fat Lenny" Caifano, to try to negotiate with Roe, he shot Caifano to death. At that point, Accardo and Giancana pulled out all the stops and designated all their possible resources into killing Teddy Roe. They finally did in August 1952, and, with his demise, officially took over the South Side and its policy operation.

Next, Accardo, with counsel from trusted boardroom

lieutenants Murray Humphreys and Gus "Slim" Alex, made the move to expand The Outfit's gambling interests outside of Chicago and into the vice hotbeds of Las Vegas and Havana, Cuba. Using the mob's access to the Teamsters Union pension fund to help finance the building of the Vegas Strip and his personal influence in political and East Coast mafia circles to infiltrate Havana, the Windy City don had now taken his crime family international. By the late 1950s, he was arguably the most powerful mob boss in the entire country. But instead of seeking to bask in the overwhelming glow of his incredible exploits, he made a decision that shocked a great deal of people, both inside the underworld and out—he sought to get out of the game all together.

**KNOWING** the heat from law enforcement was building against him and knowing that if he remained don he would most likely end up in prison, Accardo wanted to retire. Paul Ricca, now a free man, semiretired, and acting as Accardo's top counselor on family affairs, advised him against an all-out departure from the syndicate. Instead, Ricca theorized Accardo should move into the role of *consiglieri,* name a front boss, and pull the strings from behind the scenes, safely removed from the mob's day-to-day affairs and the police scrutiny that goes with it. Buoyed from his directing the successful takeover of the city's numbers business only a few years earlier, Giancana, nicknamed "Mooney" or "Momo" for his often gutsy and sometimes crazy behavior, was the logical choice to take Accardo's place atop The Outfit food chain. Holding the post for nine years, Giancana ushered in an era of excess that harkened back to the days of Capone.

Like the venerable Scarface himself, Giancana craved media attention and exploited the ability his new status as boss gave him to live as lavish a life as possible. He courted Hollywood femme fatales; cemented friendships with celebrities, most notably Frank Sinatra; and even dabbled in big-time politics, allegedly helping the Kennedy family rig the 1960 presidential election and helping the CIA in a plot to kill Cuban dictator Fidel Castro. While Accardo remained comfortably in the shadows, Giancana flaunted his mob credentials at every opportunity. And the press ate it up, making him world famous. Accardo, on the other hand, began to tire of his longtime friend's attention-grabbing routine and in 1966, with the support of several other Outfit elders, had him deposed.

Unhappy with his treatment in Chicago, Giancana fled the country for Mexico. While in exile, he established numerous overseas gambling ventures that made him even wealthier than he was when he was a don. A bearded Giancana ended up back in the Windy City in 1974, only to be killed shortly thereafter by his former mafia partners for intending to testify in front of a Senate committee investigating the Castro assassination plot and for not sharing profits from the gambling operations he ran while out of the country.

**BETWEEN** 1966 and 1970, The Outfit would go through three bosses, all while Accardo sat in the background silently directing family affairs from his slot as *consiglieri*, living half the year in Chicago and the other half in Palm Springs, California. First, Accardo chose Sam "Teetz"

Bataglia, a West Side crew chief who made his name on the streets as a feared enforcer, to take the reins. When Battaglia was sent to prison, he appointed Felix "Milwaukee Phil" Alderesio, the head of The Outfit's enforcement unit, as the new boss. After the government nailed Alderesio on charges of trying to defraud a local bank, Accardo called on his former driver and ace protégé John "Jackie the Lackey" Cerone to take over as don. But he too was soon removed from life as a free man, convicted on a charge of transportation of stolen goods across state lines when one of his lieutenants, Lou Bombacino, flipped and testified against him in court.

For the next few years, Joe Batters was forced to come back to Chicago full-time and retake the mantle as leader of The Outfit. He did so carefully, assigning Gus Alex and Joseph "Joey Doves" Aiuppa as "council members" and attempting to supervise the syndicate as a group. In 1973, when he believed that the crime family had stabilized, he stepped back once again and named Aiuppa the new front boss. After Jackie Cerone was released from prison, he joined up with Aiuppa in The Outfit hierarchy, taking the position of underboss, while Accardo settled back in as *consiglieri*.

The Outfit in the 1970s was highlighted by Aiuppa and Accardo's decision to go after the city's non-mob-connected car thieves and chop shops. Known as "The Chop Shop Wars," it took a period of several years to get all of the independent auto boosters and their operations under the mafia's umbrella. Many of the operations' leaders bristled at the notion of paying a street tax on their business, cutting the mob in for a percentage, and not getting anything in return. Some outright refused and were killed. By the end of the decade, however, The Outfit—specifically the South Side crews, led first by James "Jimmy the Bomber" Catuara and then by Albert "Caesar the Fox" Tocco, who were both overseen by caporegime Al Pilotto—successfully reigned in all the chop shops, giving the syndicate another racket in their pocket and considerably more cash to add to their bottom line.

The 1980s brought new technology and, with it, a new way for the Chicago mafia to make money—the video poker machine. They placed the electronic games in as many restaurants and bars as they could muscle into, and in just a few years, it became one of the family's biggest rackets. The decade also brought the end of The Outfit's run in Las Vegas, as a result of a shift in leadership. An extensive indictment of the entire Outfit hierarchy, minus Accardo, on charges of pension fund fraud and stealing from four casinos they secretly owned and operated resulted in convictions that sent Aiuppa, Cerone, and Joseph "The Clown" Lombardo, the syndicate captain responsible for looking after Nevada, to prison for lengthy sentences. Accardo selected West Side caporegime Joseph "Joe Nick" Ferriola to replace Aiuppa as boss; Ferriola's leadership came to an end three years later when he succumbed to cancer. His biggest claim to fame during his tenure as don was that Tony Spilotro, the family's lieutenant in Las Vegas, who had gradually gotten overly drunk on power and whose behavior had become totally out of control, was killed on his watch.

Tony Accardo died in 1992, leaving behind an epic legacy in the annals of mob history. Remnants of Accardo's

lengthy reign weren't hard to find in the years to follow—
Sam "Wings" Carlisi, a top messenger of The Big Tuna's
orders, took over for Ferriola, although his stay on top
was short lived: He was jailed in 1993 on a racketeering indictment and eventually convicted in 1996. Three
more Accardo protégés—Joey Lombardo, John "No Nose"
Di Fronzo, and John "Johnny Apes" Monteleone—diligently
looked after The Outfit in the 1990s and into the new millennium, carrying on their mentor's reputation for solid leadership and maximum respect from those they lead.

"Due to their savvy way of doing business, their unique
leadership structure, and their geographical placement
within the United States, The Outfit really was the most
powerful crime family in the country for a majority of the
twentith century," says former FBI agent Richard Stilling.
"The families in New York might have had Chicago on
pure numbers and general perception, but on influence
and ability to get things done, The Outfit takes the cake.
Their hierarchy lends itself to a more harmonious existence. Power flows more laterally than vertically, and in
most cases that protects against members getting too ambitious. Plus, Chicago is the heart of the Midwest and, as a
result, the epicenter of our nation's commerce. Every truck
and plane making their way across the country must pass
through Chicago. This gives the mafia there a lot of clout.
They can shut everything down with the snap of a finger,
and they know it. The New York mafia may control the
East Coast, but the boys from The Outfit have everything
else."

# 3.

## Clown Prince of the Mob
### The Rise of Joey Lombardo

Many would argue that Joseph Lombardo's arrest in Family Secrets marked the end of an era in the Chicago mob. He's an underworld personality like no other in the history of organized crime—recognized for his quick wit and humorous charm just as much as for being a highly feared mob enforcer and top-grade gangland administrator. Cagey, resilient, and cunningly deceptive, Lombardo endeared himself to the residents of his longtime West Side neighborhood while at the same time becoming one of Chicago law enforcement's most sought after targets and toughest adversaries. The man is truly an enigma of epic proportions, the Second City's own Jekyll and Hyde. Everyone has a different opinion regarding the mafia's one and only clown prince. To some, he was a heartless killer who preyed on the ills of society to make his living. To others he was a community leader and grandfatherly mentor whose presence in their neighborhood was indispensable. But no matter what your thoughts on the man are, the fact is, until his recent incarceration, Lombardo was a staple on the streets of Chicago for over 50 years and remains one of the final links to The Outfit's glory days of the mid-twentieth century—a true man's man and a presence in the fabric of the city with few equals.

It was a long road to the top for Joey Lombardo. He was born to Italian immigrants Michael and Carmela Lombardi on New Year's Day 1929 as Giuseppe Lombardi, the sixth of eleven children. Money was scarce in the Lombardi household. Coming to the United States from the tiny town of Bari, Italy, in 1919, and settling in "The Patch," a West Side Italian neighborhood, they scraped by with Michael working a number of menial jobs to support his wife and ever-growing bevy of children. He would work a few years as a butcher and then a few years as a printer. No matter what his employment situation, Michael was always able to make just enough money to put food on the family table. It wasn't the life Joey wanted.

Sent to work at a young age to make money for the family, Joey was a paperboy, shoe shiner, boxcar loader at the local train station, and bell boy at the Blackstone Hotel off Michigan Avenue. It wasn't long before he realized there was fast money to be made participating in certain black market ventures. Once he hit the tenth grade at Wells High School—where he walked the same halls as future Outfit lead John Di Fronzo—Joey began taking wagers on sporting events and then taking the money he made from his betting operation and loaning it out to classmates who needed a little extra cash to fix up their cars or to take their girlfriends out for a night on the town. Active in high school sports, he was a member of the basketball, wrestling, and swim teams. After high school, Lombardo even did some amateur boxing, before turning in his gloves for a set of clubs, spending a good chunk of time in his early twenties hustling less talented players on the links.

Lombardo's career as a professional criminal began in 1947, when at the age of eighteen he burglarized an area grocery store to pay for a medical procedure for his sick mother. After that, there was no looking back. He jumped full-fledged into the life of a hoodlum. Introduced to rising mob capo and Tony Accardo protégé John "Jackie the Lackey" Cerone when caddying for him on the golf course and put under his wing, Joey the Clown was off to a fast start. Displaying a knack for the seedier side of business, Lombardo adapted quickly to making a living on the streets and soon became known as a jack of all trades in the Chicago underworld as he worked his way up The Outfit ladder. His versatility as a crook became his calling card and paid substantial dividends for the notoriously wisecracking mafia lieutenant, earning him several promotions and an anointment by the sitting mob hierarchy as a future Outfit leader. Although known to many people as The Clown, he also went by the nickname "Lumpy" for the many lumps he placed on the heads of his enemies when he took on the role of gangland enforcer.

Throughout the 1950s and 1960s, he developed a reputation as a shrewd card sharp and gambling operator, running high-priced poker and craps games across the city, and as a top-notch thief, pulling jobs with the area's best burglary crew. He was a hijacking specialist, taking down truckloads of goods from the cargo section of O'Hare Airport, and a highly efficient strong arm, who was sent on the toughest collection and enforcement assignments by The Outfit administration. On the side, he ran profitable sports book and loan-shark businesses, and to curry favor with his mentors in the mob, often continued to caddy for the likes of Outfit heavyweights Tony Accardo and Fiore "Fifi" Bucceri. Various police reports list him as owning a trucking company and maintaining interest in a number of construction-related businesses.

**TO** be a successful criminal you have to be smart, but you also have to be lucky. Early on in his career on the street, Lady Luck always seemed to be on the side of The Clown. When he was indicted in 1963 along with several other local wiseguys for allegedly running a wide-spanning loan-sharking operation, the state's star witness—an indebted money borrower who claimed he was taken into the basement of an Outfit-owned saloon, tied to a support beam, and violently beaten unconscious—developed a sudden case of amnesia while on the witness stand. Just like the previous ten times he had been arrested, Lombardo skated on the charges. In order to become a made man, Lombardo is alleged to have killed a Chicago-area hotel owner and bookmaker named Manny Sklar, stalking him for several days before ambushing and gunning him down in front of his Lake Shore Drive apartment in 1965. According to FBI files, it is believed he was inducted into the crime family just a month later, sponsored by Jackie Cerone.

Marrying a local girl named Maria Nigro at the Holy Rosary Church on Western Avenue in 1951, Lombardo set down his adult roots in the same area of the city in which he had grown up—near the West Side at the intersection of Grand and Ogden Avenues. The newlyweds moved into Maria's family's apartment at 2210 West Ohio Street and never left. Real estate records show that the Lombardo family eventually purchased the entire apartment building; Lombardo's wife and daughter are currently listed as co-owners.

While rising through the ranks of the city's crime syndicate, Joey Lombardo managed to build a nice, but modest, life for him, his wife, and his in-laws in the three-story brick building on West Ohio Street. The couple had two children, Joseph Jr. and Joanne, and Lombardo was a doting father, attending almost all of his daughter's dance recitals and even coaching his son's Little League baseball team. Maria's parents lived upstairs and became very close to Joey, even going as far as calling him their "son."

He started to hold court daily at a coffee and sandwich shop up the street from his apartment and over the years became a fixture of his West Side community. Like a stop sign or a fire hydrant, he was always there. He walked the streets with regal flair. Despite continually being pegged by the police and the press as a rugged, short-tempered gangster, Lombardo had the community's utmost respect, quite often being turned to in times of need by neighborhood residents in the same way others would seek counsel and guidance from the area's politicians or clergymen.

When by the late 1960s and early 1970s, a majority of his Outfit brethren began moving from the city into the surrounding suburbs, he stayed. Not a huge fan of travel, Lombardo was a typical homebody, rarely leaving Chicago, let alone his comfort zone in the area around Grand and Ogden. This loyalty to his surroundings endeared him even more to the locals.

"The neighborhood was old school all the way," recalls former FBI agent Jack O'Rourke. "A lot of the people there were immigrants or sons and daughters of immigrants. It was a comfort thing with them. They wanted a don-like figure to be there and help look after the area. The kind of guy who had the juice to help people with their problems. Joey was drawn to that mentality like a moth to a flame and was happy to play the role."

The older Lombardo got, the more responsibilities his superiors in The Outfit bestowed on him. By the time he turned forty-five, he was hitting his full stride, a force to be reckoned with in national—not just local—underworld circles. Upon the death of Sam "Teetz" Battaglia in 1973, Lombardo was named captain of the entire West Side of the city and given a crew of over three dozen soldiers to command. He was also given authority over Tony Spilotro and his crew operating in Las Vegas and was tapped to look after the crime family's interest in the Teamsters Union pension fund and its official supervisor, longtime mob associate Allen Dorfman. After the imprisonment of Milwaukee Phil Alderesio, he is alleged to have been put in charge of The Outfit's enforcement team and asked to oversee the coordination and carrying out all of the mob executions in the area. At this time, he was also given the job of corralling all the city's pornography and strip clubs under The Outfit umbrella. The Clown was a very busy man.

**UNTIL** the 1980s, although having been arrested well over a dozen times and having faced some pretty heavy charges a few times to boot, Joey Lombardo had never been convicted of any crimes. This made the government angry and made The Clown a top priority. The FBI saw its best opportunity at nailing Lombardo was through his and The Outfit's foothold in the Las Vegas hotel and casino industry via its control of the Teamsters pension fund. Although the feds knew of the relationship between Sin City, the Outfit, and the labor union for quite some time, they had never been able to prove it. That all changed in 1978 when an FBI surveillance team in Kansas City listened in on a very damaging conversation that opened up the floodgates in the government's investigation and signaled the beginning of the end for the mob's reign in the desert's gambling Mecca.

A court-authorized wiretap installed in a mafia-run restaurant—put in place to gather information on a recent unsolved murder committed in the area—picked up a discussion between Carl "Corky" Civella, the acting boss of the Kansas City crime family, and Carl "Tuffy" De Luna, his second-in-command. The discussion discretely laid out a wide-spanning conspiracy that involved several Midwest mob syndicates silently managing, financing, and stealing from various Las Vegas casinos. This information led to another wiretap being installed in Civella's home that recorded yet another, more in-depth conversation between

Civella, De Luna, and a lieutenant of theirs stationed in Nevada. They described in detail how never-ending piles of cash made it from the casino's count room into the pockets of several mob bosses located thousands of miles away, insulated from the deed by several layers of underling.

Acting on the evidence culled from the two wiretaps, the FBI was able to indict and eventually convict the sitting administration of the Kansas City mafia syndicate. Combining the wiretap evidence from Kansas City with meticulous handwritten records of Las Vegas–based mob activity confiscated from Carl De Luna's residence during his arrest, the FBI was able to jump-start a similar investigation into the Chicago Outfit and their illegal interests in the desert—interests that at that time were the responsibility of Joey Lombardo.

By bugging the insurance company office of Allen Dorfman, a frequent visiting and conversation spot of Lombardo's, for a six-month period in 1979, the feds accumulated additional incriminating audio surveillance. With the cooperation of real estate entrepreneur Allen Glick, whose Argent Corporation fronted ownership of the Stardust, Hacienda, and Freemont hotels and casinos on behalf of The Outfit, the government's case was airtight. But they weren't done yet.

Things continued to get worse for Lombardo. While in the process of investigating him for the massive skimming operation being conducted at the triumvirate of mafia-backed casinos, the FBI stumbled on his involvement in a bribery scheme that implicated a Nevada senator. Acting on behalf of the Teamsters, Lombardo had arranged to sell a 5.8-acre lot that was owned by the labor union and located next to the Las Vegas Hilton to U.S. Senator Howard Cannon at a decreased rate in exchange for Cannon's aid in squashing a trucking industry deregulation bill that was being proposed by the House Judiciary Committee in an upcoming vote. Convicted in both cases, he was sentenced to a pair of ten year prison terms, that, lucky for him, the judge ordered were to run concurrently.

However, even after Lombardo left Chicagoland for his extended stay behind bars in 1982, turning over responsibility for his crew to his top lieutenant, James "Jimmy Boy" Cozzo, there were some loose strings to be taken care of. Certain members of The Outfit felt that Allen Dorfman, who was convicted of aiding Lombardo in the bribing of Senator Cannon, would not be able to complete his prison time. They were worried he was soft and would be prone to turn witness for the government. In their minds, it was time to cut ties—in the mob vernacular, kill him to ensure silence. The fact that Dorfman had been incarcerated less than ten years earlier for an Outfit-related scheme and had not caused any problems for Lombardo and his mob associates didn't seem to matter. Leaving a lunch meeting at a suburban hotel coffee shop in January 1983, Dorfman, who was out on bond pending his sentencing, was gunned down in the parking lot of the Lincolnwood Hyatt by two assailants wearing ski masks.

**RE-EMERGING** from incarceration in 1992, Joey Lombardo returned to his old stomping grounds—the West Side of Chicago—and wasted little time making his presence felt in the local press. In the weeks following his release from prison he placed an ad in several Chicago area papers that stated: "My name is Joey Lombardo. I've been released on parole from federal prison. I never took an oath with guns and daggers, pricked my finger to draw blood, or burned paper to join a criminal organization, If anyone hears my name used in connection with any criminal activity, please notify the FBI, the local police, and my parole officer, Ron Kumke."

A free man for the first time in ten years, Lombardo's primary goal was to keep as low of a profile as possible while still being able to take care of his duties for The Outfit. He took a job at a furniture upholstery business and then at a West Side tool and dye shop and tried his best to stay off the government's radar. It was a daunting task, to say the least. When FBI surveillance teams cruised his territory, he was easily found with a cigar clenched between his teeth, tending to his garden, doing maintenance on his automobile, or enjoying a meal at his favorite Italian restaurant, La Scrola on Grand Avenue. However, despite his continued presence in the community, law enforcement was hard-pressed to build another case against him. It appeared, at least for the time being, Lady Luck was back on his side.

Upon Tony Accardo's death in May of 1992, Lombardo, then sixty-three years old, was appointed to take his place as the crime family's *consiglieri*. With the exception of two incidents, Lombardo was able to keep his name out of the newspapers and his wrists out of handcuffs for over a decade. First, in 1993, his driver, Christopher "Christy the Nose" Spina, was fired from his job working for the city as foreman of a sanitation yard as a result of spending portions of his workday chauffeuring The Clown around town (Spina would later be reinstated in his job by a judge and allotted back pay for his dismissal). The second incident was when Joseph Jr. was kicked out of the Teamsters Union in 1998 for his alleged associations with the mob.

Then in 2003, signs began to indicate that his time out of trouble with the law would be short lived. The FBI showed up one morning at the tool and dye shop where he worked and requested a hair and saliva sample in an attempt to match his DNA to a ski mask recovered in the abandoned getaway car used in the 1974 Danny Seifert murder. They also warned him of a potential murder plot thought by the government to have been hatched by then Outfit heir apparent, Jimmy Marcello, to remove any possibility that Lombardo would deal himself out of any future charges brought in the nearly thirty-year-old Seifert homicide. For the next two years, Lombardo went about his day-to-day routine unfazed—walking his dog, Fluffy, around the neighborhood, counseling old and young alike in the community on any and all problems that were plaguing them, and holding court at La Scrola or Carmine's on Rush Street. It appeared to the naked eye that he had not a care in the world. And then the other shoe dropped.

Imprisoned Outfit hit man, Nicholas "Nicky Breeze" Calabrese, began cooperating with the FBI in 2002, and with the information he provided authorities, Joey Lombardo found himself indicted in 2005 on murder and racketeering charges. The extensive pretrial procedure in the landmark case took over two years, leaving The Clown with a lot of time on his hands. Known as a man of action, he could do little but wait, stewing in his cell following his detention, biding his time until his trial was to begin, and being forced to contemplate the very real possibility of never walking the streets again as a free man.

"Joey is a throwback," said Jim Wagner, former FBI agent and one-time president of the Chicago Crime Commission. "He learned the game from some of the best the city of Chicago has ever had to offer. There aren't a lot of people like him left. He was groomed by the likes of Accardo, Aiuppa, Cerone, and Bucceri to take The Outfit into its next life. They taught him how they did business, and he was a good student. He liked his nickname and enjoyed playing the whole Clown thing up to the press and the police. But, believe me, deep down the guy is no clown. As a street figure, he's as dangerous as they come and a lot smarter than he wants people to believe. When he got out of prison back in the nineties he was smart to not jump into the boss' seat and start playing godfather. Hiding behind the scenes, letting others do much of the heavy lifting served him well. He had a nice run. But on the street, the law is almost always going to catch up with you no matter how good of a criminal you are. I think he knew that, yet still chose to live his life in The Outfit for better or for worse."

# 4.

## A Darker Shade of Pail
The Daniel Seifert Murder

The murder of Daniel Seifert was one of the most tragic of the eighteen gangland slayings charged in the Family Secrets trial and one of the most horrible of Joey Lombardo's crimes. Of the nearly two dozen killings as part of the 2005 indictment, Seifert's was one of only two murders of someone not personally involved in any underworld activities. He was merely a young and aspiring entrepreneur who happened to befriend and eventually go into business with the wrong people. By the time he realized he had gotten in over his head and that his business partners were likely to get him into scalding hot water, it was too late. Seifert became a pawn in a game of cover your ass or else. And when that game is played with members of the mafia, people die. Plain and simple. Furthermore, if you are a meek and harmless person like Daniel Seifert was and the people you are playing the game with are hardened criminals and higher-ups in one of the most powerful and lethal crime families in the world, you are certain to be the one that ends up dead. And that's exactly what happened.

Small in stature and always sporting a goatee to commemorate his one-time identity as a self-proclaimed beatnik, Seifert, was born and raised in the greater Chicagoland area. In the mid-1960s, he lived with his wife in suburban Elk Grove and worked as a carpenter. He had previously owned and ran a fiberglass factory that had gone bankrupt. While doing carpentry work in 1967, Seifert struck up a conversation with a customer about how lucrative an industrial plastics and fiberglass business could be. The owner of the house was a man by the name of Irwin Weiner, a local bail bondsmen and top-tier Outfit associate who was known to dabble in a number of mob-affiliated trades.

Within months, Seifert was being bankrolled by Weiner and Outfit boss Milwaukee Phil Alderesio in a plastics business known as the International Fiberglass Company. A few years later, Weiner sold his interest in the company to Tony Spilotro, Joey Lombardo, and Frank Schweihs and the group of wiseguys started using the business as a hang out spot. Things were going so well that in 1969 Alderesio, Lombardo, Weiner, Spilotro, and another Outfit figure named Ronald "Ronnie the Balloon Head" De Angelis, helped finance another business with Seifert—this time with the aid of $1 million loan from the mob-controlled Teamsters pension fund—in Deming, New Mexico, called the American Pail Company.

As it turned out, Lombardo, Weiner, Spilotro, and company, despite their designations as silent partners, were not all that silent. They used the businesses as a front for their own underworld activities, specifically taking out loans on the companies' credit as a means of illegally lining their own pockets with cash they didn't intend to pay back. Before he knew exactly what was going on, Seifert was in bed with some very dangerous people.

Despite being portrayed by law enforcement as a ruthless and cunning mafia enforcer, Joey Lombardo could be quite charming and affable. These personality traits were one of the reasons Seifert was caught totally off-guard when the nefarious behavior of his partners began to come to light. Over their time of doing business together, Lombardo and Seifert became quite close. They dined and vacationed together, and it's alleged that Seifert's son Joey was named after Lombardo. It's said that Lombardo even babysat for the Seiferts. By 1972, however, it was obvious to Seifert and his wife, Emma, that Lombardo, Weiner, and their friends were really gangsters and probably not the best people to be doing business with. Emma Seifert advised her husband to sell his interest in International Fiberglass and he did. With American Pail having gone under, the Seiferts thought they were free from the mob. They weren't.

In late 1973, Seifert's seedy business connections finally caught up with him. The FBI began nosing around and asking questions about the company and its finances. Seifert, who didn't have anything to hide, began answering them. By early 1974, he went in front of a grand jury and told them everything he knew about his Outfit-affiliated partners in the then-defunct American Pail Company. Soon

Lombardo, Weiner, Spilotro, De Angelis, and Allen Dorfman, the gatekeeper to the robust union pension fund the mafia often used to finance business opportunities, were indicted for attempting to defraud the Teamsters of $1.4 million in connection with American Pail.

**A** major problem was on the horizon. When The Outfit found out Danny Seifert had turned government witness, the syndicate as a whole was forced to immediately go into damage control mode. Joey Lombardo and Tony Spilotro knew that if their former partner got up on the stand during their trial, they were both finished, most likely destined for a lengthy prison sentence. This was no laughing matter, even for a clown. Although he considered Seifert a close friend, Joey Lombardo wasn't about to let him send him up the river. In his mind, there was only one solution: kill Danny Seifert.

For a murder contract to be issued on Seifert's life, Lombardo had to get it sanctioned by Tony Accardo. This put Accardo in a precarious position. Unlike other similar situations that had arisen in the past, this would not be an easy decision for The Outfit don to make. On one hand, he knew the killing of ordinary citizens was bad for business. Accardo thought, like many of his mob boss brethren, that law enforcement could tolerate gangsters murdering other gangsters to a certain degree. But when regular civilians and non-wiseguys began getting shot down in cold blood, it attracted negative attention and public outcry. It was the kind of behavior that caused the police to want to take down the mafia even more than they already did.

On the other hand, Accardo was a pragmatist and knew how much he and the entire Outfit had to lose if the government proved their case against Lombardo and his associates. Specifically, he knew that the case put The Outfit's entire investment in Las Vegas and all the millions and millions of dollars they were receiving from the skim directly at risk.

As often happens in life, in the end it was money that ultimately did the talking. A large portion of Accardo's yearly net income came from money being siphoned from the many casinos that had been built via pension fund loans and whose count rooms, in turn, became open bank vaults for mobsters like The Big Tuna, who arranged those loans. Seifert's testimony would put the entire skimming operation in jeopardy and would almost certainly end up taking copious amounts of cash out of Accardo's pocket. After it was all said and done, Accardo, despite knowing that the murder would bring the ire of the government down upon him and his crime family more fiercely than ever before, signed off on the hit.

With the trial three months away, Seifert, fully aware his life was in danger, began carrying a gun. Without him, the government had no case and those indicted were likely to skate on the charges. Signs were everywhere that the mob wanted him dead and he knew it. He also knew The Outfit would stop at nothing to accomplish their goal. In late September 1974, Emma Seifert told Danny she saw Joey Lombardo driving up and down their street and sitting in the parking lot of her husband's new fiberglass factory. No longer on speaking terms with her and her husband, Emma was certain Lombardo was either trying to intimidate them or case the locations for a possible kill opportunity. Shortly after Lombardo's unwelcome drive-bys, Ronnie Seifert received a phone call from The Clown, who advised him to "straighten out" his older brother Danny or else.

At approximately 8:30 A.M. on September 27, 1974, Seifert, his wife, and their four-year-old son, Joey, arrived at the office of his new business, Plastic-Matics Products, located in a small industrial park off Foster Avenue in Bensenville. The Seiferts sent their other two children, Nicholas, ten, and Catherine, eleven, off to school that morning, but young Joey was feeling under the weather so they decided to bring him along for what they thought would be a typical day at work. Unfortunately for the Seifert family, the day would be anything but typical.

When the three of them reached the modest headquarters of Danny's recently incorporated plastics company, Emma began to prepare a pot of coffee and Danny ran back down to the parking lot to retrieve a vacuum cleaner he had forgotten in the car. Alone in the office with her son, Emma was startled by two assailants in ski masks, who barged through the backdoor brandishing pistols and handcuffs.

"This is a robbery," one of the men shouted.

"Where is the son-of-a-bitch?" the other one asked.

Emma screamed to try to warn her husband of the pending danger, but it was no use. As Danny came back through the office's entrance he was struck in the head by one of the weapon-wielding men and tumbled to the ground in agony. It took very little time for him to realize his life was in the balance. The Outfit had dispatched a hit team to finish him off.

Running to her desk, Emma tried to find the gun Danny had stashed there. However, before she could get the gun, one of the masked gunmen grabbed her and ushered her and Joey into the bathroom, telling them not to worry, this will be over fast.

A shot was fired, but Danny was able to get away. Leaving Emma and Joey alone in the office lavatory, the pair of gunmen sprinted toward their fleeing target. With his wife, child, and several other people in neighboring offices watching from the window, Seifert ran from one end of the industrial park to the other, thinking he could get away from his assailants by taking refuge in a connecting building. This was not the case, as another member of The Outfit hit squad was there waiting for him and shot him in the knee. Wounded and frightened, Seifert fell to the ground. While Seifert was still on his hands and knees, the assassin moved in to finish the job, putting his shotgun to the back of Seifert's head and pulling the trigger. Danny Seifert died instantly. The Outfit had solved its problem.

**AFTER** the bloodshed, the execution squad fled to two waiting vehicles that were stationed in the parking lot waiting for them. One was the getaway car, the other a "crash car," or "trail car," used by mob hit men to run interference and aid in averting capture by disrupting any attempts to follow the shooters. Speeding from the scene in a Dodge Charger and a Brown Ford LTD, the group of assassins headed to a suburban Elmhurst Pontiac dealership. Abandoning the LTD and piling everyone into the Charger, their hurried departure from the dealership caught the eye of two

Elmhurst policemen sitting in a nearby cruiser, who began to pursue the vehicle. A short high-speed chase ensued. The hit team successfully eluded the cops by ducking into a residential area of interconnecting subdivisions in the neighboring town of Northlake. The job was complete. The Outfit breathed a collective sigh of relief. The mob's prized possession, its stranglehold over the Teamsters pension fund, was safe. At least for the time being.

According to FBI reports, the Charger was stored in Outfit member Nicholas "Buddy" Ciotti's garage before it was destroyed. In spite of accomplishing the goal and eliminating what had become a significant thorn in his side, Outfit boss Tony Accardo was displeased about the way the hit went down. It was exactly what he had feared— too extreme, too high profile, and too much of a mess left behind. Informants would later tell the FBI that Lombardo and Spilotro were ordered in front of Accardo to answer for their behavior and were given a stern tongue lashing for their antics.

Seifert's heinous slaying dealt the government's case a devastating blow it would not be able to recover from. Minus Seifert's testimony, the case fell apart and all the defendants were acquitted. Over the years, however, more extensive information came out, implicating Lombardo, Spilotro, and others in the vicious mob murder, and it was included in the eighteen killings charged in the 2005 Family Secrets indictment.

In her testimony at the trial, Emma Seifert said she believed that Joey Lombardo was one of the masked gunmen who stormed into her husband's office and ushered her and her son into the bathroom. She claimed she could

\* \* \*

**BORN** on May 19, 1938, Tony Spilotro was raised on Chicago's West Side. Specifically, at the corner of Grand and Ogden, where his father, Pasquale, owned and ran a restaurant called Patsy's (the nickname friends and family used to refer to Tony's dad). Immigrating from Trigano, Sicily, in 1914 as a teenager, Patsy quickly learned that the skill of cooking he had adopted from his mother as a young child would serve him well in making a living for himself. Not long after settling in the Windy City, after several years in New York, Patsy married a young Italian girl named Antoinette, bought a home on Melvina Street, and started a family. In the midst of having six children with his wife, all boys, he opened up his restaurant and soon it became a favorite neighborhood haunt.

Famous for the homemade meatballs Patsy himself prepared every day for his loyal customer base, to go along with very popular veal and pasta dishes, the restaurant quickly became a hang out and gathering spot for the local mafia. Considering the restaurant's location was in a residential area filled with people of Italian descent and the fact that quality food from the old country was hard to come by—Patsy was known to get many key ingredients shipped directly from Sicily via contacts in Detroit—this development was not all that surprising. Notorious Chicago gangsters like Tony Accardo, Sam Giancana, Sam Battaglia, Joseph Aiuppa, and Jackie Cerone frequented Patsy's for its authentic Italian food as well as for use of its back room and parking lot for important meetings to conduct their secret underworld business affairs.

identify him by the way he moved. Turncoat Nick Calabrese testified at the Family Secrets trial that he was informed by one of the assassins himself that the five men who took part in the top-priority mob rubout were Lombardo, Spilotro, Joey Hansen, James "Jimmy the Lapper" La Pietra, and Frank "Frankie the German" Schweihs, with Hansen delivering the head shot that killed a dazed and bleeding Seifert. Furthermore, a witness identified Tony Spilotro as driving one of the escape vehicles that sped out of the factory parking lot.

The bottom line was that Danny Seifert, a father of three young children and not yet thirty years old, was dead—brutally slain so that villainous and cold-hearted men like Joey Lombardo and Tony Spilotro could avoid incarceration and The Outfit could maintain a stronghold over a union pension fund. For Seifert's wife and children, there was little solace to be taken. It was an insurmountable price to pay to benefit people and a crime syndicate that had such minimal regard for human life in the face of illegal profit.

# 5.

## Desert Don
### The Ant Makes His Move to Vegas

Whereas **Danny** Seifert didn't mean to get so heavily entrenched in mafia business, Tony Spilotro knew what he was getting into and what the consequences could be all too well.

Las Vegas had been a mob cash cow since the 1940s when notorious wiseguy, Benjamin "Bugsy" Siegel was sent out west by the New York mafia to create an environment that would become a continuous waterfall of illegal profits for organized crime syndicates across the country for nearly fifty years.

In 1971, The Outfit's primary liaison in Vegas, Marshall Caifano, was on the outs with the organization's leadership. Sent to Vegas in the mid-1950s with an edict to keep

a low profile, Caifano, a career criminal who was tapp lead The Outfit's regime in the desert by former don "Momo" Giancana, had developed a reputation as som who was unable to stay in the shadows. Caifano, know his peers as "Johnny Marshall" or "Johnny Shoes," loud, incorrigible, and apt to make a scene whenever wherever he felt like he was being slighted.

This type of behavior had become very bothers to the powers that be in Chicago, and by the start of 1970s, with Giancana out of power as well as out of country, the table was set for Caifano's removal. The Ou wanted their interests in the sand-filled oasis—prima in the form of tens of millions of dollars being illega siphoned from hotel and casino profits in an operati known as "The Skim"—looked after with as little fanfa and controversy as possible.

Enter Anthony "The Ant" Spilotro, a thirty-one-ye up-and-comer with the Windy City mob's enforceme who at the time was viewed by most in the Chicag world as a standup wiseguy who knew how to foll and had loads of leadership potential. Although eventual legacy in Las Vegas would end up worse than that of Caifano in terms of being and out of control, this was not the case in point in time, The Ant elicited a great de from his superiors within The Outfit and feelings that he was sent to Vegas to repl Chicago mafia's overlord of the Strip golden boy and its most lucrative and i It appeared to be a match made in h at first.

It was in his father's restaurant, while working as a busboy during his early teen years, that Tony was introduced to The Outfit, men he would end up working for for the rest of his life. Tony's mob involvement started at the age of fifteen, when he dropped out of Steinmetz High School and, along with a childhood pal Frank Cullotta, started a street gang. Made up of other young juvenile delinquents whom they had met around the neighborhood while skipping school and causing trouble, the gang specialized in stealing anything that wasn't bolted down. If they could get their hands on it, they tried to steal it.

Tony was tiny in stature but had a demeanor that was as ferocious as a lion, and on January 11, 1955, at age sixteen, he experienced an underworld rite of passage—in hoodlum terminology he "popped his cherry," meaning he was arrested for the first time. The charge was petty larceny as he was caught attempting to steal a men's dress shirt from a department store in the upper-class suburb of River Forest. Fined ten dollars and placed on six months' probation, Tony's criminal career was off to an inauspicious start. Nonetheless, it was the beginning of something big. By the end of the decade, Tony had become a fixture at local police stations around town, having been arrested fifteen times by his twenty-first birthday.

"Spilotro got a quick start on the streets," said Jim Wagner. "From the time he was young, he knew he wanted to be a gangster and he did everything in his power to make fulfilling his desire a reality. Eventually, the cops and the crooks took notice. He figured if he got on the cops' radar and made enough noise, he'd get The Outfit's attention. And that's exactly what happened."

\* \* \*

**LEADING** his street gang for a few more years, making a name for himself as a top-grade tough guy on the city's West Side, Spilotro eventually got noticed by some of the very men he used to encounter while working for his dad at the restaurant. For criminals in Chicago, The Outfit was the big time. Getting recognized by them was the underworld equivalent of a Minor League Baseball player getting called up to the big leagues. That's what happened for Tony when Outfit powers James "Jimmy the Turk" Torello and Vincent "Vinnie the Saint" Inserro took a liking to him and began using him for jobs. Things for Tony and the Second City's nationally renowned crime syndicate started off small but gradually began to grow. After a few years under Torello and Inserro, Tony was recruited by Salvatore "Mad Sam" DeStefano, a well-known and highly feared gangster who gladly welcomed The Ant into his crew of henchmen and under his mentorship.

A protégé of former Outfit boss Paul "The Waiter" Ricca, DeStefano had built a reputation for being one of the area's top mob enforcers, a sadistic hit man with few equals in the nation's underworld. Not only would Mad Sam kill his victims for sheer pleasure, he would also torture them in the most heinous ways possible.

As a result of the overwhelming joy he derived from his duties on behalf of the Chicago mafia, DeStefano, although a highly valued commodity on the street, was never officially asked to join The Outfit or get made. In a nutshell, the syndicate hierarchy thought he was too mentally unhinged to become an official part of their rank and file and would likely be impossible to control. Using his skills as a leg breaker and assassin was good enough for them. And Mad Sam didn't seem to mind either, since he enjoyed being his own boss and felt that being initiated into the crime family would force him into adhering to too many rules and regulations for his liking.

Under DeStefano's tutelage, Tony undoubtedly developed his own taste for killing. It was widely suspected by local law enforcement that a young Tony Spilotro aided DeStefano in the murder of local Outfit strong-arm William "Action" Jackson. Working as a collector for a loan-shark operation being run by Outfit heavyweight William "Willie Potatoes" Daddano, Jackson was thought to have been moonlighting as a police informant. Whether he actually was is still up for debate; however, the fact that he was suspected to have been working for the other side of the law was, and still is, reason enough to get you killed in the Chicago underworld.

According to FBI informant reports, DeStefano, his younger brother Mario, and Spilotro grabbed Action Jackson when he was leaving a local bar and took him to a meat plant where they tied him to a meat hook and began beating him with baseball bats and steel hammers. Then they applied an electric cattle prod to his testicles until he passed out from the excruciating pain. While unconscious, the trio of hit man continued beating their victim mercilessly. Leaving him hanging on a meat hook, the group went out for a cup of coffee. When they returned, Jackson was dead. His corpse was discovered days later in the trunk of a car on Lower Wacker Drive.

**HAVING** thoroughly impressed The Outfit's leadership during his tour of duty with DeStefano and his crew, Tony caught the eye of then–boss Sam Giancana. One day during the early months of 1962, Spilotro was approached by Vinnie Inserro, a top lieutenant of Giancana's, and asked to go to a face-to-face meeting with the much-revered don. The purpose of the meeting, which took place at Giancana's headquarters, the Armory Lounge, was reassignment. Realizing his talent as a first-class enforcer and labeling him a fast riser on the local streets, Giancana told The Ant he was placing him under the guidance of legendary Outfit assassin Felix "Milwaukee Phil" Alderesio.

In charge of the crime family's enforcement unit, Alderesio was The Outfit's go-to guy for all the Chicago mafia's top murder assignments and a large majority of its strongarm work. After telling Spilotro of his new assignment and how impressed he was with the work he had been putting in, Giancana dismissed him. Not long after the conversation, Inserro picked Spilotro up from his house and took him to a personal introduction to Alderesio and his partner in crime, Charles Nicoletti. Giancana then called for a meeting with Alderesio and Nicoletti and told them to look after the syndicate's newest young star and teach him the finer aspects of the killing trade—things a wild card like DeStefano often neglected to do in his work.

After Tony had worked with Milwaukee Phil for several months, the Windy City mob brass, as well as Alderesio himself, felt The Ant had put in enough work for his crime family superiors to be initiated into The Outfit. It was every young Italian hoodlum's dream to "receive his button" and Tony took the honor very seriously. Before the initiation was to take place, Tony was given instructions to participate in another high-profile murder that would cement his status as a future made man. In the mafia, this was called "making your bones." Most of the time when up-and-coming mob initiates make their bones, it is the first time they participate in a murder. This wasn't the case for Tony, who had put in wet work for The Outfit before. But because this killing—a double homicide—was so important, he was included and told that after it was completed, he would get his wish—full membership in the legendary crime syndicate that dated back all the way to the nation's most notorious mobster ever, Al "Scarface" Capone.

The victims were Billy McCarthy and Jimmy Miraglia and the hit took place in May 1962. It would go down in infamy as "The M&M Murders" and would be depicted in its full gruesome nature in the motion picture *Casino*.

McCarthy and Miraglia were independent burglars and wannabe wiseguys who worked out of the city's North Side. Being partners in crime, one was rarely seen without the other in tow. While having drinks in a local bar one night, they got into an argument with the Scalvo brothers, two of the bar's owners. The bar's third and final owner was a close associate of former Outfit boss Paul Ricca, which made the bar and all of it owners off-limits to any funny stuff or violence. But Miraglia and McCarthy were each only twenty-four years old and wet behind the ears when it came to local underworld protocol. They didn't adhere to that rule and decided to kill the Scalvos.

One night in early May, McCarthy and Miraglia tracked down the Scalvos and killed them, along with a waitress from their bar that just happened to be walking with them. To add to the duo's problems, the killings took place in the tree-lined suburb of Elmwood Park, an area that was off-limits from criminal activity because so many of the area's top gangsters lived there and an area in which the "M&M" boys had been pulling robberies. The triple murder brought a great deal of media attention to the bedroom community, the exact thing The Outfit's upper echelon was trying to avoid by residing there.

Needless to say, this incident didn't place McCarthy and Miraglia in good standing with the Windy City mafia. Within hours of the murders, hit contracts were issued on both of them. Tony was put in charge of setting the whole thing up. He called his old pal Frank Cullotta, who was known to associate with the intended targets, and told Frank to bring Billy McCarthy with him to a meeting in the parking lot at a Chicken House restaurant on North Avenue. Cullotta obliged and when they arrived, Tony took McCarthy inside for a meal. When they exited the restaurant, Tony pulled a gun and ordered McCarthy into a waiting car occupied by Alderesio and Niccoletti. He was transported to a nearby warehouse where Tony's old boss, Mad Sam DeStefano was waiting for them.

McCarthy was beaten severely with hands, fists, and bats. He even had ice picks put through his testicles. But despite the continuous savagery, he wouldn't give up the whereabouts of his partner. At that point, Tony impressed his superiors and made his mentor DeStefano proud by putting McCarthy's head in a vise and popping the Irishman's right eye out of his skull until he finally told his tormentors where they could find Jimmy Miraglia. Only then did Tony finally put McCarthy out his misery by slitting his throat.

Miraglia's murder was somewhat less complicated.

Tony located him and took him at gunpoint to an Outfit-owned liquor store and locked him in the store's storage room until Alderesio, Niccoletti, and DeStefano arrived. While they waited, Miraglia, sometimes called "Sonny," got drunk on some of the liquor. When the rest of his murderers arrived, he was three sheets to the wind and begging for Spilotro and the rest of the killers to get their job over with as quickly as possible. Not putting up a struggle, Miraglia was beaten, strangled, and eventually killed by having his throat slit just like his partner.

Within months of the M&M murders, Tony earned his proverbial seat at the table. In the fall of 1963, with Phil Alderesio as his sponsor, he was formally inducted into The Outfit by Sam Giancana and Anthony Accardo. For the next several years, Tony continued to make a name for himself on the Chicago streets as a man to be reckoned with in the strong-arm game. During that time, he also worked as a bail bondsman throughout the city's court system, bailing out his many criminal associates from various local lockups, and was a suspect in almost a dozen gangland homicides.

In between trips to Florida to look after a variety of Outfit interests, including its most profitable odds maker, Frank "Lefty" Rosenthal, Spilotro kept busy handling a great deal of the Chicago mafia's dirty work.

Alderman Ben Lewis; bookmakers Irving Vine, Kenny Gordon, and Arthur "Boodie" Cowan; jewel thief Guy "Lover Boy" Mendola; and Outfit enforcers Leo Foreman, Al Romano, and Angelo Boscarino were all murdered between 1963 and 1968, and in all nine homicide investigations, the name Tony Spilotro appeared as a prime suspect. Even his former mentor, Mad Sam DeStefano, made it onto The Ant's hit list; he was shot to death in April 1973.

FROM as early as the 1930s, long before Las Vegas became the city of sin it is known as today, the Chicago mafia had representation in Nevada. Even back to the days of The Outfit's most notable mob boss of record, Al Capone, the Windy City crime syndicate held numerous interests on the West Coast. Capone and his cohorts had money tied up in movie studios in Los Angeles and in gambling houses in Nevada outposts such as Reno and Lake Tahoe.

Before Capone went to prison for tax evasion in 1933, he sent a lieutenant of his named John "Handsome Johnny" Roselli to oversee these various business ventures. In California and Nevada, Roselli soon became recognized as the man you needed to see if you wanted to deal with the Chicago mafia out west. After over thirty years holding down the post for his bosses in The Outfit—a job that then included looking after the large investment the Chicago mafia had made in the Las Vegas hotel and casino industry—Roselli was forced into semiretirement due to law enforcement hassles brought on mainly as a result of his high-profile behavior.

With Roselli unable to continue his duties for The Outfit because of tight scrutiny from the police and the FBI, Sam Giancana and Anthony Accardo dispatched Marshall Caifano to Las Vegas to aid Roselli. Within a few years of landing in Vegas, Caifano fell victim to the same fate as Roselli and came under too much heat from law enforcement as a result of failing to keep a low enough profile; he was called back to Chicago by his superiors in the mob in the early 1970s.

That brings us to 1971, when fast-rising Outfit golden boy Tony Spilotro was pulled from his job on the streets as an enforcer and placed in Las Vegas as the Chicago mafia's new man out west. This suited Spilotro just fine because his face was becoming a fixture in local newspaper headlines and television broadcasts, which pegged him as a top area hoodlum and future mafia leader. The heat was on heavy and that prevented him from being able to maneuver unfettered through the Second City's underworld as he once could. Vegas, he thought, would be a perfect place to reinvent himself.

His job, just like Roselli's and Caifano's before him, was to look after and protect the crime family's interests on the West Coast, most specifically their investments in the lavish and star-studded world of Vegas casinos. These gambling palaces had few equals in the world and accounted for major cash flow into the pockets of Outfit royalty.

Tony, his wife, Nancy, and their four-year-old son, Vincent, arrived in Las Vegas in early May 1971. Once there, he was re-paired with Outfit gambling specialist and boyhood friend Lefty Rosenthal, who had left Florida in the late 1960s and relocated to the Nevada gaming paradise. Around the time Tony surfaced in the desert oasis, Rosenthal, who started out his life in Vegas running his gambling operations out of the Rose Bowl Sports Book, was placed by The Outfit in the Stardust hotel and casino, in an attempt to have an authority running things inside the casino for them.

If Lefty was Mr. Inside, then Tony was Mr. Outside, sent there to make sure nobody interfered with Rosenthal or the illegal profits being stolen from their various casino count rooms controlled by the Chicago mob. Like his predecessors, Spilotro was instructed to keep his head down and out of the view of the public, the media, and most important, the police. And for a very short period of time, he did.

Attempting to maintain a facade of run-of-the-mill domesticity, the Spilotros moved into a modest three-bedroom home on Balfour Avenue in a middle-class section of town and, with the help of Rosenthal, joined the prestigious Las Vegas Country Club. Tony and Nancy enrolled their son in a local highly regarded Catholic school and signed up for the PTA. When Vincent was old enough to play Little League Baseball, the couple didn't miss a game and sat alongside the other parents in the grandstand cheering on the team. As a front, Tony bought space in the newly built Circus Circus hotel and casino, a gambling and entertainment complex geared toward families, and opened up a gift shop.

Unfortunately for Spilotro, the act didn't play for long. Within months he was being hounded by the cops in Vegas just as much, if not more so, than when he was back home in Chicago. Tony had wasted little time imposing his will on the city's underworld. He was quick to make certain every big-time criminal and half-ass wiseguy alike knew he was the new boss in town. Unlike Roselli and Caifano before him, who made a lot of noise acting like gangsters but pretty much just benignly romped around the desert playground, milking their position of authority for all it was worth, Tony saw the city as an untapped gold mine. With such fertile ground for illicit gains and unsupervised debauchery, Spilotro invisioned creating his own personal mafia empire and immediately went to work showing the whole town what a real Vegas kingpin could and, in his mind, should be. The fact that this type of behavior was the exact opposite of what was desired by his bosses in Chicago failed to deter him.

"Las Vegas had never seen anybody like Tony Spilotro," said a former law enforcement agent. "A lot of guys came out to the desert and liked to play gangster and lot of real gangsters came out there too but, for the most part, left their criminal affairs behind them wherever they came from. This guy was a hard-core wiseguy through and through, and when he came to town and didn't have anyone looking over his shoulder, he went wild. I mean real cowboy stuff that the cops and public weren't accustomed to. He probably killed a dozen people just to let people know he was serious and that a new regime was starting up. Back in the day, when Bugsy and lot of the New York and early Chicago guys got there, they were trying, at least on the surface, to act like businessmen. Tony was a gangster and he didn't know any other way to act, nor did he care to try to sugar-coat his persona for anybody. He was just a typhoon of illegal activity that came in and stayed for fifteen years to everybody's great dismay."

Bringing in a group of close to thirty men from the Midwest to make up a crew of subordinates and help him to get the city in order, it wasn't long before he began shaking down anyone he could find. He sent for Herbert "Fat Herbie" Blitzstein, a Jewish enforcer from the North Side of Chicago known for his mutton-chop sideburns and loud clothing selection, to be his right-hand man and primary buffer between him and the street. He took old friends Paul "Paulie the Indian" Schiro, Joey Hansen, and Chris Petti, and stationed them in Arizona, Los Angeles, and San Diego, respectively, to act as fences for stolen property and look after Outfit interests on his behalf. It wasn't long before three of his brothers, John, Victor, and Michael, had at least partially relocated to Nevada and joined Tony's crew as well.

Doing something that had never before been done in Vegas, he imposed a citywide street tax—strong-arming every bookie, loan-shark, drug dealer, pimp, and thief he could get his hands on into paying him a piece of their profits in order to operate. From his office inside his gift shop at Circus Circus, he started his own bookmaking and juice loan racket, eventually getting dealers and casino employees from every casino on the Strip—most of whom were degenerate gamblers, alcoholics, and junkies themselves—indebted to him in one way or another. Recruiting a cadre of professional card cheats and burglary experts to be part of his crew, he began taking down big-money poker games in a number of the casino's card rooms and robbing out-of-town bigwigs in their hotel suites via tipsters he had stationed across the city.

Anyone who resisted Spilotro and refused to get with the program was outright done away with—killed in cold blood. During Tony's first six months in town there were six unsolved homicides of local loan sharks who scoffed at the notion of lining up behind the new regime. Over the next five years, there would be more gangland-related murders than in the previous twenty-five years combined. Jerry Delman, a Vegas-area bookmaker and former Chicago associate of Spilotro's; Joseph "Red" Klimm, a casino pit boss; Marty Bucceri, an Outfit-connected blackjack dealer; Rick Manzi, an Outfit associate; and Tamara Rand, a silent investor in one of the mob-run casinos and hotels, were all suspected to have been murdered either by Tony himself or by his crew on his orders.

The Ant also put a number of police officers and casino executives on his payroll, and soon he knew the skinny on all of his biggest adversaries. As a result, he was able to combat much of what they were trying to do to stop him. Everybody fell in line. It became crystal clear who was running Vegas. It wasn't the mayor. It wasn't the city council. It wasn't the cops. It was Tony "The Ant" Spilotro. The desert had its first don.

# 6.

## Boosting the Boss
### The Big Tuna's Revenge

Bodies were popping up everywhere—mangled and tortured corpses being found in cars and the trunks of cars all over Chicago in the frigid early months of 1978. One person disappeared all together, conspicuously absent from his everyday life in the Windy City, but never found. When all was said and done, ten people were murdered or presumed dead, each of their lives taken in the wake of a daring burglary that took place in a suburban River Forest home on January 6. But, this was not just any home. This was the residence of the city's reigning mafia don, Tony Accardo, a man of very few equals across the nation's gangland landscape. A person who could have a life ended with one phone call or even a simple nod of his head. Unfortunately for the men who planned and carried out the risky and ill-advised home invasion, he was also a man of little patience when it came to being disrespected. For a mafia head of state like the Big Tuna, brazen acts of defiance and breaches of mob protocol resulted in swift and often painful retribution. As most in the city were acclimating themselves to the new year, reentering the workforce after a few days off to celebrate the holidays, the relatives of the murder victims were spending the first portion of 1978 making funeral plans. Ten men. All of them the victims of what was one of the most horrific and bloody purges of mafia dissidents in the history of the underworld.

The fateful break-in at the home of Tony Accardo that set this string of nearly a dozen gore-ridden homicides in motion was preceded by another audacious break-in of sorts—a daring diamond heist that was carried out at one of the biggest jewelry stores in Chicago in late December 1977 and deemed by authorities in local law enforcement as the most lucrative jewel robbery of the decade. During the week before Christmas, a Saturday to be exact, a crew of Outfit jewel thieves, led by thirty-one-year-old career criminal and alarm expert John Mendell, invaded Levinson's Jewelry Store. After almost twenty-four hours of work inside, they walked away with over $1 million in cash, jewels, and fur.

Under most circumstances, a score of this magnitude, pulled off by a veteran and skilled crew like the one headed by Mendell would be greeted by The Outfit with great cheer and fanfare. However, due to some key lapses in judgment on Mendell's part, this was not the case.

The owner of Levinson's Jewelry Store, located on Clark

Street in the north end of The Loop, was Harry Levinson. In addition to owning and operating his jewelry store for over fifty years, Levinson was rumored to operate an Outfit-backed sports book and loan-shark operation on the side. He also was known to be a good friend of Tony Accardo's. Brought up during Prohibition in a Jewish section of the city, Levinson once worked for Hymie Levin, who, in his heyday, was one of the biggest bookmakers in Chicago. Levin was a close acquaintance of Accardo's, kicking up a large amount of tribute payments from his wide-scale booking operation to the Midwest mob boss. This was how Levinson was introduced to and became friendly with Accardo, and this is why his business was off-limits to The Outfit's vast network of professional thieves.

But John Mendell didn't play by the rules. He foolishly bypassed the crime family's standard chain of command and neglected to get an okay to knock over the jewelry store from his direct superiors in The Outfit. If he had, he would have been informed to stay away from Levinson's store due to the owner's relationship with Accardo. Mendell—known as one of the best high-end burglars in the city, and for being arrogant and stubborn—saw the score, took it down, and decided to deal with the repercussions of his actions after the job was done. This decision, along with the one to take his frustrations out on Accardo's personal property that followed, cost him and his crew their lives.

**JOHN** Mendell was born in South Dakota in 1947. His family came to the United States at the turn of the twentieth century from Ukraine and settled in the center of

America's Badlands. Dropping out of a small South Dakota high school during his junior year, Mendell relocated to Chicago in the mid-1960s, planting his roots on the city's rugged South Side. Quick to meet up with members of The Outfit's theft unit, he cut his teeth as a professional criminal throughout the late 1960s and early 1970s. Although he spent a portion of his twenties doing a couple of stints in prison for drug dealing and burglary, he actually established a sterling reputation as one of the best in the city at circumventing complex alarm systems. Thus he became a valuable commodity in underworld power circles across the area and was often tapped by The Outfit to take down top-end scores on its behalf.

"Mendell was as one of the premiere burglars in Chicago during the 1970s," said former FBI agent Jack O'Rourke. "He was known as a great entry man and knew all the security systems department stores and jewelry shops used like the back of his hand. He had a crew behind him, and they were all real professionals. These guys were taking down only top scores, nothing small scale. If the mob was looking to pull off big-time smash-and-grab jobs, the Mendell crew was one of the first places they turned."

In 1967, Mendell's name showed up on the Chicago Police Department (CPD) blotter for the first time when he was arrested and charged with the murder of an underworld associate he believed to be cooperating with law enforcement against him. The charges were eventually dropped when the prosecutor failed to find enough credible witnesses for the case, but the incident put Mendell on the CPD's radar as a possible up-and-comer with the Chicago crime family—someone willing to pull the trigger to rid himself or his bosses of a problem. By 1971, he had taken his first Outfit-related bust, when he was arrested, along with syndicate heavies Sam Bills and Ronnie Jarrett, for hijacking a quarter of a million dollars of aspirin off a delivery truck near the Wisconsin border.

Soon, he was making enough money to move out of the down-trodden south suburbs to the more ritzy north suburb of Lincolnwood, where he purchased a nice-size two-story house with his new wife, who was over a decade his senior. With his new influx of cash, he began dressing in more expensive clothes and driving nicer cars. He was able to do all this while hiding under the guise of being a floor manager at his father-in-law's West Side tool and die shop.

As a matter of practice, Mendell used to attend trade shows in the jewelry industry to case potential victims. At one particular show in the early autumn of 1977, he spotted Levinson, a master salesman, showing off his newest acquisition—the Idol's Eye, a highly coveted seventy-carat hulk of a diamond that he had recently purchased from a jewelry magnate in London. Levinson's asking price: a cool million dollars. Upon seeing the Idol's Eye, Mendell, the master crook, had his mark.

If Mendell knew of Levinson and his connections within The Outfit before targeting him for the job is a question still up for debate. Whether he knew and didn't care or didn't know and just failed to check his proposed heist with the powers that be in the crime family, the fact is he planned the complicated score for over two months. He cased the store for over three weeks and recruited just the right group of thieves to make up his crew. By late December, he was ready to make his move.

On December 21, Mendell and three others broke into the jewelry store via a bathroom window, using an acetylene torch to cut through the rusty steel bars that guarded the store from intruders. In order to remain undetected, Mendell used his trademark skill and bypassed myriad exceedingly complex alarm systems. Spending close to twenty-four hours inside the store, the crew made its way into and through four separate safes, looting as much cash and merchandise as they could get their hands on. To Mendell's dismay, the largest safe the group encountered, the one containing the prized Idol's Eye diamond, couldn't be cracked, and the group had to leave behind the one piece of jewelry they had gone in trying to get.

Nevertheless, it was a monumental score, the biggest of all of the burglars' careers, and they celebrated accordingly. According to FBI surveillance reports, Mendell and several others were observed partying late into the night in the days before Christmas at the posh and celebrity-filled Pump Room, as well as in a number of other fancy restaurants, bars, and discotheques in and around the city's Rush Street nightlife district.

**UPON** arriving at his store on the Monday morning after the break in and finding it in shambles, Levinson was in a state of shock. He had never been burglarized before, probably because he was known to be too close to the city's crime syndicate to touch. However, there he was, smack dab in the middle of a disaster site. The showroom was a mess, extensively rummaged through and filled ankle deep in water, which had been used by the bucketful during the heist to cool the steel as it was cut through by the invaders' blow torches. He called the police. He called his insurance company to inform them of what had transpired and that he would soon be filing a claim on the stolen merchandise. And then he made his most important call of all: he called the Big Tuna.

Meeting with his old friend Tony Accardo the day after the robbery at one of Accardo's favorite haunts, the North Side bistro Chez Paul, Levinson expressed his extreme displeasure. Not one to mince words, Accardo echoed his friend's sentiments and assured him that he would take care of the problem immediately. What happened next is another matter still up for debate. Some believe Accardo had his lieutenants reach out to the group of bandits and numerous fences to whom they had already laid off some of the merchandise, reclaim the stolen goods, and return them to Levinson only a few days later. Others believe that after retrieving the stolen items, Accardo returned a portion of them, fenced the rest through his most trusted vendors, and split the cash among his inner-circle.

Regardless of the specifics, it's known that Mendell and his crew lost their monumental score and were severely reprimanded in the process by Accardo's underlings. With the situation seemingly resolved, Accardo and his wife left Chicago and headed to their winter home in a plush, secluded area of Palm Springs, California.

Though most people involved in the incident thought the matter was done and over, John Mendell apparently failed to receive the memo. He was seething with anger and resentment. Despite being told who Levinson was connected to, he couldn't understand or accept the fact that

Accardo would favor a Jewish associate over people who had been tirelessly working for him on the street, grinding out a living in the lurid underworld to fill his bank book. As the New Year came and went, Mendell hatched a plan for revenge.

Getting his crew back together, Mendell decided—in an act of supreme stupidity and contempt—that they would break into Accardo's house while he was away in California and retake what was still there from their score. Why he would tempt fate by taking his aggressions out on a person as dangerous as Accardo probably will never be determined. But the fact is that on January 6, Mendell and his crew broke into The Big Tuna's residence, again bypassing an intricate alarm system, and took anything and everything they could find. Fortunately for Accardo, they missed his biggest hiding spot: a ten by fifteen foot chrome steel vault that housed most of the Big Tuna's prized possessions, including over a quarter of a million dollars in cash, hidden in a basement-size cove concealed behind a mirror in the home's foyer.

Nonetheless, the damage had been done. When the estate's caretaker, Michael Volpe, arrived the next morning, he was greeted by overturned furniture, vandalized art work, and strewn drawers. Immediately calling his boss in Palm Springs to inform him of the incident, Accardo jumped on the first flight available and high-tailed it back to Chicago to deal with the situation. The mafia kingpin had been violated in a display of supreme defiance. Accardo was fuming. And from that point forward, Mendell and his cronies were living on borrowed time.

"When I heard about the Accardo break-in, there was no

question in my mind it was Mendell and his crew that had pulled it off," said Jack O'Rourke. "Everybody knew that Johnny Mendell was the only guy who could probably pull something like that off. Not many people could outsmart an alarm system like he could. In a lot of ways that skill served him well on the street. He got a lot of jobs because of it. But in this case, it worked against him. I mean if we knew who did it, Accardo and his boys did too."

**TONY** Accardo was no stranger to killing in the name of protecting his property. He had done it before. Specifically, close to fifteen years earlier, when Accardo was suspected to have ordered a murder contract on a man named Van Corbin. A builder, part-time thief, and former neighbor of the don, Corbin had been hired by the Accardo family to oversee construction on their home. Accardo, a man who liked to keep his affairs as secret and discreet as possible, made it clear to Corbin that he was under no circumstances to divulge the floor plans or blueprints of the house he was building for him. Corbin, who was generously compensated for the job, agreed. However, two years after the residence was completed, Corbin found himself in financial crisis and the target of an investigation by the Internal Revenue Service. In an effort to ease the pressure the government was putting on him, Corbin offered to show the FBI his copies of the Accardo home blueprints. The FBI gladly and with great eagerness accepted the offer. Word of what his ex-neighbor had done made it back to Accardo—some actually believe that Corbin himself, in hopes of mitigating the damage of his mistake, told the mafia boss of his indiscretion—and suddenly the man who used to dine and occasionally go on fishing trips with the Big Tuna was in much more trouble with the mob than he had ever been with the government. His life was no longer worth the cost of the paper that his death certificate would eventually be printed on. Within a month, Corbin was gunned down by two masked assailants in the parking lot of the motel where he was hiding.

Like in the case of Van Corbin, it didn't take long for mob justice to be meted out to the perpetrators of the Accardo home invasion. Two weeks to be exact. The first body of the break-in team to be discovered was that of Bernard Ryan, a three-time convicted felon and close associate of Mendell's. On January 20, two weeks to the day after the burglary, he was found in the driver's seat of a Lincoln Continental on a side street in the western suburb of Stone Park, his throat slit and four bullet holes lodged in the back of his skull.

Thirteen days later, Ryan's well-known right-hand man, Steve Garcia, also a close associate of John Mendell's, was found in the trunk of his car, which had been left in a Sheraton Hotel parking garage. Enjoying the first few weeks of 1978 in Miami, Garcia had been lured back to the Windy City by the prospect of another score. Authorities in law enforcement believe it was Ronnie Jarrett, a sometime associate of Mendell's, who had made the call to set him up. It's believed Outfit hit man Anthony "Little Tony" Borselino helped carried out the execution. Garcia, like Ryan, had his throat slit from ear to ear. However, unlike Ryan, who had been shot in the head, he had been stabbed numerous times in the chest and stomach with an ice pick.

The proverbial hit parade continued when, on February 4, just two days after authorities found Garcia as trunk music, the police found an abandoned Cadillac in the south suburban parking lot of Esther's Place restaurant, which contained two more bodies: Vincent Moretti and Donald Renno. Moretti was a former cop who was kicked off the force after a felony burglary conviction and had become a feared Chicago-area hoodlum, not to mention one of The Outfit's top fences. Renno, who some speculate may not have been involved in the break-in at all, was a small-time thief who often did jobs with both Mendell and Moretti.

Both Renno and Moretti had their throats cut, but it was obvious the mob assassins had paid special attention to the ex-police officer who was seen wearing a pair of the Big Tuna's prized gold cuff links around town in the days after the burglary. Moretti had been beaten so severely that the blunt trauma to his chest had caused several of his ribs to break and one of his kidney's to rupture. He also had been castrated and his penis had been placed in his mouth, the ultimate sign of disrespect in gangland slayings.

The murders of Moretti and Renno took place several days before at a Cicero bar, located at Twenty-second and Laramie, which was owned by an associate of South Side mob chief John "Johnny Apes" Monteleone. Moretti and Renno were called in after the establishment had closed for the night under the pretense that they would help Accardo's lieutenants retrieve some of their boss' stolen property. According to Nick Calabrese, the pair were beaten and strangled to death by Calabrese himself, his brother Frank,

Johnny Monteleone, Tony Borselino, and Frank "Goomba" Saladino, while Joe Ferriola and Jimmy La Pietra acted as lookouts. Among Chicago mob circles, the brutal double homicide became known as the "Strangers in the Night" murder, since the famed Frank Sinatra hit song was playing on the jukebox in the background as Moretti and Renno were slugged and stomped into oblivion.

The next body to be found was that of the heist crew's mastermind and leader, John Mendell. Mendell was probably the first victim to be killed because he disappeared on January 15, just over a week after the Accardo house break-in. But he wasn't found until five weeks after the fact, on February 20, when police officers came across an abandoned vehicle sitting parked on the street of a South Side neighborhood, covered in ice and snow, its windshield plastered with parking ticket violations. When the police opened up the car's trunk, they discovered Mendell, frozen stiff, half-naked, and hog-tied. He had been stabbed numerous times in the chest with an ice pick and, according to the autopsy report, most likely died by strangulation as a result of being tied up in such a way that if he moved his legs or arms he would tighten the noose wrapped around his neck.

After another two months passed, Accardo's henchmen succeeded in eliminating the rest of Mendell's crew. On April 14, Johnny McDonald, a suspected member of the group of thieves and someone the police believed aided in the setup of the Bernard Ryan hit, was found murdered in a West Side alley, his throat cut and a gunshot wound in the back of his head. On April 26, twenty-two-year-old Robert Toggs, the final and youngest member of Mendell's crew, was discovered in the trunk of his car in a grocery store parking lot off Grand Avenue. His throat had been slashed and he had been shot several times in the back of the head and neck.

**WITH** Mendell and his men eradicated in the first third of the year, things slowed down for a while. The killing rampage temporarily halted. However, there were still loose ends to be tied up, roadways that could lead back to the Big Tuna that had to be closed down. In October 1978, Michael Volpe, the seventy-five-year-old Sicilian immigrant that Accardo had looking after his home while he vacationed on the West Coast, disappeared. To this day, he's never been found. Five days before he was reported missing by his wife, Volpe, a slight man who spoke broken English, had testified in front of a grand jury that was investigating the January break-in and its bloodstained aftermath. The FBI is of the belief that Accardo ordered his caretaker to be killed for either divulging too much information to the government in his testimony or for possibly aiding Mendell's crew in the robbery.

Trying to do whatever he could to disassociate himself from the series of retribution killings, Accardo is alleged to have ended his epic purge by ordering the murders of two of his hand-picked executioners; First, often-used Outfit hit man Tony Borselino was found dead on May 22, 1979, in a desolate cornfield in Will County, Illinois, shot four times in the back of his head. Then finally, in mid-September, Gerald "Jerry the Dinger" Carusiello, a top lieutenant to Accardo's second in command, Joey Aiuppa, was slain in suburban Addison, seemingly in the midst of carrying out what he believed to be a burglary, but what was in fact a setup to kill him.

The FBI had traced phone records from Carusiello to some of the victims in the hours leading up to their murders, and they were pressuring him to cooperate in their investigation. To prevent any information he had from getting into the wrong hands, Accardo and his inner circle decided he had to be done away with. The Outfit's reign of death was at last over. Ten bodies in twenty-one months. Mob justice had been rendered.

"It was just a gruesome bloodbath that took place for about a year after the Accardo burglary," said Jack O'Rourke. "I would bet some of the guys that got killed had nothing to do with the break-in at all. A couple of them were just made examples of because they were known burglars and friends with John Mendell. I wish I could tell you what the guys who did [the break-in] were thinking. These guys had worked with The Outfit for years, so they had to know what the end game was. Sometimes I guess you just outsmart yourself. You think you're so good at something; you'll never have to answer for your actions. But with the mafia in Chicago, you're always going to answer. They're brutal killers, looking for excuses to kill. Mendell gave them that excuse. And for Accardo, I think this string of homicides says all you need to know about him. He was quiet and unassuming, yet this showed how vicious he could be if and when you crossed him."

If there was anything positive that came from the string of treacherous gangland homicides that encompassed the final two years of the 1970s, it was the search warrant the

FBI was able to obtain that gave it access to Tony Accardo's River Forest residence. The disappearance of Michael Volpe provided the government with the probable cause they needed, arguing to a judge that Volpe's employment at the house was sufficient reason to believe a search of the premises could potentially bear fruit for the investigation. On November 11, 1978, the FBI agents assigned to the case got their wish and were granted access to the mafia don's prized abode at 1407 Ashland Avenue.

Once inside, they were quick to uncover a hidden panel in the foyer that led to a secret basement encampment, the size of a moderately sized home. It encased a full-size, modern kitchen, a bedroom, an office, and a cavernous conference room, nearly fifty feet in length. Surrounded by thirty-four chairs, with a full-length movie screen on the back wall, the entire room was constructed in top-grade marble and finely polished oak. They also discovered the monstrosity of a safe that the Mendell gang failed to find and a rather large, almost oversize furnace room, revealing a half dozen incinerators. Agents wondered how such a room could be used.

Although some curiosities were fulfilled, nothing of significance was found that could be used in solving the murders or making a case against The Big Tuna. It wasn't until more than twenty-five years after the final body dropped in Accardo's spree of revenge killings that three of the homicides—Mendell, Moretti, and Renno—were put at the doorstep of Outfit hit man Frank Calabrese, who was charged in the 2005 Family Secrets case.

# 7.

## All in the Family
### The Breeze Brothers

Frank and Nick Calabrese came from humble beginnings. They grew up on the city's predominantly ethnic West Side, the area around Grand Avenue and Ogden, at that time known as "The Patch." With immigrant parents who barely spoke English, Frank, the eldest child—born March 17, 1938, had to quit school at a young age and work to help the family survive. Selling newspapers and shining shoes on the corner of State and Grand Avenue went a long way toward putting food on the family's table. As a teenager he was a petty thief, sometimes doing odd jobs and running errands for Frank "Feech" Furio, a street lieutenant under West Side mob boss Fiori "Fifi" Bucceri and his protégé and future South Side mob czar, Angelo "The Hook" La Pietra.

"Growing up, Frank was always a bully," said one former neighbor who chose not to be identified by name. "He was big and strong and, in my mind, got his rocks off by picking on those around him who were weaker basically because he could. Nick was quieter in his demeanor and followed Frank around a lot. You could talk to Nick, and he would try to look out for you, sometimes even try to protect you from his brother. Frank was closed off. Nick wasn't like that, he wanted to be your friend. But Nick still idolized his brother, and it was obvious he wanted to chase his path. . . . It didn't surprise me to see what they eventually became."

Spending some time in the U.S. Army and stationed in North Carolina, Frankie Breeze went AWOL when he didn't get let off from duty after the conclusion of the Korean War like he had been promised by his recruiter. Incarcerated in a Missouri military stockade, he escaped twice, the final time taking his first arrest as a civilian when he was busted stealing a car from the St. Louis airport in 1954. Stuck back in jail until he was twenty-one, Calabrese eventually returned home to Chicago and within a few years developed into a well-respected presence in the local underworld.

Frank started out as a truck driver, ferrying dairy products all across the city and into the suburbs, while moonlighting as a top-notch burglar, cargo hijacker, and all-around strong arm. He was married in 1961 and through his father-in-laws' connections gained employment with a local Teamsters Union. Still moonlighting, he became a commodity on the street and was called up for duty by The Outfit. At first, he worked for Steve Annerino, a go-to guy for rising mob capo Angelo La Pietra, and then graduated to working for La Pietra directly.

When La Pietra moved his base of operations to the South Side's Chinatown district, an area of the city in which he had been authorized by The Outfit brass to create his own sub-crew, Calabrese followed him. With the help of Cheech Furio and a street mentor of his named Larry Stubich, Calabrese opened up a loan-sharking operation, a racket that would eventually turn into his bread and butter, and a sports gambling business. Furio ran a series of back-door card games on his behalf, and a street tax was eventually imposed on legitimate businesses he deemed ripe for the picking. Patrons of Calabrese's gambling operations who got in over their heads were steered to his juice loan racket to take out a street loan. It was a vicious circle that would end up making him a multimillionaire.

Influence in local labor politics arrived via his new brother-in-law, Ed Hanley, the president of the local Culinary Workers and Bartenders unions. He then began dabbling in construction and real estate purchases. By the late-1960s, Frankie Breeze was known throughout the city as a top racketeer, and by early in the following decade, he was given permission to head his own subcrew under the new La Pietra regime on the South Side. Earning the dual reputation as a money-maker and genuine tough guy, he was labeled a rising star.

Benefiting from The Outfit's unique power structure, a highly respected solider such as Frank Calabrese, could head a crew without being a captain. The Outfit hierarchy allowed for capos to break their individual crew down into subcrews and appoint a street boss for each. This method of command distribution was put in place under Tony Accardo in the 1940s and resulted in maximum insulation for the crime family's administration. The theory was that by having faith in the lower ranks of the syndicate and adding more leadership positions, you boost troop morale and decrease the chances of jealously and in-fighting among the chain of command.

Soon, Frank developed himself a second niche in the local underworld: murder. The Calabrese street crew emerged in the late 1970s as a primary enforcement unit for La Pietra, at that time probably The Outfit's most powerful capo. Unlike some other often-used mob assassins in the area, Calabrese didn't flaunt his reputation as a hit man. He preferred to keep that profession on a need-to-know basis; most thought he was just a loan shark.

Around Halloween 1969, Nick Calabrese approached his big brother Frank about the prospect of employment. He was sick of working at the series of Teamsters jobs Frank had gotten him—one of them was as an ironworker on the construction of the John Hancock Tower—and he wanted to go to work for the family business. He wanted a spot in his brother's crew. Called to a meeting in May 1970 at Slicker Sam's, an area restaurant owned by reputed Outfit soldier Salvatore "Slicker Sam" Rosa, Nick was told by Frank that La Pietra said it was okay for him to join up with his operation.

Frank started Nick off doing collections, and within three months had him involved in the plot to murder Michael "Hambone" Albergo. Nick, who married the niece of reputed Outfit member, William Louie "The Printer"

Tenuta, established himself as a sturdy and reliable man of honor in his own right, impressing La Pietra with his workmanlike effort on the street. Throughout most of the 1980s, he held a no-show job at a forklift company in the heavily mob-influenced McCormack Place industrial park, getting a paycheck without having to report for work. He began a collection of antique cars and often took fishing trips with his nephews in Wisconsin at a cottage he owned.

Pleased with their work, La Pietra sponsored both Frank and Nick for membership within the crime family, and in October 1983, in the bas nent of a closed restaurant near the corner of Roosevelt and Manheim, the brothers were formally initiated into the Chicago mafia by don Joey Aiuppa.

All wasn't peachy keen though and over time, a growing animosity started to fester between the pair of siblings: Frank was jealous of his brother's close relationship with his own sons, and Nick suspected Frank of holding back on his kick-up cash to La Pietra and holding out on properly compensating him and the rest of his underlings.

**IN** the 1980s, Frank Calabrese set up shop at M&R Auto and Truck Repair Service, a River Grove–based repair garage that would act as his headquarters through the next decade and a half. His crew was tight knit, if only for the fact that its members shared an equal fear and hatred of their boss.

"With Frank, you saw two distinct sides to him," said Tom Bourgeois. "One minute he could be laughing and joking with you and seem to not have a mean bone in his body. The next minute, with the snap of a finger, he could turn on you and have a demonic look in his eyes like he wanted to strangle every inch of life out of you with his bare hands. He was menacing. A lot of his subordinates walked on eggshells around him because they couldn't predict his moods."

The core of Frank's crew was made up of Cheech Furio, Frank "Goomba" Saladino, Louis "Louie the Baker" Bombacino, Phillip "Philly Boy" Fiore, Terry Scalise, Philip "Philly Beans" Tolomeo, Nick Calabrese, and Frank's two sons, Kurt and Frank Jr. The crew became masters of the old-fashioned bust out. Whenever one of Calabrese's customers got substantially indebted, the crew would take over the business—skimming cash and running up charges on company accounts with no intention of repaying any of it—and seize the customer's personal assets as a way of making up the debt.

Cheech Furio acted as Frankie Breeze's top lieutenant, handling daily affairs for the crew's operations until his death in 1985, at which time Philly Boy Fiore took over those duties. Divorced from his first wife in 1984, Frank next married Diane Cimino. Accumulating a mountain of moola from his cluster of rackets, he invested in real estate and silently backed several restaurants, where he enjoyed holding court, retelling war stories, and playing the role of mob boss. He even expanded his crew's operations outside of the Chicagoland area, starting a satellite gambling business in Rockford headed by Goomba Saladino, who had relocated there, along with his cousin Joseph "Big Joe" Saladino and Frank "Frankie the Fireman" Geraci, a boyhood pal of the Calabreses.

Alleged to have orchestrated close to two dozen gangland homicides, the downfall of Frank Calabrese ultimately resulted from the way he treated those he surrounded himself with. When his degrading antics caused loyalty to wane among his inner circle, he was through.

His overall demise would eventually come in the form of betrayal by his own flesh and blood, his son, Frank Jr. and his brother, Nick. But before that, a large part of his downfall came in the form of two scorned former friends, Philly Beans Tolomeo, a one-time Chicago cop turned crook, and Matt Russo, a business partner who thought his friendship with The Outfit king could protect him from his wrath.

Joining the Calabrese crew in 1978, Tolomeo became Frankie Breeze's point man on the crew's behemoth-size loan-sharking business. At his peak, Tolomeo had over a hundred customers on juice, reaping the crew the benefit of huge interest payments on their original loans. These funds were collected on a weekly basis by the crew's street heavies, Louie Bombacino and Terry Scalise.

Five years into his career working for Calabrese, Tolomeo was accused of skimming profits from his numerous collection routes, not turning in full shares of the ever-thickening till. He was beaten severely for the indiscretion by Frank Calabrese himself, who broke his nose and several ribs while dealing out the punitive assault. He was also forced to sign over the title to his mother's Elmwood Park home to Nick Calabrese's father-in-law. Upset with the treatment he received, Philly Beans turned to the FBI and began providing information on the Calabrese crew, and by the mid-1990s, he had entered the witness protection program.

Matt Russo was the owner of the crew's headquarters, the nerve center of the city's biggest loan-sharking racket, the M&R Auto and Truck Repair Service. He bought the business with startup money provided to him by Frank Calabrese, so Calabrese considered himself a silent partner. Behind on bank loan payments, Russo borrowed $20,000 in cash from his partner. He then got behind on the payments for his street loan and was quickly devoured by Calabrese's predator-like instincts.

Even though he was close friends and business partners with Frankie Breeze, he wasn't spared the usual treatment. Always looking for quick-and-easy ways to line his pockets with cash, Calabrese decided to bust out Russo's most lucrative asset, the auto repair business, which was his own headquarters. In fact, Frankie Breeze had been starting to exploit M&R even before Russo got into debt. including using it as a site for meetings and for cash distribution sessions.

As a means of repaying his debt, Russo was instructed to begin filing false invoices for repair work never performed and eventually was forced to sell his home to Calabrese. Fearing for his safety, he fled to the FBI. Wired for sound, Russo began making what would end up being hundreds of hours of tape recordings of life in and around the ruthless Chinatown mob chief. The tapes would be devastating court evidence.

"The instant we got Russo wired up and on the street, the case against Calabrese was sealed," said Bourgeois. "He talked his way into the indictment. I don't think he suspected that Russo was cooperating so he was more loose lipped in his presence. The information we got from

Philly Beans Tolomeo got the investigation jump-started, but after Russo started to cooperate we had him cold."

The icing on the cake in the case being built against the Calabrese crew came when Louie "The Baker" Bombacino, a protégé of both Tolomeo and the late Louie Eboli who took Tolomeo's place after his defection, ordered one of his street toughs to assault an undercover cop believed to be a recalcitrant customer. Then The Baker got arrested for attempted jury tampering. His blunders made it a slam dunk: Frank Calabrese, tough guy, killer, and Outfit mob chief, was falling. And fast.

The indictment for what the government categorized as a multimillion-dollar loan-sharking operation came down in 1995, ensnaring the entire crew. Plea agreements followed, and guilty pleas were entered the following year for all four Calabrese men: Frank, Nick, Frank Jr., and Kurt.

The Calabrese family shared Christmas dinner together in December 1996, where upon leaving for the night Nick gave Frank a rare kiss on the lips. Maybe he knew things were never going to be the same again. Maybe he just had too many cocktails at dinner and was just in an affectionate mood. Either way, it would be the last time the two brothers would ever see each other outside the confines of a federal courtroom.

In early 1997, Frank and his kids were incarcerated in Milan, Michigan, and Nick was sent to do his sentence in Pekin, Illinois. Spending a lot of his time behind bars socializing with Outfit power James "Jimmy the Man" Marcello, who was serving a stretch for a racketeering conviction, Nick immediately began vocalizing his displeasure with the conditions under his brother's regime. Apparently, he was also bothered by his brother's treatment of his nephews, who Nick believed had been physically and emotional abused by their father.

Marcello sensed that Calabrese might be a weak link. He worried that because Nick could tie him to the Spilotro brothers hit as well as possibly others, he would be personally vulnerable at the first inkling of Calabrese's discontent. When scuttlebutt about the reopening of a previously unsolved gangland homicide that had the recent addition of physical evidence pointing to Nick reached Jimmy the Man, he was downright petrified.

Jimmy tried to remedy his vulnerability by sending Nick Calabrese's wife cash payments of $4,000 dollars per month via his contacts on the outside, specifically through his half-brother, Michael "Big Mickey" Marcello. In the end, it wouldn't be enough. With the amount of physical evidence thrown in his face by the FBI, Nicky Breeze was in too tight of a corner. No amount of money could have bailed him out. The avalanche was coming down and Jimmy Marcello and Frankie Calabrese, were about to get crushed. Nick Calabrese was ready to sing like a canary and the FBI was waiting with open arms. Hello Operation Family Secrets!

# 8.

## Chinatown
### The Twenty-Sixth Street Crew

Both Frank and Nick Calabrese were members of the Twenty-sixth Street crew, one of The Outfit's most notoriously ruthless and violent subfactions. Also known as the South Side crew and the Chinatown crew, the group had a rich and storied history in the city's underworld.

"The guys from Chinatown have always been the heavy hitters, the ones you went to when you needed some serious work done," said former FBI agent Jack O'Rourke. "They have the most influence in local politics and almost all of the crew's soldiers are deep in the trenches, not afraid to get their hands dirty. It's a lunch pail, working-class group of criminals down there on Twenty-sixth Street. That's the way they are now and that's the way they've been forever."

The crew's first capo, Bruno "The Bomber" Roti, dates all the way back to the days before the rule of Al Capone. Roti was one of Chicago's original Black Hand extortionists—a racket that swept across major American cities in the early portion of the last century, threatening Italian and Sicilian immigrants in handwritten letters with physical harm if they did not immediately fork over money. He also became one of the inaugural batch of initiates under Capone when The Outfit was created in 1931.

Getting his nickname The Bomber early on in his criminal career due to a propensity to blow up the cars and homes of those who refused to give into his demands in the Black Hand racket, Roti was named one of the crime family's first territory bosses. He was given authority over the near South Side, which included the vice-filled Chinatown district at Twenty-sixth Street and Wentworth Avenue. Over the years, the crew became known for its deep ties in the local government and the people to come to if you needed a job with the city or a city-based contract. Roti's son Fred became the alderman for the extremely influential First Ward and one-time First Ward political powers Pat Marcy and John D'Arco are rumored to have been made members of The Outfit. As a result of these ties, the crew developed into a hotbed of labor union infiltration. Roti's family, friends, and criminal associates alike all benefited with jobs and perks. Reporting directly to The Outfit's political fixer extraordinaire, Gus "Slim" Alex, Bruno Roti and the mob's men from Twenty-sixth Street made life as smooth sailing and as hassle free as possible for Tony Accardo and his crime family.

When Bruno Roti died in 1957, the reigns of the Twenty-sixth Street Crew fell to his son-in-law, Frank "Skids"

Caruso Sr., who made a name for himself in the Chicago underworld by running one of the biggest sports wire services and horse-betting operations in the entire area. Caruso's wire room was located at Twenty-second Street and Wentworth Avenue, right next door to a fire station. It was run by two of his top gambling lieutenants, Anthony "Tony B" Bova and Anthony "Blind Tony" Vinci, and became a breeding ground for up-and-coming young South Siders and aspiring hoodlums, like Frank Calabrese, the La Pietra brothers, and Caruso's own sons and nephews. If he wasn't at the wire room, Skids could most times be found at the Bowery Lounge on Twenty-second Street. The Bowery was where Caruso and Gus Alex were known to hold court with their subordinates and collect tributes from their numerous rackets, which included gambling, juice loans, extortion, and jukebox and vending machine businesses.

Caruso's oldest son, Frank Jr., also known as "Toots," "Tootsie," or "Tootsie Babe," was intent on following in his father's footsteps. He started at a young age as a runner for his dad's wire service. Soon, he graduated to making collections for the family loan-sharking and bookmaking businesses. And then, alongside one of The Outfit's top burglars, Richard "Richie the Rat" Mara, he is alleged to have begun doing armed robberies, overnight heists, and home invasions.

Being groomed to eventually take over his father's South Side empire, Toots Caruso set up a headquarters at a restaurant he opened called The Hungry Hound, in the heart of Chinatown and used it as a base of operations for himself, his brothers, Bruno and Peter, and his first cousin, Leo. By the early 1980s, Toots was ensconced in the president's chair of Local 6 of the Laborers International Union of North America, and was a delegate to the city's district council. Toots's younger brother Bruno would become president of Local 1001 of the County, Municipal Employees, and Foreman's Union, in 1994 and shortly thereafter was made president of the entire Chicago District Council, before being ousted for his mob connections in 2003.

As Skids Caruso began getting up in age during the 1970s, he started to prepare for the inevitable transition in leadership his crew was going to undergo in the coming years. With his son Toots still too young to become a capo, Skids tapped Angelo "The Hook" La Pietra, to take on the role on a temporary basis, as he primarily stood on the sidelines and offered counsel from semiretirement in Florida. La Pietra had come up under and was tutored in the ways of The Outfit by West Side crime boss Fiore "Fifi" Bucceri, before moving his own burgeoning vice empire south to Chinatown.

After Skids Caruso died in 1983, La Pietra, sometimes called "The Bull," took over as full-time capo of the crew, and his headquarters at the Italian-American Brotherhood social club became the epicenter of the area's criminal commerce. Under La Pietra, Frank Calabrese, one of the Hook's top protégés, built his loan-sharking operation up to become the biggest and most lucrative in the city. Calabrese put so much money into La Pietra's pocket, that he and Nick ascended to the rank of the crew's premiere enforcement team, collecting from the toughest debtors and being assigned the most important hit contracts.

"Angelo La Pietra was a real pro," said O'Rourke. "He

was well versed on every aspect of being a gangster, and he made no bones about who he was. In the history of the South Side of Chicago not many wiseguys held more stature than La Pietra. He was small, only about five five, five six, but incredibly intimidating,. He carried himself with tremendous moxy. When he walked or drove through the neighborhood, everybody took notice. The Calabrese brothers learned everything they knew from him. Especially Frank, who tried to emulate him in every way possible."

**IN** the 1980s, the Chicago underworld saw growing profit margins due to a robust economy, but these were also tumultuous times for the Twenty-sixth Street Crew and The Outfit as a whole, in the form of a boatload of rats. Chinatown crew members Richie Mara, Charles "Guy" Bills, and Gerry Scarpelli as well as Outfit regulars Lenny Patrick, James "Jimmy the Panda" La Valley, William "B.J." Jahoda, James "Jimmy the Duke" Basile, Joseph "Joe the Undertaker" Granata, and Ken "Tokyo Joe" Eto all turned on the mob, testifying against members of The Outfit in court.

Without a doubt, the biggest blow dealt in the plethora of defections was that of Ken Eto, the most powerful Asian gangster to ever walk the streets of Chicago. Running a massive gambling empire for over twenty years out of the Golden 8 Ball Pool Room on Rush Street, Eto, who reported to North Side capo Vincent "Innocent Vince" Solano, made a fortune for himself and The Outfit by gaining a monopoly over the city's Bolita racket—a policy lottery ran out of Asian and Hispanic neighborhoods. At his peak, Eto, known for his snazzy custom-made wardrobe, was clearing over $1 million per month in gambling profits.

Although Eto didn't work directly under Angelo La Pietra and his South Side crew, his decision to become a turncoat nonetheless threw a major wrench into the survival rates of a number of Chinatown criminals. Eto laid off a good deal of his gambling action to members of La Pietra's crew and was partners with The Hook himself in several different weekly card and dice games around the area.

When he flipped, his debriefing by the FBI led him to divulge a great deal about La Pietra and helped them strengthen their epic Las Vegas skim case, titled "Strawman II," against him and fellow Outfit superpowers Joey Lombardo, Joey Aiuppa, and Jackie Cerone. His testimony in court in 1985 at the trial was one of the final nails in the proverbial coffin, aiding the government significantly in earning convictions of La Pietra, Lombardo, Aiuppa, and Cerone.

Unlike most of the other defections, Eto's was completely self-inflicted and could have easily been avoided. Arrested in a Melrose Park motel room in August 1980 and charged with running a large-scale gambling operation, Eto faced trial and the prospect of being incarcerated. This worried his superiors in The Outfit because they felt he was not mentally strong enough to do the possible time and could be tempted to turn against them. For The Outfit, these types of worries were quelled only by a murder contract. Thus, around Christmas 1982, one was issued for Eto by his captain, Vince Solano.

On February 10, 1983, only a few months before his trial on gambling charges was set to begin, Eto was called to a meeting with fellow North Side crew members Joseph "Big Joe" Arnold and Joseph "Little Caesar" Di Varco at the Hideaway Bar and Lounge, a mob gathering post on Wabash Avenue. While at the meeting, he was informed that Solano wanted to have dinner with him that night and he was to pick up John Gatuso, a Chicago cop who moonlighted as an Outfit strong arm, and Jasper "Big Jay" Campise, a high-level North Side bookie and loan shark, on the way.

Doing what he was told, Eto scooped up Gatuso and Campise in his Ford El Torino and made his way to the parking lot of the Montclare Theatre located on Grand Avenue, where he had been instructed they were to meet up with Solano. After turning off the engine, Gatuso, who was sitting in the backseat directly behind him, pulled out a 22-caliber pistol and put three shots into the back of Eto's head. With Eto slumped over the steering wheel, Gatuso and Campise exited the vehicle and fled to a waiting automobile that whisked them away from the scene. Unfortunately for the two assassins and The Outfit in general, Eto was not dead. Somehow the bullets had only grazed his skull and once his assailants had left, he was able to get out of the car and walk to a nearby pharmacy and call for help.

As soon as the FBI, got wind of what had happened and that Eto was in the intensive care unit at Northwestern Memorial Hospital, a fleet of agents ran to his bedside. Feeling betrayed by the mafia family he had worked so loyally on behalf of for over two decades, not to mention disrespected in lieu of the tens of millions of dollars he had made for them in his years of service, Eto had a lot to say.

The following day, Gatuso and Campise were arrested and charged with attempted murder. Just over a week later, Solano, Arnold, and Di Varco were called in front of a grand jury convened to investigate the incident—all three pled the fifth.

Freed on $1 million bail, the unlucky pair of mob executioners for some reason didn't seem that worried about their own fate. When asked by an associate if he was afraid for his safety Jasper Campise is alleged to have responded, "No, they told me they don't do that kind of stuff anymore."

He was wrong. They do. Five months later, on July 14, the heavily battered bodies of John Gatuso and Jasper Campise were found, stabbed and strangled to death, in the trunk of a car in a west suburban parking lot.


**ANGELO** La Pietra's imprisonment from his conviction in the Strawman II case left a power void atop the Twenty-sixth street crew that was quickly filled by his younger brother, James "Jimmy the Lapper" La Pietra. Keeping The Hook's rackets in check while he was away serving his time behind bars, Jimmy may not have been as feared as his elder sibling, but he was just as effective as a leader. The crew's financial bottom line kept booming during his seven-year reign as capo. The Lapper passed away in 1993 and John "Johnny Apes" Monteleone was simultaneously bumped up to Chinatown captain and overall Family street boss. In order to effectively look after the Outfit's daily affairs and oversee all the other syndicate capos, Monteleone broke his South Side crew into three sub-factions. According to a late '90s Chicago Crime Commission report, he allegedly assigned command over them to Frank Calabrese, "Jimmy" Di Forti, and Michael "Handsome Mike" Talerico. A nephew of both La Pietra brothers, Talerico was only thirty-one years old when he is alleged to have receieved the promotion. Under Monteleone's reign, the Chinatown crew expanded and took over the former crews in the south suburbs, Chicago Heights, and Northwest Indiana.

Regaining his freedom in 1996 after serving ten years in prison, The Hook was immediately bumped up in The Outfit's hierarchy to an "acting underboss" post that he would hold in the John Di Fronzo administration until his death in 1999.

Monteleone died in 2001 and it is alleged that Chinatown's prodigal son, Toots Caruso, then assumed the throne his father and grandfather once held. Officially named captain over the South Side in 2002, Caruso is currently the youngest of all The Outfit's territory bosses. He quit his position on the city's LIUNA District Council in the early 1990s due to pressure from the government; when he is alleged to have become a capo, he was the assistant director of the union's board of trustees and its nearly $800 million pension fund. His reputed promotion to crew boss, however, brought unwanted attention from law enforcement, and in 2003 a giant purge of organized labor in Chicago brought an end to the union careers of the entire Caruso family—Toots, his brother Bruno, and his cousin Leo were each ousted from their positions within the LIUNA when all the union's Windy City locals went into court-ordered trusteeship.

# 9.

## The Rundown
### Dauber's Death Race

William Dauber was in a race for his life. Less than a half hour after leaving the Will County Courthouse, where he had attended a pretrial motion hearing on the morning of July 2, 1980, Dauber, one of the city's most-feared mafia enforcers, was being chased in his car down a rural stretch of highway by mob assassins sent to kill him. They were shooting at him from two sets of automobiles and closing in fast.

The irony was clear—the hunter had become the hunted. And he wasn't alone. Sitting next to him in the front passenger's seat of his light blue Lincoln was his dearly beloved wife, Charlotte. To think the group of bloodthirsty hit men would spare her life if the couple were caught was foolish. The man they called "Billy the Chopper," or simply

"Choppers," knew the only way to save both his and his wife's lives would be to outrun them.

He floored the accelerator, but he could not lose his pursuers. The hit men knew if they failed in their assigned mission, they too could become the targets of future mob hits. It was a vicious circle and both Dauber and the men chasing him knew it all too well. The death race continued for several more miles, neither vehicle giving an inch. Then the executioners made their move. Dauber's fate hinged on his ability to triumph in the road battle he found himself entangled in. As the two cars behind him pulled alongside him with guns drawn, it was not looking good.

**DAUBER** was born and raised in Orland Park, Illinois, a South Side suburb of Chicago. He was a high school dropout who went to work as an Outfit debt collector before his eighteenth birthday. Hailing from German descent, he was fast to make a reputation for himself as a highly efficient strong arm; gamblers and juice loan clients would shudder with fear at the very thought of seeing him at their doorstep. By the time he had reached his early twenties, all the diligent work he had put in on the hardened streets of the Windy City paid off when he caught the eye of powerful South Side Outfit lieutenant James "Jimmy the Bomber" Catuara. Looking to fill the roles of driver, body guard, and personal one-man wrecking crew, he selected Dauber.

"Billy was one tough son of a bitch," said former FBI agent Richard Stilling. "He was an undeniable force on the streets, and people cowered at the mere mention of his name. The guy was a true mobster, someone who would do anything for a buck and wasn't afraid to get his hands dirty in the process."

Dauber's prominence within the mafia would come to a zenith throughout the 1970s, when Jimmy Catuara was assigned by The Outfit to lead an infiltration of the city's car theft racket, specifically the chop shops used by thieves to dissemble vehicles they had stolen so they could sell off the individual parts. Being Catuara's closest ally and most used strong arm, Dauber was tapped to act as the point man for the Chicago mob's plan to muscle in on what would end up becoming one of the crime family's most lucrative underworld trades ever.

Up until approximately 1971, independent car thieves in Chicago were allowed to operate in the city without paying tribute to the mafia. Dons Tony Accardo and Joey Aiuppa, realizing they had been missing out on extreme proft potential by virtually ignoring such a cash-friendly racket, sought to impose a street tax on any and all car thieves and chop shops doing business in the area. Because the majority of the city's chop shops resided on the South Side, the job of getting everyone in the business in line behind the Outfit fell to Catuara, Dauber, and Angelo "Little Angie" Volpe as well as a group of fearless and deadly mob enforcers known as "The Wild Bunch."

The Wild Bunch consisted of William "Butchie" Petrocelli, Jerome "Jerry the Witherhand" Scalise, Harold "Harry the Hook" Aleman, Anthony "Little Tony" Borselino, James "Jimmy the Ice Pick" Inendino, and Gerry Scarpelli. Almost all of these men were seasoned killers who willingly and sometimes eagerly engaged in acts of violence with the normalcy of a regular law-abiding citizen washing a load of laundry. Their activities and assignments were overseen by West Side caporegime Joe Ferriola—Aleman's uncle.

Even though most of the area's car thieves and chop shop operators were not in the mafia, they were far from criminal lightweights. The majority of them were hardened felons, men who didn't take well to being told what to do. This was especially the case when what they were being told to do significantly sliced into their bottom line, as was the situation when The Outfit decided to move into the previously unregulated racket.

In response to the new edict, a portion of these men scoffed at the prospect of cutting the mob in for a piece of their business. Known as an organization that didn't take well to insubordinates, those who refused to go along with The Outfit's agenda were killed with little hesitation or thought.

"Percentage-wise, the stolen car and chop shop racket would end up being the Chicago mafia's biggest money maker of the era, in terms of an overhead cost perspective," said Stilling, who oversaw the bureau's investigation into the mob's takeover of the industry. "The chop shops were such a valuable commodity. They were mainly a South Side thing, and the guys who were assigned to bring them all under The Outfit's flag were real hard-core gangsters. These guys were killers with not many equals. They were smart too, though, and really knew how to insulate themselves from us."

**THE** first salvo in what the local press would dub "The Chop Shop Wars" was launched in late June of 1971, when Robert "Bobby the Racer" Pronger was murdered after refusing to yield to The Outfit's demand to pay a street tax on his stolen car operation. Like many of the area's car thieves, Pronger maintained a career as a race car driver on weekends and owned an auto parts supply and repair business in the suburb of Blue Island as his day job. Employing a stable of about a half dozen fellow professional racers who went out at night looking for vulnerable automobiles to hijack, Pronger's business also served as an after-hours chop shop.

When he was first approached in the early days of April by Wild Bunch members Jerry Scalise and Gerry Scarpelli and told that the mob was going to begin requesting a monthly tribute starting immediately, he laughed in their face and told them to get lost. A few weeks later, Billy Dauber, flanked by Butchie Petrocelli, showed up at Pronger's business and reinformed him of The Outfit's new policy. After again not agreeing to pay the requested street tax, he was pushed to the ground by Dauber, kicked several times in the back by Petrocelli, and threatened with his life if he didn't comply.

The month of May came and went and still no tribute came from Pronger. Reported missing on June 17, the championship race car driver was never seen again. He was allegedly tortured, doused with acid, and killed, his remains found in a garbage pit in northwest Indiana almost two weeks later on June 29.

Pronger's murder was only the tip of the iceberg, the first of over two dozen homicides committed as a result of The Outfit's foray into the stolen car business. Guido "The Weed" Fidanzi, a notorious South Side car thief, was killed in August 1972. Michael Regan and Roger Roach, two associates of Fidanzi's operation, were both done away with in a hail of bullets as they entered a private residence a month later.

After a nearly three-year hiatus from the bloodshed, The Outfit murder spree resumed on June 16, 1975, when Harry Holzer, business partner of longtime chop shop operator Steve Ostrovosky and his girlfriend, Linda Turner, were shot to death in the garage of the duo's headquarters, South Chicago Auto Parts. Donnel Crawford and James Small, both chop shop specialists, were killed in November and December of 1975, respectively. Ostrowsky, who was a close friend of Dauber's, had been a top-rate earner for the mob for a good decade, but his reluctance to give up additional tribute to his bosses in The Outfit ended with his slaying on October 10, 1976.

Around 1977, Salvatore "Sammy the Mule" Annerino, one of Jimmy Catuara's enforcers and the owner of an extremely profitable chop shop racket himself, got into a beef with Joey Lombardo and was gunned down behind the wheel of his car in July 1977. That same year, Pat Marusarz, Joe Theo, Earl Abercrombie, Timmy O'Brien, Norman Lang, Richard Ferraro, and Jimmy Palaggi, all of whom worked for Annerino and Catuara, were done away with.

Some of these murders didn't sit well with Catuara. He was also upset with having a portion of his responsibilities and percentage of his rackets shifted to South Suburb mob power, Albert "Caesar the Fox" Tocco while he was away serving a short stint in prison. Never one to hold his tongue, Jimmy the Bomber, the original leader of The Outfit's chop shop takeover, opened his mouth to voice his complaints one too many times and found himself a victim of the blood-ravished purge as well. Catuara ended up being found in the trunk of his car in July 1978, his throat slit and two bullets in the back of his head.

The Chop Shop Wars lasted another five years; it wouldn't be until approximately 1983 that the city's entire car theft industry was completely controlled by the Chicago mafia. Over that period of time, more and more bodies continued to pile up: Don Lawson in July 1979, Edmiro De Jesus and Robert "Chick" Kurowski in May 1980, Charles Monday in July 1981, Harry Rosenbloom in November 1982, and Michael "Monk" Chorak in March 1983.

"The fallout from the takeover was pretty messy," said Stilling. "There was blood and guts all over the place. Anybody who even thought of disobeying orders was hit and hit hard. The entire operation showed just how brutal The Outfit can get when they want to or feel like they need to. If they want something done, it's going to get done, and people are probably going to end up dead as a result. It's hard for regular, everyday civilians to understand that, but that's the name of the game and the business these people are in."

**AFTER** close to a decade of terror that came down upon the South Side's chop shop operators, courtesy of Billy Dauber and his death squad, the law finally caught up to The Chopper. In November 1979, Dauber was indicted on gun and drug charges after he was caught attempting to make a large-scale narcotics deal with an undercover cop. Getting busted dabbling in the drug trade is to break one of the mafia's most cardinal rules, and Dauber knew he was going to have to answer for his behavior. With Jimmy Cataura, his biggest protector, long gone, he saw few options for himself and began cooperating with the Bureau of Alcohol, Tobacco, Firearms, and Explosives (ATF) in building a case against his cohorts in The Outfit. It was long rumored that Billy had been a Top Echelon informant for the FBI, but it was simply a theory, something that was never confirmed. His work with the ATF, on the other hand, was a different story altogether and one that led to his eventual demise.

Albert Tocco was worried that Dauber's drug bust might make him cooperate with authorities, so he assigned James "Jimmy the Duke" Basile, a veteran mob foot soldier, to keep twenty-four-hour surveillance on Dauber's activities to get a better gauge of his intentions. Sticking to his target like glue for a period of several weeks, Basile witnessed Dauber conduct various clandestine meetings with people he suspected were members of law enforcement. Once Tocco learned of Basile's findings, Dauber's fate was sealed. Dauber's duties as point man on the chop shop racket were reassigned to John "Johnny Hot Dogs" Manzella, and after Tocco consulted with Joe Ferriola, it was decided that Dauber would be killed. Clearing their plan of action with Tony Accardo and Joey Aiuppa, Tocco and Ferriola issued the murder contract and gave it to The Wild Bunch to be carried out as soon as possible.

For whatever reason, The Wild Bunch put the killing on hold for a few months. This did not sit well with their superiors in The Outfit. After witnessing an unscathed Dauber walking around town as if it were business as usual, Ferriola and Tocco turned their ire at the would-be assassins. Calling several members of the hit squad to a meeting, Albert Tocco reamed them out and told them that Frank Calabrese, a well-versed hit man from the Chinatown crew, was coming onboard to help them complete their task.

Jimmy Basile was again assigned to follow Dauber

around and get a feel for his daily schedule and habits so the killers could plan their assault. Meeting with Calabrese, Butchie Petrocelli, and Gerry Scarpelli for biweekly briefings on the status of his work at local diners, Basile made it clear that The Chopper's lack of a consistent routine would make the plotting of his execution difficult. Then, in an incredible stroke of good luck for the hit team and, in turn, bad luck for Dauber, a member of The Wild Bunch stumbled on the perfect setup. While attending a meeting at his attorney's office, an attorney he coincidentally shared with Dauber, he happened to glance at the secretary's appointment book and noticed that Dauber was scheduled to be in court at the Will County Courthouse on the morning of July 2 for a motion hearing on a gun charge. With the knowledge of his definite whereabouts secured, Dauber's murder contract was a full go, and his time left on this earth limited.

**WHEN** July 2 came around, Calabrese and The Wild Bunch were ready. They staked out the courthouse in two separate cars, waiting for Dauber to emerge from his hearing in front of the judge. Scarpelli, Petrocelli, and Ronnie Jarrett, Frankie Breeze's right-hand man, sat idling in a cream-colored van in a parking lot adjacent to the courthouse steps. Parked next to a meter down the street, Calabrese himself sat in a Mustang car nicknamed "Little Casey." Communicating via walkie-talkies they had purchased the previous day, the two cars of assassins patiently bided their time until they caught sight of their intended victim.

At around 10:30 in the morning, Dauber, alongside his wife and attorney, appeared outside the courthouse, their judicial proceeding just completed. Together with ATF agent Dennis Laughrey, Dauber's handler during his cooperation with the government thus far, the foursome walked down the street to a doughnut shop to eat breakfast, having no idea their every move was being watched. After finishing their meal, the Daubers' said good-bye to Laughrey and the lawyer, turning down an offer by the hard-nosed ATF agent to follow them home to make certain they hadn't been tailed. The decision to decline Laughrey's escort would be the wrong one and the couple would pay dearly.

Pulling away from downtown Joliet, where the Will County Courthouse is located, the Daubers began driving east bound on Manhattan-Monee Road. Under normal circumstances, Charlotte Dauber would be spared the same fate as her husband. But she had been on The Outfit's bad side for quite some time and the thought of killing her only sweetened the pot for the crazed-executioners. Known for aiding Billy in his street rackets and running her mouth constantly and to anyone who would listen about how she thought his services and performance were undervalued by the local mafia, Charlotte wasn't your typical gangster's girl. She liked to get her feet wet and her hands dirty. And it was that attitude and behavior that found her included in her husband's murder contract.

Cruising undisturbed on Manhattan-Monee for a few miles, the road quickly became a barren, two-lane highway. Billy lit up a cigarette and rolled down his window. He took a drag of the tobacco and for a brief period of time enjoyed the quaint silence and fresh air blowing into his car. The silence was short lived.

Without much warning, the two automobiles carrying

The Outfit hit squad came speeding up behind them. All of a sudden, one of the assassins fired a gun several times in their direction, trying to strike the Daubers' tire and halt their progress. It didn't take long for Billy to realize what was happening. The marker on his life was being cashed in.

Racing bumper to bumper for close to ten miles, neither vehicle would yield. When the oncoming traffic disappeared, the Mustang driven by Frank Calabrese passed the Daubers' Lincoln, getting in front of it in order to try to slow it down. The hit team's van, being driven by Jarrett, then pulled alongside the Lincoln, and Butchie Petrocelli, riding shotgun, fired at Billy with a semiautomatic pistol. Gerry Scarpelli opened the van's sliding door and took aim with a sawed-off shotgun, putting several rounds into the Lincoln backseat door panel. Undeterred, Dauber kept driving at as high of a speed as possible, doing everything he could to elude the shooters. Despite a valiant effort to save his and his wife's lives, the Chopper's luck was about to run out. Maneuvering the Mustang to the other side of the Lincoln, Frankie Calabrese swung in front, forcing the car holding Billy and Charlotte Dauber into an apple tree at the side of the road and eventually into a ditch.

Getting out of the van, Scarpelli walked over to the bullet-pierced automobile and dispensed shotgun blasts into both husband and wife, killing the Daubers instantly. Both work cars—the van and the Mustang—were driven into a set of bushes several miles down the road, doused with lighter fluid, and set ablaze. The weapons used in the hit were wiped clean of any fingerprints, dismantled, and thrown into the Cal-Sag Canal, a body of water that rests directly off Route 83. Although the brutal double homicide

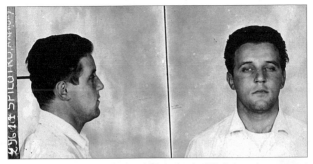

Chicago mob lieutenant Anthony "Tony the Ant" Spilotro, who was sent to Las Vegas by The Outfit in 1971 to oversee their interests in Nevada and the entire west coast. His execution set off a chain of events that led up to the Family Secrets arrests.
*Courtesy of the Chicago Crime Commission*

Michael Spilotro, slain younger brother of Tony Spilotro. Fearing future reprisals, the younger Spilotro, who idolized his big brother and, to his detriment, emulated much of his behavior, was included in Tony's execution in June 1986.

*All photos courtesy of the U.S. Department of Justice, unless noted otherwise*

Outfit crew boss Frank "Frankie Breeze" Calabrese, who for much of the 1970s, 80s, and 90s led the biggest loan sharking racket in Chicago and was linked to more than a dozen gangland slayings. Calabrese was so despised that both his son and younger brother turned against him and testified for the government against The Outfit at the Family Secrets trial in 2007.

Circa-1970s photo of Nick (fourth from left) and Frank Calabrese (arm around him) taken at Nick Calabrese's wedding.

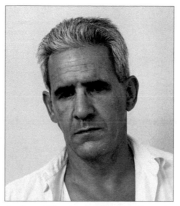

Nick Calabrese, brother of Frank, who became the only made member of The Outfit to ever turn government informant and testify against the syndicate in court, tying his older brother to over a dozen of the eighteen murder charges in the Family Secrets indictment.

Frank Calabrese, Jr., whose decision to turn on his father while the two were serving prison time together for racketeering and his subsequent letter to the FBI in 1998 were the sparks that ignited the Family Secrets case.

Anthony "The Big Tuna" Accardo, the nation's longest serving Mafia don, sitting atop The Outfit for nearly fifty years.

FBI mug shot of former Outfit boss Joseph "Joey Doves" Aiuppa, the Chicago mob stalwart with ties back to the day of Al Capone.

The infamous "Last Supper" photo of longtime Outfit don Anthony Accardo (sitting closest to the camera) and all of his top lieutenants, snapped at a mid-1970s dinner held in honor of dying mob lieutenant Dominick "Bells" Di Bella (second from left). Pictured (left to right, far side of table): Joseph Aiuppa, Dominic Di Bella, Vincent Solano, Albert Pilotto, John "Jackie" Cerone, Joseph Lombardo, (near side) Anthony Accardo, Joseph Amato, Joseph "Little Caesar" Di Varco, James "Turk" Torello.

FBI surveillance photo of (left to right) then–Outfit boss Joe Ferriola, Sam Carlisi (back to camera), Jimmy Marcello, and Rocky Infelice taken July 21, 1986.

LEFT: Early photo of reputed Outfit boss John Di Fronzo taken after a 1949 arrest for burglary during which he had a small part of his nose shot off and earned the nickname "Johnny No Nose."

RIGHT: Angelo "The Hook" La Pietra, now-deceased Chinatown capo who mentored both Calabrese brothers in the ways of the underworld. Released from prison in 1996, La Pietra became an "acting underboss" under John Di Fronzo until his death in 1999.

Crime scene photo of the Billy and Charlotte Dauber double homicide. The Daubers' car was run off the road and into a crab apple tree following a multi-mile chase with the execution squad—the notorious "Wild Bunch"—sent to kill them. Frank Calabrese was convicted in the Family Secrets case for taking part in the Daubers' murders.

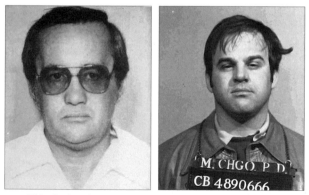

LEFT: Slain Outfit enforcer William "Billy the Chopper" Dauber, who was killed gangland style along with his wife following a high-speed chase in 1981 for being a federal informant.

RIGHT: 1970s mug shot of former Chinatown crew enforcer and Frank Calabrese, Sr., confidant Ronnie Jarrett, who was part of the group that murdered the Daubers. *Courtesy of the Chicago Crime Commission*

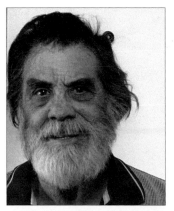

FBI mug shot of longtime West Side capo and mob boss Joey Lombardo, taken following his arrest in the Family Secrets case in 2006. Working his way up from shoe-shine boy to consiglieri of the Chicago Outfit, Lombardo was one of the most powerful and well-respected Mafia figures in the entire country.

Top Outfit associate Frank "Frankie the German" Schweihs, Joey Lombardo's right-hand man, bodyguard, and primary enforcer. Charged in the Family Secrets indictment, Schweihs died of cancer before the government could convict him for a slew of gangland murders.

The Family Secrets prosecution team following the conclusion of the trial in the fall of 2007, including top mob prosecutors John Scully (far left with glasses), Mitch Mars (center), and Markus Funk (right of Mars), whose hard work and expert courtroom battle plan led to the landmark convictions.

investigation garnered heavy media attention and several good leads, the prospect of solving the case was cold for twenty-five years.

**BILLY** and Charlotte Dauber's murderers didn't end up that much better than their victims. Falling out of favor with The Outfit hierarchy for stealing money that he was supposed to deliver to an imprisoned Harry Aleman, Butchie Petrocelli was killed six months after the Daubers. Called to a meeting at the Chinatown-based headquarters of South Side capo Angelo La Pietra on December 30, 1980, for what he thought was an assignment of another murder target for his Wild Bunch, Petrocelli was led to an adjacent office under the ruse that he was about to receive the specifics of the contract. However, as soon as he walked in the door, he was jumped by Frank and Nick Calabrese, Jimmy La Pietra, and Frank Santucci. With Gerry Scarpelli, Jimmy Basile, John Monteleone, and Frank Furio, standing lookout on the street, Nick Calabrese, La Pietra, and Santucci held Petrocelli down, while Frank Calabrese strangled him with a piece of electrical cord. To make certain the job was finished, Frankie Breeze cut his throat.

Scarpelli and Basile took Petrocelli's body, wrapped it in an old sleeping bag and put it into the trunk of a four-door Ford sedan parked outside. Per instructions from Angelo La Pietra, the car was driven by the Calabrese brothers to an abandoned tow lot under a freeway viaduct on the city's South Side and torched.

The body was not discovered until four months later. According to numerous reports, at some time during the morbid ordeal—either before he died or after—Petrocelli's head and chest were burned with an acetylene blowtorch.

Gerry Scarpelli's life lasted about nine years longer than Petrocelli's, but his ending, just like his former Wild Buncher, was far from pleasant. One of Scarpelli's long-time partners in crime, Jimmy Basile turned informant and began logging a mass of taped conversations between the two of them, concerning an abundance of illegal activity. Detained in a prison cell after he was caught red-handed by the FBI committing a home invasion in Michigan City, Indiana, and faced with knowledge of the Basile tapes, Scarpelli had little wiggle room. When word surfaced that his indiscretions had led his capo Joe Ferriola to issue a murder contract on his head and give it to his primary enforcer Ernest "Rocky" Infelice, Scarpelli agreed to become a government witness himself.

As a result of flipping Scarpelli, a mob soldier with an admitted eight murders under his belt, not to mention incredible insight into the inner workings of Joe Ferriola's West Side crew, the FBI had hit major pay dirt. Giving both written and videotaped confessions, Scarpelli divulged everything he knew, hoping the judge in his case would spare him significant prison time as reward for his cooperation.

Consumed with guilt in the months leading up to his time on the stand, he got cold feet about turning against his old buddies in the mafia and recanted the statements he had made against them. While he sat in his jail cell at the Metropolitan Corrections Center lockup in downtown Chicago, hoping that The Outfit, and especially Ferriola, who had since risen to don status, would find a way to forgive him for his misdeeds, his lawyers fought to have his confessions suppressed. In the end, Scarpelli didn't even wait for the ruling to come down and hanged himself in the shower room barely two days before he was going to get a verdict on his attorney's suppression motion.

Ronnie Jarrett would end up being gunned down in front of his home in late December 1999, dying in the hospital a month later. Frank Calabrese, the last of the Daubers' executioners left alive or not cooperating, would, in 2007, be forced to stand trial for those slayings and the murder of Butchie Petrocelli.

Although he wasn't killed, Jerry Scalise had his good fortunes undermined by a lengthy prison sentence overseas. Shortly after the Billy and Charlotte Dauber hit, Scalise, whose nickname "The Witherhand" derived from the fact that he was missing three fingers on his left hand, found himself in a London jail, after being convicted of a $3.6 million jewel heist that took place in Knightsbridge, England. The heist included the theft of the Marlborough Diamond, a $960,000 stone that had once been the property of Winston Churchill and was considered the most prized piece of jewelry in all of Great Britain. Returning to Chicago after his prison bit in London, Scalise, who also went by the street name "One-Armed Jerry" or "Jerry the Hand," stayed out of trouble for a while, but he was back behind bars in the late 1990s on a drug conviction. Recently paroled, Jerry the Witherhand, is back in his old stomping grounds of west Chicago and in the summer of 2008 acted as an on-set consultant for the feature film, *Public Enemies*. To this day, the Marlborough Diamond has never been recovered.

# 10.

## Terror at the Tee
Pilotto's Botched Execution

Going into the summer of 1981, Al Pilotto had a lot of factors working against his job security and personal safety. A capo of the south suburbs and The Outfit's territory in northern Indiana, Pilotto had recently been indicted in Florida alongside Outfit boss Tony Accardo, for allegedly receiving over $2 million in kickbacks from a labor union insurance policy. Notorious for wanting to cut ties with anyone and anything that could possibly lead to a criminal conviction and subsequent time behind bars, Accardo was not beyond putting murder contracts on even his closest and most respected lieutenants if he thought it was in his best interest. Accardo worried that Pilotto, already into his seventies, might not want to spend his remaining golden years in prison and could turn government witness. He was also quite upset because he believed Pilotto's poor mob management skills had led him into the legal mess in the first place. Pilotto was well aware of this and knew if his boss thought there was even the slightest possibility of him cooperating with the government in their case, he was a dead man.

Adding to his problems was the fact that with the knowledge of his precarious situation, certain members of The Outfit leadership sought to take advantage of his weakened position and started to plan a siege on his turf. Many wanted Pilotto out of the picture so they could start profiting from dealing drugs, an activity he was known to vigorously prohibit. The sharks were circling, and he could do little to combat the issue other than attempt to wait it out and hope it passed without incident.

According to FBI agents who worked the south suburbs, West Side capos Joe Ferriola and Joey Lombardo were scheming to get Pilotto out of the picture so they could take over his rackets. Some even believe Albert Tocco, Pilotto's trusted second in command, was plotting with Ferriola and Lombardo to kill his boss, so he could take over as capo while splitting the crew's assets and illegal business endeavors with his allies on the West Side.

Enemies were coming out of the woodwork. If he was to be safe from harm, he was going to need eyes in the back of his head. Given the storm of chaos that was gathering around him, it comes as no surprise that Al Pilotto's summer was anything but relaxing.

* * *

**BORN** in the city of Chicago in 1915, Pilotto grew up on the South Side, making money as early as the age of sixteen working for a bookmaking business ran by Outfit heavyweight Francisco "Frank La Porte" Liparota. His first run-in with the law came in June 1935, when he was arrested in a bar in Calumet City and charged with aiding an illegal gambling operation. La Porte, a former top lieutenant under Al Capone, took a liking to Pilotto and eventually made him his bodyguard and driver. In 1942, when Pilotto was only twenty-seven, La Porte, via his Outfit political connections, got him appointed president of Local 5 of the International Hod Carriers Building and Common Laborers Union. The local was based out of Chicago Heights, a city traditionally known as a hotbed for mob activity. Shortly thereafter, he was elected to the city labor unions' district council, eventually rising as high as vice president.

As La Porte's criminal empire grew throughout the south suburbs and parts of northern Indiana, Pilotto, his right-hand man, benefited greatly. In 1947, with La Porte sponsoring him, don Tony Accardo officially initiated Pilotto into The Outfit. Throughout the late 1940s and into the 1950s he saw his own stock grow significantly in mob circles due to his relationship with La Porte. The pair of wiseguys opened up a series of bars and strip clubs in Calumet City and taxed all independent criminals conducting business in the area. Out of several of these taverns and topless bars, they ran prostitution, juice loans, and gambling operations, even setting up a back-door casino at the

Owl Club, a restaurant and lounge that became the duo's headquarters.

Most evenings Pilotto could often be found at either the Palace Tap or the Club Palace, both of which he owned and both of which held high-stakes late-night poker games that he oversaw. Pilotto and La Porte's legitimate business front was the Co-Operative Music Company, which provided jukeboxes and slot machines to all the local mobbed-up watering holes, strip clubs, and restaurants.

For a period of time, Pilotto held a no-show job at Tony Accardo's Premium Beer distributorship, which sold his own brand of beer called Fox Head. On a tax return he filed in the late 1950s, he listed that he had partial ownership of Wilco Amusement and Tobacco Company, a vending machine business run out of Joliet.

He was forced to step down as president of the union in 1962 as a result of pressure being applied by the government to cleanse organized labor of unsavory influences, but his time away didn't last long as he was reelected to the post a year later. When Frank La Porte died of a heart attack in 1973, Accardo named Pilotto to succeed him as boss of the south suburbs, a position he held without incident until that fateful summer of 1981.

"Al Pilotto came up through The Outfit the hard way," said former FBI agent Jim Wagner. "He worked the streets for over forty years until he became a boss. As a result, he was old school in the way he did business. In some ways that hurt him because he wasn't willing to adapt to the changing times and that bred some resentment in the people he had around him. Drugs were starting to become a major money maker in the 1970s and 1980s, and he wouldn't turn his head and let his guys do their thing. This was a big reason why some of his loyalists were willing to turn against him. Plus, it didn't help matters that he got Tony Accardo in trouble. And then I remember the day we brought both of them into the office to book them on their case and Pilotto called Accardo 'boss.' It was in a joking manner, but it was in front of all of us, and Accardo shot him back a look that could kill. At that point in time, he didn't have many allies standing behind him."

**WITH** Pilotto's trial date fast approaching and a number of members of The Outfit becoming increasingly worried that he was going to flip, Tony Accardo didn't have a hard decision to make. He sent for Sam "The Gobber" Guzzino, Pilotto's driver and bodyguard, and Nick D'Andrea, Guzzino's right-hand man and a reputed mob assassin. In a meeting reported to have taken place in Florida, Guzzino and D'Andrea—a top suspect in a mid-seventies gangland homicide in Milwaukee—were allegedly told to begin making arrangements to have Pilotto killed before the start of their trial. Whether Albert Tocco or Joe Ferriola and Joey Lombardo played a role in convincing Accardo to issue the murder contract is unknown but, according to law enforcement reports regarding the plot, highly suspected.

Less than two weeks before Pilotto and Accardo's trial was set to begin in a federal courthouse in Miami, Guzzino had a meeting with his former son-in-law Danny Bounds and asked him if he would be interested in undertaking an assignment. After some discussion, Guzzino informed him it was a homicide he wanted committed. As someone who was not an accomplished hoodlum and had never killed before, Bounds was a bit reluctant. Attempting to entice him into accepting the job, Guzzino offered Bounds, an employee at Guzzino's taxicab company, a $2,000 down payment, with $8,000 coming after the assignment was carried out and a promotion to a better-paying position at work. In addition, Guzzino told Bounds that he would talk to his daughter about getting Bounds more visiting time with his young child, who he did not get custody of in the divorce. When Bounds was still hesitant to take on the murder contract, Guzzino tried to intimidate him by informing him that because he already knew a homicide was about to be committed, failing to go along with the plan could end up being a dangerous move. Feeling backed into a corner, Bounds accepted the offer.

Over the next forty-eight hours, Bounds met with Guzzino two more times, once at the cab company and another time at the Vagabond Lounge in Chicago Heights, a bar that Guzzino owned and a location often used as an after-hours mob gambling den. Present at both of these meetings were D'Andrea, Richard "Fat Richie" Guzzino, Sam's younger brother, and Robert Ciarrocchi, an Outfit weapon's specialist. Bounds' compensation and further specifics of the proposed murder were discussed at more length, and he was informed, for his own well-being, that he would not know who the target of the hit would be until a later date.

After the meeting at the cab stand, the five men traveled to an desolate, roadside field in Will County to test out weapons for the job. It was decided that a rifle was too loud and that it would be better to use two pistols instead. Leaving their target practice, the foursome drove by the Lincolnshire Country Club and it was pointed out to Bounds that was the location of the future hit.

Supplied with work clothes and a police scanner, Bounds was then shown a videotape of the Guzzinos' mother's seventy-fifth birthday party. During the viewing, Sam Guzzino froze the tape on a frame that showed a man on the dance floor. The man was Al Pilotto, and for the first time, Guzzino identified for Bounds the intended target of their planned assassination.

When Bounds learned that it was Pilotto they wanted him to kill, he became very nervous. He was well aware of Pilotto's significant status within the Chicago mafia and the fact that his brother, Henry, was the chief of police for the city of Chicago Heights. Trying to calm his fears, Guzzino told him that the hit "had been blessed" and that Pilotto "had a case coming up in Miami," "We're afraid that he's going to spill some names," Guzzino said to him.

It was explained to Bounds that on the morning of Saturday July 25—two days before the Pilotto and Accardo trial was to start—Sam Guzzino, Al Pilotto, and two of their associates were going to be playing a round of golf at Lincolnshire Country Club and that he was "to be hit on the course." The location of the assassination attempt was selected as a way to put Pilotto at ease because the foursome had played there together every Saturday morning for the past six years. Bounds was instructed to position himself in some bushes that were to the side of the tee-off point for the eighth hole and wait for the group to arrive in two separate golf carts after completing the seventh hole. As soon as Pilotto exited his golf cart, Bounds was told to come out of the bushes and shoot him as many times as possible. Guzzino warned Bounds to be certain not to be too loud when he approached his target because Pilotto was aware of the circumstances surrounding him and, "If he hears even a twig in those bushes crack, he's going to be in his cart and taking off." After completing his task, he was to run to a rendezvous point near the closest main road and meet up with Ciarrocchi, who would be waiting for him in a car to take him from the scene.

The next day, the Guzzino brothers and Ciarrocchi took Bounds out to the country club and put him through a test run of the planned hit. When the Guzzinos' drove up to the eighth tee in a golf cart, Bounds came storming out of the bushes and pretended to empty his gun. While being timed, he then ran as fast as he could to the roadside rendezvous point and jumped into Ciarrocchi's waiting automobile. The duo sped off and met back up with the Guzzino brothers at the clubhouse, where Guzzino remarked, "That was great, that was beautiful," and then treated everybody to lunch.

After shaving off his moustache and crafting a makeshift mask out of a nylon stocking, Bounds was ready to go. He was picked up in front of his home around 2:30 in the morning by Robert Ciarrocchi on the day of the hit and transported to an Outfit associate's apartment, where Richie Guzzino was waiting to help them complete final preparations for the big event. At the apartment, Ciarrocchi provided Bounds with a knapsack outfitted with a pair of leather gloves, two automatic pistols, and the police scanner the group had purchased a week earlier. Around 5:30, Sam Guzzino stopped by and assured everyone that the hit was "still a go"; he told Bounds to be sure to be in position in the bushes by 8:30.

Ciarrocchi and Richie Guzzino dropped Bounds off at the golf course at approximately 8:00, and he immediately got into place to perform his duties. The foursome soon approached the eighth hole, and everyone exited their golf carts. Despite his instructions to the contrary, nerve-wrecked Bounds allowed Pilotto to tee off before commencing the attack. With Pilotto standing in front of his cart and another one of the golfers preparing to tee off, he rushed out of the bushes and began shooting.

Hit in the shoulder and neck, Pilotto fell to the ground and began pleading with his assailant to spare his life. Ignoring the pleas for mercy, Bounds fired three more shots into Pilotto at a closer range and then sprinted off, nearly shooting himself in the foot as his gun misfired. Finally reaching Ciarrocchi in the getaway car, he realized that he had left the knapsack with the radio scanner in it behind at his hiding spot in the bushes. Pilotto, bleeding profusely from his wounds, was driven by Guzzino in the golf cart to a nearby condominium complex where an ambulance was called.

Miraculously, the barrage of bullets fired into Pilotto's body missed any major organs, and after nearly five hours of surgery he was stabilized, and his family was informed that he would survive. His brother, Henry, the police chief, set up a round-the-clock security team to guard his room and word quickly made it back to The Outfit that the assassination attempt had been unsuccessful. Everyone involved in the botched hit immediately felt severely unsettled, ill at ease at the prospect of answering for their shoddy work.

Each knew all too well that repercussions for such a misstep were severe and very possibly deadly.

The plot to kill Al Pilotto was essentially cursed from the moment Sam Guzzino decided to use his son-in-law, a man who was not a killer, nor a member of any street crew that would normally be tasked with such a treacherous duty. Guzzino's decision not to make adequate preparations for such a high-profile hit would soon bring doom to everyone involved.

**WHEN** Bounds showed up for work the day after the golf course shooting, he was called into a meeting with Sam Guzzino in his office. After being told by Guzzino that it appeared that their target was "going to be okay," Bounds apologized for not being able to complete the task he was given and offered to do anything he could to make up for his mistake. Guzzino let him know that the police had recovered his knapsack at the scene and that people—both law enforcement and the mob—were already speculating that he was the culprit. At this point, Bounds was told that it would in his best interest if he got out of town as quickly as possible. Richie Guzzino, who was also present at the meeting, gave him a wad of cash and the number of a friend in Atlanta that he could stay with. Fearing for his life, Bounds disappeared from Chicago for the next four months.

Fallout from the unsavory incident was inevitable and started right after Labor Day. Nick D'Andrea was found beaten to death in the trunk of a burning Mercedes in a Chicago Heights trash depository on September 13. Twenty-six years later, former mob hit man, Nick Calabrese, testified at the 2007 Family Secrets trial that he and fellow Outfit members, Sam Carlisi, Angelo La Pietra, and James Marcello were dispersed by The Outfit brass to interrogate D'Andrea as to the identities of the participants in the Pilotto assasination conspiracy. According to Calabrese, they bound his hands and feet, repeatedly pistol-whipped him, and bludgeoned him with the butt of a shotgun before realizing they had accidentally killed him without getting the desired intelligence. Knowing that at the very least Sam Guzzino was in charge of the operation, The Outfit set its sights on him to exact retribution for the bungled murder attempt. Nearly six weeks later in late October, Guzzino was found in ditch on the side of the road by a farmer in Beecher, Illinois, his throat cut and three bullets lodged in the back of his skull.

Hearing what happened to D'Andrea and Guzzino and the ongoing rumors that The Outfit was looking to kill him too, Bounds resurfaced in Chicago in the days following the Thanksgiving holiday and turned himself into the FBI. With no cajoling at all, he offered to cooperate.

The FBI was happy to oblige and immediately put him to work—he was sent back onto the streets wearing a wire. Recording several conversations between himself and his co-conspirators, Bounds aided the government in building an ironclad case against Richie Guzzino and Robert Ciarrocchi. On April 11, 1984, both were indicted for attempted murder and conspiracy to deprive a citizen his right to testify as a witness in a judicial proceeding. Both eventually were convicted and issued prison terms. Guzzino was sentenced to seven and a half years in prison and Ciarrocchi ten years. Each appealed their sentences, but both sentences were affirmed by the higher court.

Fully recovered, Pilotto was able to stand trial on his charges in Miami alongside his boss, Tony Accardo. Steadfastly refusing to turn against the don and the crime family that sought to have him brutally killed, he was convicted and on Septermber 14, 1982, sentenced to serve a twenty-year federal prison sentence.

Acquitted of the charges himself, Accardo was wrong about his longtime lieutenant; Pilotto had defied expectations and even facing death from his friends in the mob, stood true to the code of allegiance he had pledged on his Outfit initiation over thirty-five years earlier. According to those who knew him, the immense irony of the situation was never lost on the Big Tuna, an always wise-don who wasn't afraid to critique his own leadership.

Although in prison, Pilotto's name would pop up again in local newspapers two years later, accused of offering to pay an FBI informant to assassinate then sitting Chicago mayor Jane Byrne for her refusal to legalize a casino he had a financial interest in. Nothing further came of the mayoral assassination plot and after serving a decade behind bars, Pilotto was released in 1992. A bid to get back into labor politics was thwarted in 1995, as he was ousted from both Local 5 and his position on the area's district council for his connections to organized crime. Pilotto died of natural causes in July 1999 at the age of eighty-eight after spending his final years living full time in Florida. In 2005, Jimmy Marcello was indicted for the murder of Nick D'Andrea in the massive Family Secrets case, but in October 2007, the jury deadlocked of that specific charge.

# 11.

## Loose Cannon
### End of the Spilotro Era

As all of the pieces that would later make up the Family Secrets case started to come together in Chicago, The Outfit's monetary foothold in Las Vegas held strong. By the mid-1970s, Tony Spilotro was the king of the desert, having risen higher in the Las Vegas underworld than anyone had before in the city's storied history. He was an overwhelming presence on the Strip and in the area's social strata, forging a presence throughout the decade as everyone's favorite celebrity gangster. The best seats at shows and the most exclusive tables at the finest eateries in town were all his for the asking. Attracted to his status and swagger, woman threw themselves at him and famous Hollywood actors, when in town for vacation, sought his company.

Infrequently did a day pass when Spilotro's name and picture didn't appear in the local newspaper or on the TV's nightly newscast. Everybody knew that the city was in the palm of his hand, and he ate it up.

Accumulating a criminal portfolio that was second to none in gangland circles across the nation, he was richer and more powerful than he could have ever imagined. And his empire was getting only bigger. This was not necessarily a good thing.

With his behavior and activities going virtually unchecked by his bosses in the Midwest, Vegas's little wiseguy—Tony stood barely five feet four inches tall—had developed a huge ego. Not to mention, career ambitions that significantly outsized what The Outfit had in store for him.

Having departed his original base of operations in Circus Circus, Tony set up shop first in the Dunes hotel and casino poker room, and then in the clubhouse of the Las Vegas Country Club, using both locations as temporary headquarters while he sought another business to purchase in order to set up his permanent office. In November 1976, he opened the Gold Rush, a multi-level jewelry store built in an Old West motif that stood on a side street off the Strip. It immediately became the nerve center of Spilotro's ever-expanding criminal regime. Around this time, he also formed the soon-to-be notorious "Hole in the Wall Gang," a high-end burglary crew made up of a dozen or so of the group of henchmen he had imported from Chicago, and began a large-scale drug distribution business.

The Hole in the Wall Gang became famous for bypassing alarm systems by simply busting large holes in the homes and stores they intended to rob. Tony appointed

Frank Cullotta, his boyhood pal who had just emerged from a six-year prison stint and relocated to Las Vegas, to be his top lieutenant on the street, in charge of the highly trained group of professional thieves. The crew would go on to pull jobs all across the West Coast.

He stationed Fat Herbie Blitzstein at the Gold Rush, where all of the stolen merchandise his crew apprehended was fenced or resold to unknowing customers, and he allegedly made his younger brother, Michael, in charge of his narcotics operation. Michael was traveling between Nevada and Chicago, where he ran Hoagies, a popular restaurant and Windy City mobster haunt. Other members of Tony's inner circle included Ernie Davino, Leo Guardino, Wayne Matecki, Lawrence "Crazy Larry" Neuman, Salvatore Romano, Peter Basile, Jimmy Patrazzo, Bobby Stella, Joey Cussamano, Sammy Siegle, Jasper Speciale, Fred "Sarge" Ferris, Tommy Amato, Gene Cimorelli, Robert Doldot, Frank Masterana, Dickie Stevens, and Gussie Gallo.

If The Ant wasn't at the Gold Rush conducting business, he could usually be found at either the Upper Crust Pizza Parlor, a restaurant owned by Cullotta; Jubilation, a nightclub run out of the Stardust; or the My Place Lounge, a bar where he did most of his drinking and socializing. Cash was flowing in at epic rates. However, in a move that would end up costing him severely in the not so distant future, too much of it was going into his pocket and not enough of it into the pockets of the powers that be in Chicago.

**JUST** as Tony's empire was reaching its zenith, things began to take a turn for the worse. And from there, they got downright ugly. The leadership of the Chicago mob was convicted of stealing millions by skimming the casinos that Spilotro was overseeing and Tony became the centerpiece in over a half dozen federal and state racketeering investigations. As Spilotro's problems with the law mounted, his behavior became increasingly insolent. He developed a bothersome cocaine habit and embarked on a dangerous and forbidden love affair with a highly placed mob associate's wife. Stories of frequent rants about his desire to violently ascend to the top spot in the Chicago mob went a long way in placing The Ant outside the good graces of The Outfit's leadership. At a time when he should have been enjoying the pleasure of having paradise in the palm of his hand, Tony Spilotro was instead digging himself a hole that even the most Herculean of mobsters couldn't find their way out of.

"After a while, Spilotro let all the power he had amassed go to his head," said a former law enforcement agent. "He was completely incorrigible, totally out of control in every way possible. At one time he was arrogant and power hungry but still able to look at things from the perspective of a smart criminal. Through the years, his behavior began to defy logic and eventually undermine his entire empire. The lifestyle he led in Vegas, the lack of checks and balances from his superiors, really took its toll."

Beginning in May 1979, the floodgates opened up on Tony's legal woes and didn't close for nearly five years. On May 16, he was indicted in Las Vegas, alongside his two top emissaries, Herbie Blitzstein and Frank Cullotta, for heading a large-scale and statewide sports betting and loan-sharking operation. A large part of the investigation that led to the indictment was the FBI's ability to have one of its agents successfully penetrate Spilotro's inner circle. Posing as a top of the line jewel thief, agent Rick Baken, using the alias Rick Calise, gained the trust of Tony's brother John and then Tony, allowing him access to a large number of invaluable conversations and firsthand transfers of stolen property. After Baken's heroics, it was only a matter of time until the government could make its case. To add insult to injury, right before the end of the year, Tony was placed in the Las Vegas Gaming Commission's Black Book, officially banning him from entering any of the city's casinos for his connection to organized crime.

Tony's affair with Geri Rosenthal, the ex-showgirl wife of his childhood best friend, Frank "Lefty" Rosenthal, was also starting to make waves around this time. The relationship between Spilotro and Geri became the worst-kept secret in town and an obvious ploy by Tony to put Lefty, who he had developed a growing feud with and whose ego was the only one in the city to rival his own, in his place. The affair, as well as Tony's expanding drug business, were extreme violations of the mafia's code of conduct. Traditional mob logic says dealing in narcotics brought harsher legal penalties and, as a result, more opportunity for its soldiers to become traitors. Sleeping with co-workers' wives was an even further dalliance into the gangland forbidden zone because it bred resentment and unrest.

Rumors of The Ant flouting the rules in both situations were slowly making their way back to Chicago and had his bosses asking questions regarding his judgment. An unauthorized and unsuccessful attempt on Lefty Rosenthal's life—a car bombing that he was lucky to survive—

rumored to have been engineered by Spilotro in the years to come didn't win him any popularity contests back home either.

The start of the new decade didn't bring much of a change to Tony's bad fortune. In June 1980, he was arrested by Las Vegas police for being seen inside Sam's Town Hotel, a modest gambling hall located a good twenty miles off the Strip. Tension between the Spilotro organization and local law enforcement, who by this time had a team of close to two dozen officers assigned specifically to tracking the Ant's every move, were about to reach its peak.

In Tony's mind it started in the 1970s with petty harassment from the cops sent to follow him, but by the end of 1980, Spilotro felt like he was under siege. Just a week following his arrest for being inside Sam's Town Hotel, one of his associates from Chicago, Frank "Frankie Blue" Bluestein, was shot and killed by two Las Vegas Metro Intelligence Division detectives in the driveway of his home. Bluestein was a maitre d' at a restaurant inside the Hacienda hotel and casino and the son of Steven "Stevie Blue" Bluestein, a Las Vegas labor union official and suspected member of his crew. Trailed home from a meeting with Tony and Frank Cullotta, Frankie Blue was shot after exiting his vehicle and allegedly waving a pistol in the cops' direction, complaining of being unnecessarily hounded. Responding to Bluestein's death, a number of Tony's crew drove by the home of a member of Metro Intelligence Division and peppered it with shotgun fire.

The drive-by coupled with word on the street that Spilotro had issued murder contracts on the two detectives who killed Bluestein, prompted Kent Clifford, the head of Metro Intelligence, to board a plane and go straight to Chicago and to the doorsteps of Joey Aiuppa and Joey Lombardo. Unable to meet face to face, he left messages with both of their wives that any retribution delivered on his men would be returned tenfold. If The Outfit hierarchy didn't know before, they were now fully aware of Spilotro's continued spiral downward.

Tony's luck wasn't getting much better and the days of his Hole in the Wall Gang—a venerable cash cow for him for the last several years—were coming to an unceremonious conclusion. At the start of 1981, Salvatore Romano, one of the gang's primary lieutenants and a longtime Spilotro crony, switched sides and began working for the government. When Frank Cullotta began planning a major score on behalf of the gang scheduled for the July 4th holiday weekend at Bertha's, a handsomely sized jewelry story on West Sahara Avenue, Romano made sure the FBI was briefed on all the details. Wanting to hold off on the bust until they caught the infamous gang in the act, the FBI staked out Bertha's on the day of the intended robbery and made their arrests as Cullotta and company were in the process of burglarizing the store.

Stocked with a mountain of evidence provided by Romano's cooperation and the undercover work undertaken by agent Rick Baken, a mere two weeks after the highly publicized Bertha's bust, Spilotro was indicted once again. This time, he was indicted alongside Fat Herbie, his brother John, and Joe Blasko, a former cop who had joined Tony's crew on a full-time basis after his dismissal from the force for providing the Spilotro organization with illegal information. The government nailed Tony on charges of racketeering and conspiracy to deal in and possession of stolen property.

By May 1982, Frank Cullotta decided to begin cooperating with the FBI against his former boss, The Ant. Facing mounting legal problems himself, learning of Spilotro's refusal to chip in for his defense fund, and knowing about recorded confirmation of a contract on his life, Cullotta was convinced to turn on Spilotro and enter the witness protection program.

Based on the information and evidence culled from Cullotta's cooperation, in January 1983, Tony was indicted for the seemingly long-forgotten M&M murders from twenty years earlier and was jailed without bond pending trial. While behind bars in Chicago, he was hit with yet two more racketeering indictments: one was regarding his command over the Hole in the Wall Gang and the murder of Jerry Lisner, a homicide committed by Cullotta at his behest when it was discovered that Lisner was working for the FBI. The other found Tony indicted alongside several other mob figures in the Midwest, including Outfit leaders Joey Lombardo, Joey Aiuppa, Angelo La Pietra, and Jackie Cerone in the legendary Strawman II case, charged with pension fund fraud and the skimming of three separate casinos.

The unbearable heat that Spilotro's brash and careless behavior had been bringing down on himself had finally hit his bosses. And they held him responsible. The thin ice he had been skating on for quite some time was about to crack.

"All the legal problems he had compiled were beginning to reflect on the authority above him and ultimately provided Chicago with an excuse to do him in," said a former agent. "He had faced bumps in the road from the law before, but by the end of his first decade in Nevada, he was immersed in arrests, indictments, and trials. People like Cullotta and Romano started to turn against him, and the totality of the circumstances made it appear that he had lost control of his crew. It was only a matter of time before either the law or the mob were going to put an end to his run."

**ACQUITTED** on the M&M murders, Tony was once again a free man. But it wasn't long before he found himself in more trouble. However, this time it wasn't with the law. It was with his health. Spilotro's drug use, heavy drinking, stress level, and increasing weight gain had given him a heart attack and the need for bypass surgery. This development let Tony's attorneys successfully sever him from the pension fund fraud trial while he recovered. During his stay in the hospital, The Ant also jumped into a May-December romance, and fell in love and eventually carried on a lengthy affair with one of his nurses. As Spilotro watched on the sidelines while his superiors in The Outfit all got convicted in the Strawman II case, he readied himself for his own upcoming battles in the courtroom and the possibility that his ongoing antics had now made him a target for mob reprisal.

As Tony had begun to suspect, The Outfit had tired of his routine. When he began his first racketeering trial in Las Vegas in January 1986—which would end in a mistrial—the mafia family he had been a member of for over twenty years started making preparations for his murder. Spilotro's primary backer in the Chicago mob hierarchy, Joey Aiuppa, was so upset with his own conviction that he abandoned his support of Spilotro and sanctioned his execution. Spilotro's second most powerful advocate, Joey Lombardo, might have been able to help, but he was out of the picture at the time, sitting hundreds of miles away in a federal prison cell.

When Joe Ferriola, an avid anti-Spilotro advocate, took Aiuppa's place as boss at the start of 1986, the table was all set for The Ant's downfall. Ferriola, also known as "Joe Nagal," "Joey the Chinaman," or "Joey Spoons," is alleged to have tasked his protégé, John Di Fronzo, with the job of making arrangements for and setting up the heavily anticipated hit.

On two separate occasions in the coming months, hit teams from Chicago consisting of the Calabrese brothers, Jimmy Di Forti, Frank Santucci, Frankie Schweihs, and Giovanni "Big John" Fecoratta made trips out West to try to take Spilotro out, but each time had their plans thwarted by The Ant's unpredictable movements. Finally, in June, The Outfit was able to lure Tony back home, with the promise of a promotion for him and an initiation ceremony for his brother Michael. Although he found it strange that his recent behavior could warrant such an accolade, he boarded a plane on Friday, June 13 and landed at O'Hare Airport at around 7:30 in the evening.

With his retrial in Las Vegas slated to begin the following Monday, Tony was already on edge. Picked up at the airport by Michael and his wife, Ann, Tony and his wife were taken to their former residence in suburban Oak Park, a home now occupied by his brother and sister-in-law. A phone call from Jimmy Marcello later that night taken at Hoagies, Michael's restaurant, confirmed the ceremony the next day where Tony was supposed to be upped to captain status and Michael was to be formally initiated into the crime family.

Neither brother was extremely confident with the validity of the alleged events set to take place the following evening, but both know they had no choice but to do what they were told. When they were instructed to meet Marcello late Saturday afternoon at a hotel parking lot in Schiller Park, they hesitantly went, skipping Michael's son's Little League Baseball game. Armed with the full knowledge they could be walking into an elaborate sabotage, the Spilotro brothers bucked up and followed orders. They appeared to be accepting the inevitable.

The siblings' worst fears were confirmed when they were brutally beaten and strangled to death at the faux ceremony the next day by a ruthless group of hit man later identified in court testimony by Nick Calabrese as himself, Joe Ferriola, Sam Carlisi, John Di Fronzo, Jimmy Marcello, Jimmy La Pietra, John Fecoratta, Louie Eboli, and Louis "Louie Tomatoes" Marino. One of the most storied eras in Outfit history had concluded, almost appropriately, in a sadistic rage of violence.

Tony and his brother had become rouges. They were clearly operating by their own rules, and this was unacceptable to their bosses. Their murders would resonate with the public, press, and various law enforcement agencies for much time to come, and in some ways, make Tony Spilotro more famous in death than he had been in life—

movies like *Casino* and television shows like *Crime Story* were inspired by his legacy.

And in the classic fashion of The Ant, the overly heinous double homicide reached far beyond the grave, demonstrating that not even death could stop Tony Spilotro from causing the Chicago underworld major headaches. In the ultimate act of fate, the execution of the two Spilotro brothers would unknowingly start a chain of events that nearly two decades later would bring a storm of chaos upon The Outfit and threaten to bring the entire crime syndicate to its knees.

# 12.

## Burial Blunders and Farm-Side Follies
### Big John Pays the Price

Tony and Michael Spilotro were lying bludgeoned, battered, and very dead on the basement floor of Louie Eboli's Bensenville home as the nearly dozen participants and witnesses in the vile slayings were slowly shuffling out the door and on their way. Some would go enjoy a hardy dinner after the exhausting execution, others would retreat to their suburban estates to spend the rest of the Saturday evening with their families. For these men, it was merely just another day at the office. However, even though the murder of the Spilotros was completed, there was still work to be done. The two bodies had to be buried, transported from Eboli's house to a makeshift grave site somewhere far away from the Windy City suburbs. The duty of making certain this job got done as quickly and cleanly as possible fell upon Giovanni "Big John" Fecoratta, one of the Spilotros' killers and a highly tenured Outfit enforcer and hit man from the Chinatown crew. A longtime leg breaker for the mob-controlled Local 8 of the Industrial Workers Union, Fecoratta was one of the La Pietra Brothers' most trusted lieutenants.

Instructed to bury the bodies outside the state of Illinois in northern Indiana, Fecoratta called for the assistance of Albert Tocco. Tocco and his cleanup crew—named in FBI reports as Dominic "Tootsie" Palermo, Albert "Chickie" Roverio, and Nicholas "Jumbo" Guzzino, the younger brother of slain Outfit member Sam "The Gobber" Guzzino and imprisoned Outfit member Richard "Fat Richie" Guzzino, arrived at the Eboli residence shortly before sunset. With the help of Fecoratta, they loaded the two corpses into the back of a work van and took off headed across the state line to a predetermined site where they would dig the grave. Before they left, Fecoratta told Tocco to call him when the job was completed.

Driving approximately 60 miles past downtown Chicago, Tocco and his lieutenants found an isolated parcel of a cornfield in Enos, Indiana, parked their van, and began to dig. It was now after midnight and the sky was pitch black. Having dug only a few feet into the earth, the foursome of wiseguys, heard a car pull up by the side of the road. Thinking it was the police, they became scared and all ran off in different directions. Lucky for them, what they thought was a cop car was just a couple teenagers looking to score some marijuana plants they knew to be growing in that particular field. After some time passed, and the teenagers were long gone, Palermo, Roverio, and Guzzino returned to the grave site. Their boss, Albert Tocco, did not. He was lost in the vast Indiana cornfield and couldn't find his way back.

Still spooked and thinking the police may be returning to the scene, Palermo, Roverio, and Guzzino hurriedly placed the Spilotro brothers' corpses into the half-dug grave and covered it with dirt. They then got into the van and sped away, leaving Tocco behind to find his own way home. Meanwhile, Tocco was furious and frustrated and had no idea where he was. When he realized his compatriots had abandoned him, he began walking, trying to locate the nearest pay phone so he could call for help. Seething with anger, Tocco, his clothes soaked in the Spilotros' blood, made his way to Interstate 41 and hiked nearly two miles until he came upon a roadside telephone booth. Out of breath, he called his wife, Betty, who was sound asleep in their south suburban home, and told her to get up and come retrieve him in rural Indiana.

Angelo Tocco was no dummy. He had been around The Outfit for a long time and knew the repercussions for such a colossal misstep would be harsh. It was well-known both in law enforcement and gangland circles that in the months following the debacle, he was very worried about his and his family's personal safety. Tocco had gained significant stature in The Outfit for leading the final stage of the crime family's successful takeover of the chop shop rackets. He was promoted to full-fledged capo in the early 1980s, but was convicted and jailed on racketeering charges in 1989. He died behind bars in 2005.

When Betty Tocco finally arrived at her husband's

location, he was boiling over with anger and on the ride back to Chicago, spilled the entire story of what had just transpired. The fact that such sensitive Outfit information was forbidden to be spoken of outside the crime family didn't seem to bother him, as Albert told his wife everything—who was murdered, who was in charge of the burial, who he rode out to the cornfield with. Tocco, not one to easily accept blame himself, appeared to place a big chunk of responsibility for the mess-up on John Fecoratta. "This never would have happened if Al Pilotto were still in charge," he remarked to Betty during his rant. Betty Tocco word subsequently testify against her husband.

The next morning, Tocco called Tootsie Palermo to ream him out and get the skinny on what he, Roverio, and Guzzino eventually did with the bodies. He then phoned Fecoratta and told him what happened. Unbothered by the news, Big John told Tocco that everything was okay and not to lose any sleep over the incident. Unfortunately for Fecoratta, everything wasn't okay and in only a few short months, he was the one that was going to have to pay the consequences for a job far from well done.

**LESS** than two weeks later, on June 23, 1986, Michael Kinz, a local farmer, came out to his cornfield to spray some weed killer. In the midst of its application, he stumbled upon a suspicious pile of turned over soil on his property. Fearing it was a dead, poached animal underneath the ground, Kinz contacted the Indiana Game Wildlife Agency, who sent a biologist to the scene to check it out. After only digging a few feet, the biologist discovered two heavily bruised and beaten dead bodies and called the local sheriff's office, who then made contact with the Chicago FBI office. Within hours, the once quiet farmland was crawling with hoards of law enforcement personnel, reporters, cameramen, and interested on-lookers. Suspecting it could be the Spilotro brothers they had found because their family had reported them missing a week earlier, the FBI compared Tony and Michael's dental records to the two dug-up corpses and got a match.

Word quickly spread that the Spilotros had been found dead, and the media had a field day with the lurid story of the high-profile gangster, who many Chicago news outlets were mentioning as a future don candidate for The Outfit, running afoul with his bosses in the crime family. For the next several days, the story made the front page of all the local newspapers and was constantly being discussed and analyzed on the area's television news broadcasts. This was exactly what The Outfit leadership didn't want to happen. Tony Spilotro, the ultimate thorn in their sides for the past several years, was supposed to disappear and never be spoken of again. Out of sight, out of mind, was the syndicate's theory. He wasn't supposed to be discovered a mere nine days after he was rubbed out, with his violent death becoming the talk of Chicago. They were mad. And they wanted someone to blame.

Even though it wasn't Fecoratta who personally bungled the burial, the fact that he was already sitting on his mob superiors' bad side as a result of previous indiscretions didn't work in his favor when The Outfit began assessing culpability. Big John had recently begun to get a reputation for slacking off on his assignments, being hard to get in touch with when he was needed, and even worse, talking outwardly subversive. There were rumors that he was the culprit behind a stick up that had taken place at a local mob-run poker game. He owed outstanding debts to John Di Fronzo, John Monteleone, and the La Pietra brothers from previous street loans he had taken out, and he was also suspected of stealing money, holding back earnings on his rackets, and pocketing cash given to him to disperse to other Outfit members while traveling on business together. Bringing his girlfriend on top-secret syndicate assignments and allegedly filling her in on the details of his activities didn't help matters either.

Everything considered, whether he was the one who actually botched the burial or not was of little consequence. Fecoratta was going to take the heat. And taking the heat in The Outfit meant you were living on borrowed time. Displeased with the entire postmortem Spilotro fiasco and Fecoratta in general, Joe Ferriola and Sam Carlisi, the primary decision makers in the Chicago mafia at that time, marked Big John for death. They informed Fecoratta's captain, Jimmy La Pietra, acting in his jailed brother's place as head of the Chinatown crew, of the situation and told him to take care of all the details. La Pietra then farmed out the contract to two of his most-experienced executioners, the Calabrese brothers.

Knowing that Fecoratta was savvy in the ways of the underworld, someone who wouldn't let himself be an easy target, Frankie and Nicky Breeze took their time in setting up his murder. Letting some time pass after the Spilotros were found to make him feel that he had escaped The Outfit's wrath, the Calabreses waited until after Labor Day to set their assigned contract in action.

In early September, Frankie Breeze called Fecoratta and said that "Brother Jimmy," another nickname for Jimmy La Pietra, had given him and his brother the task of bombing a local dentist office, and he wanted Fecoratta to go along on the job with them and act as the getaway driver. Going to lengths to make certain Big John didn't suspect a setup, Nick Calabrese went as far as taking him out on faux casings of the office located near the corner of Belmont and Austin. On September 6 at around 9:00 P.M., Nick picked Fecoratta up at a designated meeting point, and the pair headed for their target.

Before Nick had gotten into the car—a stolen 1986 Buick Century—to leave for his rendezvous with Fecoratta, his brother, Frank, gave him three guns from his garage. Two of the weapons were loaded and the other was not. He also gave him a fake bomb, made up of emergency flairs to look as if they were sticks of dynamite, carried in a crumpled brown paper bag. Frank instructed Nick to give Big John the dummy gun and to take the other two himself, hiding one in his waistband. When Fecoratta let his guard down, Nick, who was given the duty of trigger man because it was felt Big John would least expect it coming from him, was to shoot him in the head. Frank would be waiting in another car and pick Nick up after the hit was completed.

Arriving in the alley behind the dentist's office, Nick and Big John made small talk for a few moments, waiting for a pedestrian to leave the area before going into action.

Finally, with the coast clear, Nicky Breeze grabbed the brown paper bag as if he were going for the fake bomb, and instead came up with a loaded .38-caliber pistol. He started to point it at Fecoratta, but he was too slow. Fecoratta was primed for the play, and the pair started to struggle for control of the weapon, former comrades in arms, now engaged in a battle to the death. The gun went off twice, and both Nick and Big John were wounded at the same time. Fecoratta was hit in his chest and Calabrese in the shoulder. Unfazed by the shot to the chest, Fecoratta was somehow able to tilt the chamber back on the gun, unload the remaining bullets onto the floor, and bolt out of the car.

Gathering himself, Calabrese got out of the car and went after him. He chased him across Belmont Avenue, a busy metropolitan roadway, and toward a set of buildings on the north side of the street. Both men were bleeding from their wounds and blood marked their trail. Nick was almost hit by a car at one point. By the time he reached the door to Brown's Banquet Hall, a facility often used as a bingo hall at 6050 West Belmont, Fecoratta was weak and losing steam. He staggered and fell down. Just as he was trying to get back up, Nicky Breeze appeared, grabbed Big John by the hair, and put two bullets in the back of his head, killing him instantly. Running away from the bingo hall, Calabrese accidentally dropped the pair of leather golfing gloves he had been wearing during the job.

Within minutes, the cops were on the crime scene—via a 911 call from a shocked and disturbed bingo player—and discovered two separate types of blood and the gloves Nicky Breeze left behind. Although they weren't aware of it at the time, they had just found the first piece of what would be a very complex puzzle. A puzzle that began with the Spilotro execution and that would not be solved, or even known about, for close to two decades. And the result would be one of the biggest federal racketeering indictments and convictions in American history.

# 13.

## Changing of the Guard
### A New Regime

When Tony Accardo died on May 27, 1992, a void was left at the top of The Outfit that needed to be filled. Like any corporation needs a CEO or any army needs a general in order to operate at maximum capacity, the mafia needs strong leadership at the top. Accardo, buried at Queen of Heaven Cemetery in west suburban Hillside in a grave site sectioned between deceased Outfit brethren Paul Ricca and Sam Battaglia, left some pretty big shoes to fill.

Even though Accardo had let other mafia stalwarts like Sam Giancana, Joey Aiuppa, and Joe Ferriola look after the day-to-day operations of The Outfit throughout his time overseeing the syndicate, at the end of the day, the responsibility for the welfare of the Chicago mafia ultimately fell on his shoulders. He was the foundation, the pulse of the streets, and his absence from the scene made a lot of people predict peril for the Family in the future. The Windy City underworld was in a period of great transition, and for the first time in nearly half a century, the stability that had been the trademark of the local crime family was now in question.

Luckily for the Chicago mob, the Big Tuna had been actively planning for the time he would no longer hold the crown to his Midwest mafia kingdom, and in his later days he had begun grooming several heir apparents to take his place atop the throne when he was gone.

Four primary Accardo lieutenants stepped to the forefront after the Big Tuna's death and assumed the torch of power—Joseph "Joey the Clown" Lombardo, John "No Nose" Di Fronzo, Joseph "Joe the Builder" Andriacchi, and James "Jimmy the Man" Marcello, each of them reputed to have taken a significant leadership position in Outfit activities from 1992 forward. The immediate success they found in their former mentor's stead quelled any thoughts that the mafia in Chicago would crumble into disarray without Accardo's leadership. The 1990s and the dawning of the new century would bring new and untapped rackets for The Outfit to exploit, more money to be made, and a fresh perspective on mob rule implemented by Accardo's successors that would both harken back to the glory days of the Big Tuna's past and set forward a new and more prosperous road leading to a rewarding future.

Taking a page from their legendary predecessor, The Outfit's new breed hierarchy, to its overall benefit over the past two decades, has gone to extreme lengths to disguise its depth chart. To this day, nobody, not even the FBI, knows for certain what the pecking order in the Chicago mob is. Lombardo, Di Fronzo, Andriacchi, and Marcello have done such a good job of keeping their crime family's business under wraps that queries into who is the syndicate's real bosses and who are merely front bosses are asked and debated upon almost daily among the area's law enforcement, historians, and press alike.

"The Outfit's new breed of leadership has followed closely in the footsteps of their predecessors," said former FBI agent Jim Wagner. "They've learned from guys like Accardo, Aiuppa, and Alex on what it takes to have a nice run in the upper echelons of the mafia. For the most part, they know how to successfully navigate around the pitfalls that most mob bosses face on an everyday basis. Most important, they've been able to mask their overall hierarchy by using multiple fronts and insulation methods that tell us that the new Chicago mafia, despite reports of its downfall, is just as active and dangerous as the old Chicago mafia."

**RELEASED** from a decade-long prison stretch at almost the exact same time that Tony Accardo's death rocked the Chicago underworld, Joey Lombardo's timing proved impeccable. Without missing a beat, The Clown is alleged to have stepped into Accardo's role as Outfit *consiglieri*. Like the Big Tuna, Lombardo would end up carrying just as much clout, if not more, than the family's boss.

Accardo's passing also happened to coincide with the indictment a short six months later of then-Outfit don Sam

"Wings" Carlisi on racketeering charges. This development left yet another leadership spot that had to be addressed. The name most law enforcement sources say heeded the call of duty was John Di Fronzo—even though some in the know insist that Lombardo took the syndicate's number one spot. Di Fronzo was a longtime lieutenant from Elmwood Park, who had been named a caporegime in the mid to late-1970s. It's believed by most in law enforcement that No Nose Di Fronzo was selected as the Outfit's new boss in early 1993 when Carlisi was jailed as a flight risk while awaiting trial.

John Di Fronzo was born on December 13, 1928, to Michael and Dores Di Fronzo, both immigrants from Italy. He dropped out of Wells High School in the eleventh grade and took his first arrest for petty larceny in May of 1946. Di Fronzo, who was running errands for Jackie "The Lackey" Cerome as early as sixteen years old, spent two years in the U.S. Army as a paratrooper and received an honorable discharge in 1948. Returning to Chicago, he got his start in major underworld activities by being a part of a burglary and hijack team that called itself "The 3-Minute Gang" and pulled cartage thefts and jewelry and fur heists across the city. Eventually, he became a driver and bodyguard for Cerone, helping him run several West Side loan-sharking and gambling operations.

He earned the moniker "No Nose" at the age of twenty-one during a 1949 robbery of a Michigan Avenue department store when he lost a portion of his nose, depending on who you ask, either by jumping through a glass window trying to avoid being caught by the law or by being shot by a policemen while fleeing down the street. Marrying his wife, Rosemary, on December 29, 1950, he adopted her son from a previous marriage, Michael, and the couple had one son of their own, Joseph, in September of 1951. During his career in The Outfit, Di Fronzo has been arrested more than twenty-five times.

In late 1993, less than a year into his tenure as godfather, he was convicted for trying to extort a California-based Native American casino and sent to federal prison. At his farewell dinner, which took place at Agostino's on North Harlem Avenue the night before he left Chicago to serve his sentence on the West Coast, he dined with fellow reputed Outfit members Pat Marcy, Marco "The Mover" D'Amico, Donald "Donnie the Sponge" Scalise, John "Little Jackie" Cerone, Jr., and his younger brothers and top lieutenants, Joe Di Fronzo and Peter "Greedy Petey" Di Fronzo. Serving just over twelve months in a California prison, he was released in late summer 1994 when the conviction was overturned on appeal.

Since returning to the streets of the Windy City following his brief stint behind bars, a majority of mob watchers agree that it has been No Nose who sits atop the mountain peak as overlord of the Chicago mafia. He has stayed mostly free of legal hassles after being sprung from federal prison but rumors of pending indictments, none of which have come to fruition, have hounded him over the last decade. During the 2007 Family Secrets trial, he was implicated in the murder of the Spilotro brothers, yet avoided being charged in the case.

Besides stabilizing the syndicate after Accardo's death, Di Fronzo is also reputed to have led a foray for the Chicago mafia into a previously taboo terrain—narcotics. It's not that drugs had never been sold in The Outfit before, just that it had never been sanctioned from the top before. Keeping a safe distance from the actual street sales of drugs, throughout the 1990s and into the new millennium, Outfit lieutenants are believed to have been given new-found authority by mob administrators to begin financing narcotics transactions with the area's African American, Asian, and eastern European criminal groups and biker gangs. Joe Di Fronzo, the youngest of the three Di Fronzo brothers, served a federal prison sentence for marijuana trafficking.

The most significant change of protocol made by the new regime led by Di Fronzo and Lombardo, was the decision to minimize The Outfit's dispersal of violence as a deterrent to those who break the rules. Feeling the murders and beatings that had once been a syndicate calling card was bad for business and invited too much exposure for the crime family as a whole, orders from the top were now to dispatch stern warnings instead of the physical thrashings of before. The use of violent behavior would be applied only as a method of last resort.

Eerily similar to modus operandi employed by Tony Accardo during his forty-six years in charge of The Outfit, John Di Fronzo displays an extremely low-key demeanor and knows how to stay in the shadows, avoiding the spotlight at all costs. A virtual recluse, No Nose is not a fan of nightclubs or fancy restaurants but rather is described by people who know him as a homebody who enjoys the exclusive company of his family and only a few close friends. He has numerous real estate holdings—said by law enforcement to reach close to a dozen of properties, including 12.2 acres of land in Melrose Park and vacation homes in Florida, Wisconsin, and McHenry County—and alleged ownership interests in big money-makers D&P Construction, a waste hauling and construction business, and J&K Ventures, a recycling materials company. Di Fronzo has also always been said to hold ownership in several car dealerships, Elmwood Park Motors, Northwest Dodge, and Irving Park Chrysler-Plymouth amongst them. Always a man of habit, for close to forty years No Nose could be seen meeting with his driver and top proxy Eugene "Lefty" Cacciatore for breakfast at Gene's Deli in Elmwood Park every morning at around 7:30 A.M., until Cacciatore's death in 2000.

Overly cautious in his movements, he speaks to very few Outfit members and associates face to face. The FBI believes he issues orders primarily through his brother Pete Di Fronzo, a captain who reputedly commands mob affairs in No Nose's old stomping grounds of Elmwood Park, and Marco D'Amico, a former crew leader himself and one of the don's closest advisors. Much like Accardo before him, Di Fronzo is a fan of having a "street boss" to oversee day-to-day Outfit affairs on his behalf. The extra layer of protection between him and the street suits the notoriously hands-off boss well. Upon taking the reigns, Di Fronzo named South Side capo John Monteleone the syndicate's street boss and then upon Monteleone's passing in 2001, tapped Joe Andriacchi for the position. No Nose also utilizes an underboss: First, he allegedly appointed former Carlisi confidant Alphonse "Al the Pizza Man" Tornabene, who held the job until he went into a brief retirement around 2002 when he is alleged to have selected Andriacchi to

replace him. Tornabene's absence from the Outfit administration was less than lengthy and he allegedly returned to
fill the role of Family consiglieri in 2005 upon Joey Lombardo's indictment.

Di Fronzo is said to be very conscious of the Outfit's
national profile too, making sure to be on good terms with
other American mob powers. Until his death in 2002,
Frank "Frankie the Horse" Bucceri, brother of one of No
Nose's original underworld mentors Fifi Bucceri, acted
as Di Fronzo's intermediary with the other La Cosa Nostra factions, such as the crime families in New York, Los
Angeles, Detroit, and St. Louis. Even before ascending
to capo and eventually street boss, John Monteleone was
believed to be the syndicate's liason with the Milwaukee
family, and Rudy Fratto, close relatives of former Midwest
mob kingpins Luigi "Cockeyed Louie" Fratto and Frank
"Frankie One Ear" Fratto, is alleged to be in charge of all
Outfit affairs in Iowa. Joey Lombardo's right hand man,
Jimmy Cozzo, was reputed to be the Family's representative to the Cleveland mafia from the 1960s until his death
in 2007.

"Johnny Di Fronzo is very low key in terms of the public, but in Outfit life, he's assertive in his authority, and
everybody knows to defer to him," said Jim Wagner. "He's
not flashy or someone who feels the need to tell people
who and what he is. If you didn't know him personally
or through business and you met him, you'd never suspect
who he was. When I was in the bureau, you would always
be able to find him every morning at one of his dealerships,
sitting behind his desk with a paper and a cup of coffee.
He keeps a tight inner circle and talks Outfit affairs with

only one or two people, mainly his brother, Pete. Although he tries not to look the part of a crime boss, he plays it very successfully. And the way he acts and conducts business is a big part of that."

Joe the Builder, Lombardo's first cousin and a partner of both The Clown and No Nose in a robbery crew they were all a part of during their early days working in the local underworld, was a natural fit as Di Fronzo's number two man. Andriacchi replaced a deceased Vince Solano as captain of the North Side in 1992, and some Windy City mob prognosticators speculate that by the turn of the century, he actually ascended past Di Fronzo to become The Outfit's don and still holds that position today. Most likely, however, The Builder, holds the dual role as the syndicate's street boss and underboss.

Three years younger than his cousin The Clown, Andriacchi was born on October 20, 1932, and got his nickname by gaining a foothold in the Chicago area construction industry in the 1970s and 1980s and using it to The Outfit's great advantage—a feat that impressed the mob and aided him in building leverage for himself, which he was able to parlay into a swift climb up the syndicate ranks. He opened Aunt Sarah's Restaurant in River Park, which he used as a headquarters, and for a good portion of the '70s and '80s it was known as a popular Outfit hangout. Like Lombardo and Di Fronzo, Andriacchi is a low-key personality who knows how to generate cash for the mafia while not making waves. Unlike Lombardo and Di Fronzo, for the most part he has been able to avoid the ire of the law. Except for a prison bit he served between 1968 and 1971 for a burglary conviction, Andriacchi has stayed out of jail and avoided arrests and indictments in his time moving up The Outfit ladder.

Rumored to hold a silent ownership interest in the widely popular Rosebud restaurant chain, The Builder can often be found many nights of the week holding court on Rush Street. When he's not at Carmine's, a flagship establishment of the Rosebud chain, he can usually be seen down the street at Rosebud's on Rush or at the posh and popular Tavern on Rush.

**AS** the twentieth century came to a close, things at the top of the Chicago underworld became even more foggy than they already were. Reports from sources in law enforcement and on the street began to circulate that Jimmy the Man, an imprisoned capo from Cicero, had taken John Di Fronzo's place as boss of The Outfit. Whether this was true or it simply meant that Marcello, who also went by the monikers "Little Jimmy," "Jimmy the Driver," and "Jimmy Lights," was being put out into the fray as a front boss to further shield No Nose from FBI scrutiny is still not known. What is known is that at the same time as this alleged shift of power, the violence that had for the most part disappeared on the local streets during a majority of the Di Fronzo regime returned.

Whether this change in the way of conducting business can be directly attributed to Marcello's rise in stature is still up for discussion. But after several years of no murders taking place in The Outfit, in less than two years, there were two very high-profile slayings that re-established the crime family's authority.

\* \* \*

**JIMMY** Marcello was born exactly one week after the Japanese attacked Pearl Harbor, on December 13, 1941, and grew up on the city's West Side. The offspring of a Irish mother and a Sicilian father—Salvatore "Sammy Big Eyes" Marcello, who was also a member of The Outfit and eager to set the foundation for his son to follow his lead into a life of crime—at the age of nineteen, he went to work for the city of Chicago in the Streets and Sanitation Department via one of his father's connections. In the early 1970s, Sammy Marcello, a one-time lieutenant and close friend of Sam Giancana, was killed while making a street tax collection. Jimmy was devastated, and it is rumored that he might have played a role in the retribution slaying of his dad's killer just a few months later.

Employed by the city for thirteen years, in 1973, around the same time as his dad's homicide, he quit his job at Streets and Sanitation and started loaning out money. A quick study in the loan-sharking racket, Marcello was soon making a nice profit, and his skill at the trade gained him and his business the attention of The Outfit. Going to work for Joe Ferriola's crew in 1975, he was quick to make a reputation for himself as an expert shakedown artist, displaying an uncanny ability to make extortion victims part with their money with little hesitation or hassle.

Eventually all of Marcello's hard work in building up his mob profile paid off, and he was accepted into Ferriola's inner circle. By the late 1970s, he had moved his way up the food chain until he became the driver and right-hand man to Sam "Wings" Carlisi, a valued Outfit lieutenant who got his nickname by being the syndicate's primary messenger of news, decisions, and orders to other La Cosa Nostra crime families across the country.

Due to his close association and friendship with Joe Ferriola, Carlisi was on a fast track to power in the Chicago mafia. Becoming tight with Carlisi and hitching his career prospects in The Outfit to him was the best thing that could have ever happened to Jimmy Marcello. As Sam Carlisi's star in the Windy City underworld rose to meteoric heights, so did his. When Joe Ferriola became boss and selected Carlisi as his underboss, Marcello basically became the third most powerful gangster in Chicago, getting a promotion to captain status and being given authority over Dupage County.

The most significant feat accomplished in Jimmy the Man's early rise to power was his ability to take the syndicate's video poker business to an entire new level of profitability. The business was started in the 1970s by Outfit bigwigs Hyman "Red" Larner and Carmen and Salvatore Bastone and it developed into an immediate international cash cow, with Larner and Bastone taking their business to the Carribean. But by the late 1980s the joker poker racket had began to stagnate in and around Chicago. With a posse of mob soldiers at his disposal, over the next few years Marcello rejuvenated the floundering business with new machines, updated technology, and a lot of street muscle. In the 1990s, if you were a bar or working-class restaurant in the Chicagoland area, you most likely had a video poker machine there. And odds are it was put there, in one way or another, by The Outfit, and specifically those working for Jimmy Marcello. As The Outfit made its way to the start of the new millennium, the all cash business, which at one time had been a mid-level money maker for the crime family generating nowhere near the level of profits traditional gambling would, had become one if its largest rackets.

Indicted in December 1992 along with his mentor Sam Carlisi on charges of racketeering, and convicted and jailed a year later, Marcello's run on the streets came to a temporary halt. However, despite being locked behind bars in a federal prison in Milan, Michigan, he still carried some serious weight in The Outfit. While Marcello was in prison, word began to spread in the late 1990s that Jimmy the Man was on his way to the top of the mountain in the Chicago mob, the hand-selected heir apparent to The Outfit throne. In the fall of 2001, the Chicago press started to report that he was the newly anointed boss of the local mafia. Gaining his release from incarceration in 2003, a free man for the first time in ten years, Marcello took his much-anticipated spot in The Outfit hierarchy. If he wasn't the syndicate's overall don, then at the very least he was its street boss, helping reputed underboss Joe Andriacchi watch over day-to-day affairs and calling a great deal of shots.

What Marcello didn't know was that although he was in the process of reacclimating himself to the outside world, getting comfortable in his new job as mob royalty, any long-term career aspirations were dead in the water before he even stepped foot out of his Michigan jail cell. In the years leading up to his release, the FBI, with the aid of turncoat and former hit man Nick Calabrese, had started building an epic case against The Outfit, and Jimmy Marcello, its reputed new boss, was one of its main targets.

Certain that Marcello was still maintaining a good

piece of control over things going down in the Windy City, issuing orders and such from behind the barbed-wire walls in Milan, the feds decided to watch him as closely in prison as they had while he was on the streets. This meant paying special attention to his phone calls and visits, which were both recorded via federal prison policy. They hit pay dirt. Marcello was caught on tape talking about a variety of incriminating things, including the Spilotro brothers' murders, leaks in law enforcement, and his attempt to pay Nick Calabrese's family $4,000 a month as a safeguard against him becoming an informant—a venture that obviously proved futile.

Walking out of the Milan prison gate in November 2003, Jimmy Marcello was a marked man. The media, who had been speculating on his leadership status in the mob for quite some time, wanted a story, and news cameras were there to meet him at his home on the day of his return. The FBI, insistent on its belief that he had taken part in gangland murders in the past and that he was still commanding Outfit affairs from his jail cell, wanted him back in prison. They would soon get their wish. After enjoying less than two years of freedom, Marcello was indicted for his role in three murders, one attempted murder, and various charges of racketeering in the April 2005 Operation Family Secrets case and was returned to prison, where he has remained ever since.

**THERE** are a few things that are known for certain about the modern-day Chicago Outfit. First of all, although the crime family's power has been far from wilting, its numbers have been facing a steady decline. A syndicate that once boasted close to two hundred made members had been whittled down to under a hundred, and probably closer to between fifty and eighty, when the curtain came down on the last century. As a result, the approximately seven crews that had made up its organizational structure for over sixty-five years were condensed into just four. The former Elmwood Park and Rush Street crews were consolidated into one and re-named "The North Side Crew." When west suburban boss Anthony "Tony Tracks" Centracchio died in August 2001, his crew was merged with Joey Lombardo's Grand Avenue/Ogden Crew and re-named "The West Side Crew." The Twenty-sixth Street/Chinatown crew absorbed the south suburban crew and all territory residing south of the Eisenhower Expressway and in northwest Indiana—area's previously looked after by a then–ailing Tootsie Palermo—and was re-christened "The South Side Crew." Finally, all activities taking place in Cicero, Melrose Park, and Lake County came under the umbrella of one all-encompassing crew.

In addition to its traditional rackets like bookmaking, loan sharking, labor infiltration (which by 2003 had been severely limited via government intervention), prostitution, political fixing, and extortion, the onset of the new millennium brought with it new business opportunities for The Outfit. A majority of these opportunities came in the form of white-collar scams and taking advantage of the most recent advancements in technology.

The proliferation of bigger and more cost-friendly health-care plans and HMOs in the 1990s offered a perfect chance for the crime family to delve into the healthcare industry.

Typical mob scams in this arena of business included open-ing healthcare brokerage companies and then overcharging customers—in a lot of cases mob-backed businesses and labor unions—for group healthcare providers, pocketing the difference, and intimidating the administrators at the providers into approving the overcharges. The Outfit would often times strong-arm people into securing coverage through these companies and then use access to medical records they gained through ownership to blackmail their own customers. It is suspected that Anthony Centracchio, who was heavily invested in the Westside Medical Center and listed as president of the firm, led the syndicate's foray into the medical field.

Garnering a foothold in the country's financial dis-trict has been a big moneymaker for The Outfit too. Stock manipulation scams, such as pump-and-dump rackets, in which mafia-run brokerage houses falsely inflate stocks only to sell before the bottom falls out, and muscling asso-ciates involved in Wall Street for insider information to use to the crime family's advantage have turned a steady profit for at least two decades.

The advent of the Internet, the cell phone, and the international business world's increasing dependence on the computer has also brought newfound cash rewards for the mafia in Chicago. The Internet provides a place for The Outfit to launder its profits with considerably more ease and less possibility of discovery and offers a new way to make money from all forms of gambling, pornogra-phy, and prostitution. Stolen computer components retain a huge dividend on the black market, plus have an added bonus of being practically untraceable. Finally, the black market sale of cell phones and calling cards to foreigners in the Chicagoland area reaps a large benefit for the mob.

A Chicago Crime Commission report titled "New Faces of Organized Crime" sums up the modern-day Outfit best: "The new Chicago mob, like other generations before them, is like a serpent that sheds its skin. Its present appearance may be different, but beneath the surface is the same dangerous beast. The mob is more flexible and adaptable than ever before. Its power and wealth have never been more sound and difficult to penetrate."

## 14.

**The Weight Meets His Fate**
The Spilotro Crew: A Decade Later

With Tony Spilotro out of the picture in Las Vegas, for all intents and purposes the region once again became a wide open territory. Although The Outfit replaced him with a combination of Donald "The Wizard" Angelini, an Outfit lieutenant and gambling expert who lived a portion of the year in Chicago and the other portion in Las Vegas, and Chris Petti, Spilotro's man in San Diego before his execution—both of whom would be indicted and eventually jailed alongside John Di Fronzo in 1993 on charges of trying to extort a California-based Native American casino property—the desert basically became free of mafia influence after the Ant's departure. Corporate buyouts of a majority of the mob-controlled casinos and hotels coupled with the two Strawman convictions turned the one-time gangster's playground into a vacation hot spot for families and a convention destination for businesses worldwide.

By the conclusion of the 1980s, most of Tony Spilotro's crew was long gone from Vegas, either dead, in jail, under the protection of the government, or plying their trade in another city's underworld. Frank Cullotta, Tony's former right-hand man and leader of his Hole in the Wall Gang, disappeared into the witness protection program. Victor and John Spilotro, Tony's younger brothers, each moved back to Chicago and continued to work under The Outfit's protection. Lefty Rosenthal, the mastermind of The Outfit's gambling empire in the desert, left Las Vegas and relocated to Florida, he continued to be one of the country's most-respected handicappers until his death in October 2008. Paul Schiro, Tony's guy in Phoenix, remained the Chicago mafia's representative in Arizona until he was convicted in 2001, along with the former chief of detectives from the Chicago Police Department, cop Bill Hanhardt, for helping run a multimillion-dollar jewelry heist ring.

Former Hole in the Wall Gang members Wayne Matecki and Ernie Davino both ended up going legit and are currently living in Illinois and New Jersey, respectively. Leo Guardino died in 1998, after serving a prison sentence on burglary charges connected to his work with the Spilotro crew. Crazy Larry Neuman died in prison in 2002.

Out of The Ant's entire inner circle, Joey Cussamano and Fat Herbie Blitzstein were the only ones to remain in Las Vegas after their boss's murder. Cussamano, who some even claim became The Outfit's point man in Nevada after Petti's and Angelini's imprisonment, has been there uninterrupted since 1986, when Tony died. Blitzstein, who was forced to leave in 1988 to serve a prison sentence for tax evasion and credit card fraud, returned to Las Vegas in 1991 and reopened shop on a large-scale loan-sharking and sports gambling operation. According to police reports, Blitzstein was also running a series of insurance fraud scams, in which he would offer up his services to clients of his other illegal business ventures as means of clearing their debt if they agreed to aid him in filing false claims.

Setting up a headquarters for himself at a body shop he owned on Fremont Street, just off the Strip, called Any Auto Repair, by the mid-1990s Fat Herbie's various rackets had blossomed into a venerable cash cow. And he wasn't sharing. Not working for Spilotro anymore made it so it was all his. And although he kept up solid relations with his former friends and associates in The Outfit as well as the mafia syndicate working out of Los Angeles, he wasn't paying tribute to them either, which made it all the better.

However, the fact that he had no mob protection, no crime family officially watching his back, made him vulnerable. When the L.A. mafia, in the midst of harsh times due to general attrition and a late-1980s racketeering bust of most of its administration, was on the lookout for people and illegal businesses to exploit, they turned to Vegas. A crew stationed in Sin City was witnessing Blitzstein's lucrative operation up close, and he became the perfect mark. All the while, Fat Herbie was oblivious to the dangers on the horizon. He thought, despite not cutting the boys back in Chicago in for a piece of his burgeoning mini criminal conglomerate, they were still looking out for him. Which in his mind made him untouchable. He thought incorrectly.

The L.A. mafia had seen better days. It was 1996, and the crime family was just getting back on its feet after the release from prison of its boss Peter "Shakes" Milano and his brother and underboss Carmen "Flipper" Milano, both of whom pled guilty to various racketeering charges in March 1988 and were each sentenced to six years of jail time. A syndicate that once boasted well over seventy members in its heyday of the 1950s was down to less than two dozen. Turncoats like Altadena "Jimmy the Weasel" Frattiano, a one-time acting boss of the family; Anthony "Tony the Animal" Fiato, a top enforcer of Shakes Milano; and Mike Rizzitello, a powerful capo, had done significant damage.

Reduced to controlling only a small number of rackets—mostly moderate-size bookmaking and loan-sharking operations—and being afforded a general lack of respect by the rest of the L.A. underworld, the Milanos had to find new ways to generate cash. It was the Milano brothers belief that such measures were the only hope of restored power and prestige.

Pete and Carmen Milano, known as passive dons and ones who virtually refused to use violence as a means of wielding authority, were desperate. They wanted to get the family's reputation back to where it was years before, and by the mid-1990s, they appeared willing to go to extreme lengths to accomplish this goal. One of these lengths was being more flexible on their unspoken edict of nonviolence. The results of this decision would not turn out well for Herbie Blitzstein.

The Milano brothers were born in Cleveland, sons of Anthony "Tony the Old Man" Milano, the longtime *consiglieri* of the Cleveland mafia. Tony Milano came to the

United States from Calabria, a southern region of Italy, in 1900 and settled in Buffalo. After a few scrapes with the local police, he left town and headed west, finally planting his family's roots in Cleveland. Along with his brother Frank and his best friend, Alfred "Al the Owl" Polizzi, both future bosses of the Ohio-based crime family, he started a loan company and two separate importing companies, bringing in Italian and Sicilian culinary delicacies via his contacts in New York. All three businesses were run out of the Italian-American Brotherhood Club, a social club opened by Milano in the Little Italy section of the city during the 1930s and that over the years became a hotbed of mob activity. Combining forces with the area's Jewish mob, "The Mayfield Road Gang" led by Moe Dalitz, to gain a grip over all local vice, Tony and Frank Milano, rose to be the most powerful figures in Ohio organized crime throughout the early to middle twentieth century.

Tony Milano also took up interests in California starting in the 1940s, keeping residence in a posh Beverly Hills estate. Once settled in his new digs, he received the blessing of L.A. mob don Jack Dragna, to forge a small but prosperous niche for his Cleveland gangster consortium on the West Coast. For most of the 1940s, 1950s, and part of the 1960s, he split his year in half, living the fall and winter months in California and the spring and summer months in Ohio. Part of the reason Los Angeles was so appealing to Tony was that it was close to his brother Frank, who, following his stint as mafia boss in Cleveland, fled the country for Vera Cruz, Mexico, instead of facing charges in Ohio for income tax evasion.

Eventually though, in the late 1960s, Tony packed up

his belongings and returned to live out the final years of his life in Cleveland, leaving behind his sons Peter and Carmen to look after his interests in L.A. Carmen had received a law degree and for a while was a practicing attorney before being disbarred. When Dominic Brooklier, the don of the Los Angeles mafia for most of the 1970s and his underboss Sam Sciortino were convicted of racketeering charges in November 1980 and sent away to prison, two spots opened up atop the crime family hierarchy, and Peter and Carmen Milano were more than happy to fill them.

Ruling unfettered for eight years until their bust in 1988, the Milano brothers did their time and reemerged on the street in the mid-1990s ready to start anew. They were keeping their eyes open for any possible future scams and new victims to terrorize, when Carmen, who relocated his crew to Las Vegas, learned from some associates how much money Herbie Blitzstein was making in the operations being run out of his auto repair shop. He became more than a little interested. Checking to make certain that Blitzstein's ventures were not under anyone else's protection, Carmen Milano decided Fat Herbie's rackets were his and the L.A. mob's for the taking. Clearing the decision with his brother Pete in California, who desperately needed fresh sources of income for his crime family's portfolio, it was all systems go for the takeover of Blitzstein's business by the fall of 1996.

"Carmen wasn't a tough guy by any means, but he had some real dangerous guys that used to hang around him," says former FBI agent, Herm Groman, who worked the Milano's Las Vegas–based crew in the 1990s. "The crime family he belonged to was facing hard times and Carmen and his brother, were looking for ways to revitalize it. Herbie was an easy mark. He was walking around town, flashing his success, and that pissed a lot of people off. Plus, he had no formal protection, like he had back in the 80s when he was under the Spilotro group out of Chicago. The guys out of L.A. saw taking his business from him as their right. Blitzstein was Jewish. He wasn't Italian, so they didn't view him as a part of their operation. Since he wasn't giving anyone in the mafia a taste of his rackets, they felt like they were being disrespected in some way. The guy really didn't stand a chance. Once they made their decision to go after him, it was a done deal. The L.A. mob might have been on the ropes, but they were still a family and they had a number of guys working on their behalf. Herbie was just one man."

**BEGINNING** in October, the first of several meetings took place between Carmen Milano and others—mostly West Coast–based wiseguys—in order to decide how the job of muscling in on Fat Herbie was going to work. Sitting at a back table of the Sea Breeze Social Club, the California mafia's Las Vegas headquarters, Milano discussed specifics of the plan with Stephen "Stevie the Whale" Cino and Louis "Little Louie C" Caruso, both reputed soldiers in the L.A. mob, and Johnny Branco and Peter "Pete the Crumb" Caruso (no relation to Louis Caruso), both high-level associates who worked under Carmen and his brother. The group decided they would approach Blitzstein at his home and tell him of their intentions. If he refused to go along with the plan, which they believed was a likely scenario,

Milano gave them permission to beat him into submission. Although the underboss authorized a beating of Fat Herbie, it was specifically instructed that they were not to kill him. Knowing that Blitzstein also sometimes acted as a fence for stolen jewelry and often kept merchandise at his house and at the auto repair shop he worked out of, Milano ordered the group to rob him of any jewels he was in possession of too.

Thinking it would be safer to have a connection on the east coast, instead of someone local, to lay off the stolen merchandise, Cino, originally from Buffalo, suggested they bring Bobby Panaro, the Buffalo mafia's representative on the west coast as well as an associate of Blitzstein's, into the fold. Milano agreed with Cino's suggestion, offered the Buffalo mob liaison and his boss, upstate New York don Joseph "Lead Pipe Joe" Todaro, a piece of the action and invited Panaro to attend the group's next meeting, which took place at a coffee shop inside Bally's hotel and casino on the Strip, approximately a month later.

While in the coffee shop, Milano instructed Pete Caruso to reach out to Alfred Mauriello, another valued associate who worked for the L.A. mafia, and have him outsource the shakedown intended for Blitzstein to two of his subordinates. Subsequently, Mauriello, who was paid $10,000 for his efforts, gave the job to Antonio Davi and Richard Friedman, promising them each $3,500 once the work was completed. Milano then informed Peter Caruso, that he was to break in to Fat Herbie's residence in the hours leading up to the confrontation, take all the jewelry they could find, and then leave a back door open for Mauriello's thugs, who would be tailing them.

What Milano didn't know was that Pete Caruso had changed the plan. Despite not having the authority to do so, he wanted the entire Blitzstein operation for himself and was planning to kill to get it. Instead of having Maureillo tell Davi and Friedman to rough up their target if he resisted, he told him to instruct the pair to murder Fat Herbie.

At this point in time, Milano and company decided to bring one more person into their conspiracy. His name was Joe De Luca, and he was Blitzstein's partner in Any Auto Repair. It was widely known that De Luca and Fat Herbie had been feuding for quite some time. De Luca wanted a bigger piece of the business, but his partner didn't want to give it to him. He felt he deserved it. He was Blitzstein's front, and as a result he was exposed to a great deal of risk. If the police ever started nosing around the auto repair business and found out that it wasn't just a place for people to get a tune-up or a muffler replaced, he would be in a lot of trouble.

Fat Herbie continually dismissed his partner's desire to be cut in for a larger share of his profits and that frustrated and angered De Luca to no end. So, when Johnny Branco, who was aware of the friction developing in the business partnership, asked him to join the Milano organization's plan to run Blitzstein out of town, De Luca didn't hesitate and immediately jumped on board. It was a major coup to get De Luca to turn on Fat Herbie since his defection came equipped with information on their target's schedule and security codes.

De Luca told them that Fat Herbie was going to be in Mexico over the Christmas holiday, so the Milano group set their sights on the first week of January as the time to confront Blitzstein. On January 4, 1997, Pete Caruso, De Luca, Cino, Panaro, and Branco all met at a Vegas-area Denny's restaurant, to iron out the final details of their plan and discuss how exactly Fat Herbie's assets were going to be divided up following the hostile takeover.

What the plotting wiseguys didn't know was that their scheme was cursed from the outset. First of all, Johnny Branco, tapped by the Milano brothers to become a made man at the syndicate's next initiation ceremony, was working for the FBI and wearing a wire the entire time he was helping organize the Blitzstein caper. Furthermore, Carmen Milano's Las Vegas crew had been infiltrated by a pair of undercover FBI agents posing as wiseguys who were tipping off their superiors to a portion of what was transpiring in an investigation called "Operation Thin Crust."

On January 6, the long-gestating plan to forcefully acquire Fat Herbie Blitzstein's various illegal business ventures was put into motion. At around 3:00 P.M., while Blitzstein was still at work, Pete Caruso, and others armed with security codes provided by Joe De Luca, entered Fat Herbie's residence and pilfered the home of all its valuables. They got uncut diamonds worth over $65,000. They got Rolex and Cartier watches. They got twenty-five pounds of gold bullion. They got cash. When they were done raiding the place, they came away with over $100,000 dollars. Just as Milano had advised, they left the back door open for Davi and Friedman, who were set to arrive soon thereafter.

When Blitzstein got back to his home on West Vernon

Avenue around 6:00 P.M., Davi and Friedman were already there, waiting for their prey in the back of the house. Entering through the front doorway with his cell phone in hand, Fat Herbie encountered Davi, equipped with a .38-caliber revolver and Friedman brandishing a .22-caliber pistol.

Before an astonished Blitzstein could utter a word, Friedman shot him in the face. Down on one knee, a bloodied Fat Herbie looked up to his assailants and asked, "Oh no, why me?" Without a response, Friedman went to shoot him again, but his gun jammed. Showing little hesitation, Davi handed him his weapon and Friedman unloaded another shot into his target. Slumping into a nearby black leather recliner, Blitzstein was knocking on death's door. Just as they were about to leave, Friedman finished off the job by shooting Fat Herbie in the back of the head, making certain there was no chance he would survive the attack. On their way home, Davi took Friedman's cell phone and called Alfred Mauriello, telling him, "The party went well," a prearranged code to let him know the job was complete. Fat Herbie was dead and all hell was about to break loose.

**THE** fallout from the Blitzstein murder, although slow to develop, was significant. The homicide took the situation into an entirely different stratosphere—both for law enforcement and the mob. The FBI saw it as an opportunity to deliver a final death blow to the West Coast crime syndicate, and with Operation Thin Crust already in full bloom, open yet another case against the L.A. mob, this one to be known as "Operation Button-Down." The mafia and their associates who carried out the Blitzstein hit were forced to go into cover-their-ass mode and try to protect themselves against the possibility of unanticipated lengthy prison sentences. The result was myriad cooperating wiseguys aiding the government in the takedown of a large portion of the already-reeling Milano crime family.

From the moment Fat Herbie's lifeless body was discovered by Joe De Luca the morning after Davi and Friedman had murdered him, things began spiraling downward. First off, the two underworld factions that organized the plan to strong-arm Blitzstein began to fight over the riches they had inherited upon his death. Only a few days after the homicide, Bobby Panaro was informed by the L.A.-based mobsters that he and his benefactors in Buffalo would be getting shut out of receiving any percentage of Blitzstein's rackets. An incensed Panaro, who had previously negotiated a 50 percent take of Fat Herbie's auto repair shop and a share of the more than $200,000 in street loans, was told by his superiors in Buffalo to back off. He did. Less than four months later he was indicted.

Secondly, and significantly more detrimental to the Milano crew, John Branco, who was told of the killing on the afternoon of January 7 at a lunch meeting with Pete Caruso, was immediately instructed by his handlers in the FBI to drop everything else he was doing for the government and to make ascertaining who was in on the carrying out of the murder his one and only priority. Branco was fast to get to work, and on January 30 he got Caruso to admit on tape to hiring Alfred Mauriello to farm out the job to Davi and Friedman. Three months later, he got Mauriello talking on tape about his role in the plot. By May, a twenty-five-person,

101-count indictment was levied against the Milano camp, including charges of murder against Pete Caruso, Panaro, Mauriello, Davi, Friedman, Cino, and De Luca.

The first one to turn was Joe De Luca. Being locked in jail without bond for two months didn't sit well with De Luca, who was guilt ridden over double-crossing his business partner. So in June he went to the FBI and offered up his cooperation. Although it would take almost another two years for the case to go to trial, other turncoats would follow De Luca's lead.

In the beginning of April 1999, just three weeks before jury selection at his trial was set to start, Alfred Mauriello pleaded guilty to one count of murder in aid of a racketeering conspiracy, and in return for a reduced sentence, agreed to testify against his alleged co-conspirators in court. One week later, Antonio Davi flipped. He pled guilty to the murder and for the promise of a twenty-year prison sentence, also agreed to testify against his co-defendants. Then on April 27, the morning opening arguments in the trial were to begin, Louie Caruso charged with racketeering, but not the Blitzstein murder specifically and was given a two and a half year prison sentence for benefiting from the burglary of Fat Herbie's house.

Carmen Milano, facing a slew of racketeering charges, decided to turn government witness as well. Though he would eventually recant his cooperation, the underboss's debriefing by the FBI yielded a great deal of information on the West Coast's most prevalent mafia family. Pete Caruso died of a heart attack in the months leading up to the trial and Richard Friedman decided to plead guilty to being paid to commit the murder and take a promise of a twenty-five-year sentence recommendation. The only two defendants left to face the jury were Stephen Cino and Bobby Panaro, both of whom were eventually acquitted of the murder charges, but convicted on charges of racketeering. Fat Herbie's murder would yield no convictions, merely a legacy of brutality that dated back to the rotund gangster's days of running the street with Tony Spilotro, a decade earlier.

"After Blitzstein was killed, all of our other investigations stopped, and we completely committed all of our resources to solving the murder," says Groman. "It really cut us out of a lot of things. There was a lot more we could have learned and gotten involved with that could have spelled the end for the L.A. mafia for good. There's not a doubt in my mind that we would have eventually gotten to Pete Milano. The inroads were there, set up for us to take advantage of. We just never go the go-head, cause we already had enough to make a case with the Vegas crew and the higher-ups thought that was enough."

# 15.

## Dirty Blue
Mob Cops

Arguably the most important thing a highly functioning crime syndicate needs to survive and thrive are significant connections within law enforcement. Nobody knows this better than the Chicago Outfit, a mob franchise that has practically written the book on the subject matter. The Midwest mafia family has a deep, rich history of forging strong, intricate relationships with various area police departments and sheriff's offices. These relationships, along with its firmly entrenched ties in local government, have always helped The Outfit maintain a steady edge on those in law enforcement trying to bring them down. Notorious mob double-agents like Richard Cain and Michael Corbett headline a long list of men who successfully played the role of both cop and crook at the same time.

Anthony Passafume grew up on the South Side of the city, home to many of the local underworld's most vicious mobsters. It was a place where the mafia and its way of life was, well, a way of life. Raised without a father—his dad had died when he was a baby—Passafume was a bit of a problem child and spent time in an assortment of reform schools early in life. Popular on the playground for being a standout athlete and adored by the girls for his strong, athletic build and handsome face, Anthony spent his early adulthood floating by on good looks and charm. His swarthy appearance at the time elicited thoughts of a comic book superhero: dark hair, razor-sharp jaw line, bulging muscles, and all. He didn't graduate from high school, and through his late teens and early twenties roamed the streets day and night with his friends while being supported by his mother.

Adulthood finally hit the hulking Passafume in the late 1960s when his live-in girlfriend became pregnant and he needed money to support his future family. He acquired some work with the Teamsters through his budding friendship with rising South Side mobster Frank Calabrese, a man he met via his cousin. Anthony soon went to work for the city in the Water Department and then as a street sweeper in the Streets and Sanitation Department. He hung around with guys like Calabrese and other Outfit types like Ronnie Jarrett and Aldo "Junior" Picitelli and, according to authorities, helped some of his buddies out with collections duties for their respective street operations.

Passafume changed his name to Anthony Doyle in 1975 in honor of a boyhood mentor and in the hope of being accepted to the Irish-dominated police academy. He eventually acquired the nickname "Twan." Depending on who you ask, the moniker either spawned from a derivation of his first name, Anthony, or is a reference to a Chinese dessert dish—fried sugared dough on a stick, known as a Twan—since he originated from the city's Chinatown district. Accepted to the police academy in 1980 after a number of years of trying, he graduated in the fall of 1981. Twan Doyle was finally a cop.

Starting his career in blue in the Twelfth District Precinct, he worked eight years as a transit officer, dressing up as a wino to nab muggers on the subway and el train. He was transferred to a gang unit and took on a number of ruthless Latino street gangs. Appearing on the outside to be the quintessential man of the badge, he discreetly continued to maintain his ties to the mafia. He visited Picitelli, who was serving time on a loan-sharking case, in prison in Indiana and was spotted dining with South Side mob capo Frank "Toots" Caruso. In the latter part of his career, Doyle was assigned to the department's Evidence Storage Unit. Retiring with a full pension, he moved to Arizona, where he joined an auxiliary unit at his local police station.

Michael Ricci was fifteen years older than Doyle and had well over a decade more of duty for the Chicago Police Department. He started as a beat cop and worked his way up to homicide detective. From early on in his career in law enforcement, Ricci was suspected of being a little too close to the members of The Outfit he was supposedly being paid to arrest. He is alleged to have co-owned a hot dog stand with West Side crime boss, John Di Fronzo, and a topless bar with Frank Calabrese. On various occasions he was seen in the presence of local mob pillars Sam Giancana, Fifi Bucceri, and Angelo La Pietra. In the 1960s, he became a confidant of Frank Sinatra. During the Chairmen of the Board's frequent trips into the Windy City, Ricci would often act as Sinatra's bodyguard and chauffer, flanking Ol' Blue Eyes as he hit the nightclubs on Rush Street and feasted on the signature ribs at the Twin Anchors, a bar and grill that was one of his favorite area watering holes.

Ricci is also alleged to have developed into the Calabrese crew's mole at Chicago Police Department, facilitating bribes to vice unit personnel in exchange for tipoffs on raids and investigations. Leaving the force in the 1990s, Ricci, also known as "Mooney," went to work for the Cook County Sheriff's Office, but continued to provide Frank Calabrese with inside information via his contacts all the way up until the Family Secrets indictment in 2005.

Well aware of the other's reputation, Twan Doyle and Michael Ricci, didn't personally cross paths until Frank Calabrese was sent to prison on his first racketeering bust in 1997. Needing help maintaining his interests on the outside, Frankie Breeze is alleged to have used people like Doyle, Ricci, and Outfit wunderkind Nick Ferriola, son of the late mob don Joe Ferriola, to act as his conduit to the street. Sometimes Doyle and Ricci rode together to the Milan, Michigan, federal prison to visit with the jailed rackets boss.

At the behest of Calabrese, Ricci asked Doyle to use his post in the evidence lockup to find out if the FBI had removed the bloody glove found at the scene of the John

Fecoratta murder for further analysis. The answer came back affirmative. With the investigation into Fecoratta's murder reopened, Ricci provided status reports on the inquiry via intelligence he gleaned from interoffice memos and meetings between various law enforcement agencies. Federal prosecutors also alleged that both Doyle and Ricci made collections on behalf of Frankie Breeze's loan-sharking operation. Indicted alongside each other and Calabrese in the 2005 Family Secrets case, their names are now forever linked in infamy on the city's lengthy and storied résumé of dirty cops. Doyle would make it to trial in 2007, but Ricci wouldn't, dying due to complications from a heart surgery.

Demonstrating just how deeply embedded the tentacles of The Outfit stretch into high level law enforcement, more allegations surfaced before the Family Secrets case made it to trial. Highly decorated U.S. Marshall John Ambrose was suspected of passing information to the mob regarding Nick Calabrese's holding location. Ambrose, whose father was a disgraced former cop and mob associate, was alleged to have passed details on Calabrese's whereabouts and personal security schedule to a friend who then passed it on to Outfit lieutenants John "Pudgy" Matassa and Big Mickey Marcello. Time and time again, the cycle of corruption proves never ending.

"It's highly disconcerting when you find out that the same people who are supposed to be on your side in the fight against the mob are aiding and abetting your adversaries," says FBI agent Ross Rice. "Sometimes you don't know who to trust and that hurts the overall objective, which is to nail these guys and put them in jail. What the cops did in the Family Secrets case severely undermined the investigation and compromised key intelligence. It could have unraveled the whole thing, and that's scary. The corruption of certain members of law enforcement has always been an issue, and it will always be an issue. Sadly, its the dark side of human nature. But you just keep doing your job the right way and have faith that justice will prevail in the end."

**BILL** Hanhardt was one of the most decorated police officers to ever walk the streets for the Chicago Police Department. Known for his bold and brash attitude and unmatched skill and savvy as an investigator, he built a reputation for himself the size of Wrigley Field. Blessed with a photographic memory, the West Side–born and –bred Hanhardt knew every major criminal in the city like he knew the back of his hand. Lavished with praise over a career that spanned from 1953 through 1986, he headed the elite Crime Investigation Unit, leading the war against the city's best thieves and cargo-hijackers; at one point, he held the prestigious posts of deputy superintendent, chief of detectives, and commander of the burglary unit.

Racking up countless numbers of high-profile arrests while working the beat, his exploits eventually caught the eye of Hollywood. Chicago-born director/producer Michael Mann used Hanhardt as an on-set consultant and inspiration for lead characters in both *Crime Story,* Mann's TV follow-up to mega-hit *Miami Vice,* and *Heat,* his epic crime motion picture starring Al Pacino and Robert De Niro. Bill Hanhardt was a legend and he knew it.

Despite all of that, Hanhardt was constantly dogged with rumors of inappropriate and illicit behavior and accused of being a much darker individual than the one shown through his squeaky clean media image. After close to five decades dodging innuendo, the label finally stuck. The rumors, the myths, were true. In 2002, he pled guilty to masterminding a multistate jewelry theft ring that lasted for at least twelve years and used his contacts with the police department. The first theft that was part of the indictment that he pled guilty to occurred in 1984, two years before his retirement from the force. The term *dirty cop* and the name Bill Hanhardt were now officially synonymous.

As early as his first few years as a beat cop, Hanhardt was allegedly shaking down all the bookies, burglars, and loan sharks he could find. Former Outfit associate, Robert "Bobby the Beak" Siegel, would testify in court that in the 1960s, his boss, South Side numbers kingpin and mob chief "Little Angie" Volpe, was giving Hanhardt over $1,000 a month cash in protection pay, plus several new cars a year. There were allegations of him tipping off some of his more favored criminals about pending investigations in exchange for envelopes stuffed with hundred-dollar bills. The Outfit both loved and loathed Bill Hanhardt at the same time.

Heading toward retirement from the force in the early 1980s, Hanhardt started thinking about life after his days in blue, and contacted James "Jimmy Legs" D'Antonio, who he did business with on the street. A veteran thief and shakedown artist, D'Antonio was a top lieutenant to Grand Avenue capo Joey Lombardo, often acting as The Clown's personal driver and bodyguard.

Already running a profitable theft ring dating back at least ten years—pulling jewelry heists and fur shipment hijackings with a steady crew of able henchmen—Jimmy Legs cut Hanhardt in for a piece of the action. After turning in his badge in 1986, Hanhardt went full time into a life of crime. He immediately replaced D'Antonio as head of the well-established burglary crew and started to craft a legend for himself as a gangster that rivaled his reputation as a cop. Jimmy Legs, who left his day-to-day role in the crew to help fill the shoes of the imprisoned Lombardo, helped out when and where he could, but Hanhardt was the boss and he oversaw a crew that included D'Antonio protégé Joseph "Skinny Joe" Basinski, Hanhardt right-hand man William "Cherry Nose Billy" Brown, Gaetano "Guy" Altobello, Salvatore "Little Sam" De Stefano (nephew of Outfit wildman Mad Sam De Stefano), Robert Paul, and Paulie Schiro (who was residing in Phoenix holding things down for the boys in Chicago).

Using his pull as a former cop to gain access to information on potential victims' businesses and vehicles through police department computer database searches, the robbery gang focused on targeting traveling jewelry salesmen, who dealt in high volume and high cash. They were meticulous in their movements, keeping flawless surveillance records and scamming their way into a variety of manufacturers' auto codes and master keys—and sophisticated in their work, using coded language and complicated hand signals, the best possible robbery tools, and an array of disguises and identities to thwart possible detection. With Hanhardt calling the shots from his home in the posh North Shore suburb of Deerfield and only occasionally going on scores himself, and Skinny Joe Basinski quarterbacking things on the street, the newly restructured band of thieves were off and running.

The multistate burglary spree is said to have commenced in October 1984 in Glendale, Wisconsin, where $310,000 worth of Baum and Mercier watches were stolen from a Mercedes in the parking lot of a hotel when its owner, a high-end jewelry salesman, went into the lobby to make a phone call. In October 1986 in Monterey, California, they struck again and nabbed a half a million dollars worth of Rolex watches off a duped salesman on a trip for work. There were jobs in Arizona, Michigan, Minnesota, Texas, and Ohio, where they scored $1.5 million from safe deposit boxes at the Hyatt Regency in Columbus. Back in Wisconsin in 1995, they stole $750,000 worth of uncut diamonds from a jewelry salesman in his hotel room.

Through discussions with Jimmy D'Antonio, Hanhardt knew The Outfit was happy. Everyone was making money. When Jimmy Legs died as a result of severe injuries sustained in a car accident in 1993, the crew didn't miss a beat and kept chugging along at a steady pace. Hanhardt was seen in the presence of reputed high-ranking Mafioso Rudy Fratto, who investigators believed became the gang's new contact in The Outfit when D'Antonio died.

But by the mid-1990s, the FBI was on to Hanhardt and his crew. Numerous informant reports of the group's activities gave rise to a top priority investigation by the FBI. Using a former victim as bait, the feds set up a sting for a potential score in northern Indiana. The FBI was videotaping as the crew followed a previously ripped-off jewelry salesman traveling in a blue Lincoln Town Car from suburban Chicago to a restaurant parking lot in Porter, Indiana, where the crew took $60,000 worth of watches out of the trunk. One of the lookouts for the job, in a nearby idling car, was also caught on tape. It was Bill Hanhardt.

With the decade coming to an end, the bad news continued to mount against Hanhardt. In 1999, as a result of a divorce proceeding, one of Hanhardt's crew members' estranged wife discovered a safe deposit box filled with stolen merchandise and fake ID's. The FBI found out and swept in with subpoenas. That same year, Jimmy D'Antonio's nephew surfaced and turned over to authorities twenty-seven suitcases he found that had belonged to his uncle and contained burglary tools and intelligence files.

The curtain finally came down on Hanhardt in October 2000, when he, along with Basinski, Brown, Altobello, De Stefano, and Schiro were indicted for a string of robberies that spanned a decade and a half. Facing a rock-solid case against them, the entire crew agreed to plead guilty to the charges. In the weeks leading up to the highly publicized in-court plea, the pressure of the events surrounding Hanhardt proved too difficult for him to cope with and he tried to commit suicide by overdosing on pills. His attempt was unsuccessful, and he was sentenced to sixteen years in prison in the spring of 2002 at the age of seventy-three.

"Bill Hanhardt was a complex individual who leaves a complex legacy," said Richard Stilling, who worked with him throughout his career in the FBI. "It's still hard for some people like myself, who knew him in a professional setting, to understand that other side of him. He was like two different people. He was a paradox."

\* \* \*

**PAULIE** Schiro, the gang's top surveillance expert, was sentenced to twelve years. It was the first significant prison sentence the then sixty-four-year-old Shiro would have to serve; however, he knew if he stayed out of trouble on the inside and did good time, he could make it out in time to still enjoy some of his golden years in the Arizona sun. The prospect of a future as a free man died early in his sentence. Rumors of Nick Calabrese's cooperation in late 2002 led Schiro to speculate to a visiting friend that what Nicky Breeze had to offer could help the government put him away forever. The Indian was trapped in a corner it didn't look like he was getting out of and all he could do was wait for when the feds decided to drop the bomb.

# 16.

## Sins of the Father
Frank Calabrese Jr. Turns Informant

Frank Calabrese Jr. was fed up. Specifically, he was fed up with his father, Frank Sr. He was fed up with being lied to. He was fed up with being bullied. And he was fed up with having the future of an entire mob crew placed on his shoulders. After years of abuse at the hands of his dad, the mob hit man, Frank Jr., decided to do something about it. Incarcerated in a federal prison in Milan, Michigan, alongside his father—both there as a result of a 1995 racketeering conviction that took down Frankie Breeze and several underlings, including his two sons—and unhappy with his father's decision to continue living a life of crime, even behind bars, he reached out to the Chicago FBI office. In a letter dated July 27, 1998, and addressed to agent Tom

Bourgeois, Frank Jr., offered up his cooperation in constructing yet another case against his father. One he hoped would keep him in prison for the rest of his life.

> *I am sending you this letter in total confidentiality. It is very important that you show or talk to nobody about this letter, except who you have to. The less people that know I am contacting you the more I can and will be able to help you. What I am getting at is I want to help [you] and the GOVT. I need you and only you to come out to Milan FCI and we can talk face to face. NOBODY, not even my lawyers, know that I am sending you this letter, it is better that way for my safety. Hopefully, we can come to an agreement when and if you choose to COME HERE. Please if you decide to come make sure very few staff at Milan know your reason for coming because if they do they might tell my father and that would be a danger to me. The best days to come would be TUES or WEDS. Please no recordings of any kind, just bring pen and lots of paper. This is no game. I feel I have to help you keep this sick man locked up forever.*

Bourgeois, a 22-year veteran of the FBI, was familiar with both Calabreses, as he had worked feverishly through the late 1980s and early 1990s putting together the case that would eventually send both of them to jail. Born in Baltimore, his dad was a Maryland-based FBI agent who was killed in the line of duty when Tom was just two years old. Moving to New Jersey with his mother and new stepdad when he was six, he attended high school in suburban Redwood and then college at Marquette University in

Milwaukee. Joining the FBI in 1981, Tom spent his first three years of service in Wisconsin and then South Carolina, before being assigned to the Organized Crime Unit in the Chicago office in 1984.

"When I first got Frank Jr.'s letter, we immediately sat down as a unit and mapped out a plan to parlay his possible cooperation into a major investigation and hopefully a big bust," Bourgeois recollects. "I wasn't necessarily surprised that Frank Jr. wanted to come over to our side, but at the same time, the letter took me a little off guard because I wasn't expecting to receive it. Needless to say, it was a big deal and had to be dealt with very carefully. We had a hunch that Frank Sr. didn't treat his sons that well. Informants told us about Frank Jr. being berated in public by his dad for being too soft on debtors he was collecting from and stuff like that. So we definitely saw him as a possible weak link in the fence that surrounded his father. I think he saw in the way we handled him through all the stuff that went down with the original bust that we weren't monsters, like his dad might have made us out to be. We treated him like a gentlemen and did some stuff like return some of the items we seized in a raid of his house, that we thought might endear us to him. After his sentencing in the mid-1990s, I approached him when his father wasn't looking, and gave him my card. From that point on, the ball was in his court. Luckily for us, he decided to do something about it."

**BROUGHT** into the Chicago mafia at a very early age, Frank Jr., had little choice what line of work he would go into as an adult. Frank Sr. figured if The Outfit life was good enough for him, it was good enough for his oldest son. The fact that Frank Jr. was a Golden Gloves boxing champion as a fourteen-year-old convinced Frank Sr. even more that the street life was the right fit for his son. Frankie Breeze started sending Frank Jr. out on collection assignments while he was still in high school. First, he gave him a series of adult bookstores and movie theaters to go to on a weekly basis to collect street tax profits. Then he promoted him to collecting juice loan payments from clients of Frankie Breeze's loan sharking business, even personally teaching him the best way to rough up those who either refused to or couldn't pay. Following his teenage years, his father got him on the payroll at the City of Chicago's Sewer Commission and began mentoring him in the tricks of loan sharking, bookmaking, and arson for hire.

The older Frank Jr. got, the more he got involved with his dad's work for The Outfit. The more involved he became in mob affairs, the more money he made and the crazier his life became. He developed a cocaine problem and was prone to fits of rage, behavior he picked up from his father. And the violence his dad exhibited in his job and tried to teach his son to emulate was not always confined to the street. Sometimes it came home. When Frank Jr. told his dad that he was dating a girl that his father did not approve of, Frank Sr. beat him up. When Frank Sr. discovered that Frank Jr. had stolen over a half a million dollars in cash from his personal stash, he stuck a gun in his face and told him, "I'd rather kill you than have you disobey me."

Eventually, Frank Jr.'s work with his dad got them both sent to prison, convicted on charges of running a large-scale juice loan racket—one of the biggest loan-sharking rings ever to operate in the city's history—the case that was built by Tom Bourgeois and his fellow agents who worked the Calabreses' South Side crew. Before they left to serve their prison terms, Frank Jr., sick of living a life of crime and being terrified of his gangster father all the time, asked Frank Sr. to give up his racket empire once he returned home and go straight. Father and son embraced and Frank Sr. promised to abide by his wishes.

However, once the pair got to prison in Michigan, Frankie Breeze was singing a different tune. Despite his son's reservations about spending the rest of his life in The Outfit, he began to speak often about eventually turning over control of his crew and loan-sharking operation to him. He desperately wanted Frank Jr. to carry on the Calabrese name in the Chicago mafia long after he was gone. The fact that Frank Jr. had no desire to follow in his footsteps and had made it clear that he wanted him to retire from the mob after his release from prison, didn't seem to deter him from steering his son in the direction of a future in the underworld.

Coming to the realization that his father had no intention of leaving The Outfit behind as he had promised, Frank Jr. felt he had no other option but to turn against him. He had a lot to offer the FBI, including shedding insight into the long dormant John Fecoratta murder investigation.

"I went out to Milan to see Frank Jr. for the first time in August of 1998," said Bourgeois. "Things had to be kept real quiet because we didn't want Frank Sr. to have any idea about what was going on. The staff at the prison was real helpful in that regard and did everything in their power to make sure our business with Frank Jr. went as smooth as possible. When I got there, he told me about the Fecoratta hit and how he knew that it was his father and uncle who did it and how his uncle got shot in the process. His dad used to tell war stories and that was one of the ones he talked about a lot. I knew if it checked out, it would be a major development and could lead to some big things. You see, Frank Jr. was terrified of his father. I think he thought he was going to kill him or eventually get him killed somehow. He basically knew his dad was a menace and didn't want him doing any more harm. His thinking was it would be better for everyone if he was to stay behind bars for the rest of his life. From that conversation with Frank Jr., we opened up the Family Secrets investigation."

**WITH** Frank Jr.'s cooperation secured, the next step for the FBI was to see if they could use the recently attained information to flip Nick Calabrese and to get Frank Jr. to get his father on tape and talking about life in The Outfit. Visiting Nicky Breeze in Pekin Federal Prison, in Pekin, Illinois, where he was doing his time, Bourgeois and fellow FBI agent Mike Hartnett explained to him the situation.

"I went in there and I didn't play any games with him," said Bourgeois. "I said to him point blank: 'We got solid information that you killed John Fecoratta, and we have a court-ordered DNA test, blood test, and X-ray, that's going to prove it.' I told him, 'There was blood at the scene that wasn't Fecoratta's, and we know it was yours. There was a glove left behind, and we know it has your DNA on it. And we know that you got shot while pulling the job, and when we x-ray you, we're going to see it.' He just sat there and turned white. Didn't say anything, just nodded his head, like he knew he was in big trouble.

So, we get the X-ray back and it lights up like a Christmas tree. You can see the chipped bullet fragments from in his arm clear as day. And then the DNA and blood tests come back, and they're both positive matches for what we had at the crime scene. We had Nicky boxed in, and he was fully aware of his predicament without us having to spell it out for him. I go back to Pekin and tell him the news. I say, 'We got all this evidence, and its pointing directly at you.' I also tell him, 'We're not stupid, and we know you weren't alone on this, and we know there were people a lot higher up then you on The Outfit food chain that were involved with ordering the hit. That said, unless you want to help us, you're gonna end up taking the rap.' And in this case, the rap meant the government was going to seek the death penalty against him. He still didn't really respond, other than simply acknowledging the situation. We left there, and told him if he wanted to talk, we'd be there to listen. We broke contact after that for a while."

The following February, they had Frank Jr. wired for sound, recording conversations with his dad behind the prison walls, trying to get him to divulge as much incriminating information as he could without arousing suspicion. Since Frank Jr. was a big music fan and known for walking the prison yard and recreation areas with headphones attached to his ears blaring his favorite tunes, Bourgeois and the Bureau's technical support staff thought it would be best to bug his portable Walkman.

At the same time, in a move to get Frank Sr. to gear his conversations toward certain specific subjects, like past murders that could possibly be pinned on him and to inject an overall climate of paranoia into The Outfit as a whole, the FBI began a disinformation campaign. They sent their agents and informants out into the street and told them to imply to as many people as possible that they had more people cooperating with them in some large, unnamed investigation than they actually did. Frank Jr. also knew the best way to get his dad talking was to use his uncle Nick—a person Frank Sr. had developed simmering tensions with since their conviction—as a catalyst to goad him into discussion.

For the next year, as Frank Sr. held court with his son in their time away from their cells, almost every word he spoke was making its way back to the government. And once Frankie Breeze began to talk, he didn't stop. And boy did he like to talk. He talked about the past—how his brother Nick came to him and asked to be brought into the family business:

> **FRANK SR.:** One time we were talking at Slicker Sam's. This was in the sixties. '66. After Larry died. Was it after Larry died, let me think a minute. No, yes it was after Larry died. So it had to be '67 or '68. I would think it was either '68 or '69....Yeah, so we were talking and he says to me, I'd like to get into something like you know what you're doing. I said, Nick, I said, I would like to have you with me, but you know, this is a rough life, Nick....I says I can't promise you what we're going to do. But in the mean time,

I always got him all of his jobs. Any job
that Uncle Nicky had, I got him.

**FRANK JR.:** I mean I was just wondering
like what made him decide, 'cause I really
think that once he started doing that, he
didn't want to be there no more. It just
seemed like it.

**FRANK SR.:** I wish he would have told
me...ya know, if he would have told me,
if he'd been honest with me and said
listen, I only want to do this part. I
don't want to do that part...I would have
respected that.

He talked about the present—his fear that his brother is
going to end up cooperating with the government against
him and The Outfit:

**Feb 14, 1999**

**FRANK JR.:** I'm talking about in his own
mind. Its his biggest enemy, ya know.

**FRANK SR.:** Yeah, because you know what,
Frankie? He created fear in himself.
He created fear because he knows his
thinking ain't right. You don't see me
fearing anything do you? I'm not scared

of dying in prison, if I have to. I don't want to. Believe me, I don't want to.

**FRANK JR.:** Well, I don't think anybody does.

**FRANK SR.:** But the thing is, if I have to, if I have to. But am I gonna, am I gonna put other people away. No, I can't do that. No.

**March 13, 1999**

**FRANK SR.:** Isn't uncle Nicky acting funny?

**FRANK JR.:** See, that's what scares me. So, what are they gonna do? What do you think? They're gonna come to you and see if you got a problem....

**FRANK SR.:** Frank, remember one thing. When you make your bed, you better sleep in it.

**FRANK JR.:** I understand that. Okay. I understand.

**FRANK SR.:** And in his case, in his case, he's been doing a lot of shooting his mouth off....I told you before, I put it in God's hands. That's the only thing place,

that's the only person we have going for
us. I don't want to see anything happen
to him, but I'm gonna tell you something.
If somebody feels that its them or him,
he's gone. That's the bed he's made.

**FRANK JR.:** ...Are they gonna make sure
that you got no problem with that, if they
had to go to that extreme, because they
don't want a problem with you? That's your
brother.

**FRANK SR.:** Frank, with all due respect,
how I feel about that....No, I would,
that, that, in fact if something did
happen, I will send my blessing.

He talked about the future—what he wanted his son to do
when he got released from prison:

**FRANK SR.:** What I'd like to see here done,
is maybe when you get on the street, talk
to the big guy about this guy getting his
fucking legs broken.

**FRANK JR.:** I'll do that

**FRANK SR.:** Because he didn't do it once,
he did it twice

**FRANK JR.:** Yeah, right.

**FRANK SR.:** ...But the thing is, he put his fucking hands on the kids once after being told don't do it again. He went back a second time. So, he deserves what he gets.

He talked about his initiation into the mafia and being made:

**FRANK SR.:** Their fingers got cut and everybody puts the fingers together and all the blood is running down. Then they take pictures, put them in your hand and burn them

**FRANK JR.:** Pictures of?

**FRANK SR.:** Holy pictures

**FRANK JR.:** Oh

**FRANK SR.:** You stand there like this. There are the holy pictures. And they look at you and see if you budge while the pictures are burning. They wait till they're getting down to the skin. Then they take them out of there.

**FRANK JR.:** What happens if you budge?

**FRANK SR.:** Then it shows your fear That you have fear. You stand there like that

with your hand cupped like that. Then they
say okay. Then you take them and go like
this....One guy at a time. You don't see two
up there. One guy, when one guy's on it, the
other guy's sitting somewhere else. In the
same place, but in a different room. There's
a panel like that, about nine guys.

**FRANK JR.:** Ah, I thought, I always
thought it was just in the movies

**FRANK SR.:** Very, very close, very close,
very close. And the guy that's the second
guy in charge is the guy that talks to
you. Everybody else is the capos.

**FRANK JR.:** They just sit there?

**FRANK SR.:** They're watching you

**FRANK JR.:** And what do you got to do...
the guy that brought you in, he's there
with you, too?

**FRANK SR.:** The guys that brought you
in there is a capo. He's sitting at the
table too.

He talked about mob politics, which people and crews in
The Outfit wielded the most power, made the most money,
and treated their men the best:

**FRANK SR.:** Okay, he was even commenting about it. That the Bull [Angelo La Pietra], that he won't give us nothing. We ask for this and he won't give us that. It was fucking him by fucking us. Because we were loyal to him and we were getting fucked.

**FRANK JR.:** Yeah

**FRANK SR.:** I'll give you a for instance. Look what Johnny [John "No Nose" Di Fronzo] did for every one of his guys. He got them all legitimate businesses. He made it a point for them all to get legit. Every time we wanted to open a legitimate business, he [La Pietra] would talk us out of it. Okay, Johnny out of everybody, Johnny was the smartest.... Johnny thought in all directions.

**FRANK JR.:** Oh

**FRANK SR.:** ...Joey [Joseph "Joey the Clown" Lombardo] and Johnny are partners

**FRANK JR.:** Right, right

**FRANK SR.:** See, anything that went on between them, they always got a piece of it.

**FRANK JR.:** What do you think he's worth?

**FRANK SR.:** Joey? Oh, Johnny's worth more.

**FRANK JR.:** Oh, really?

**FRANK SR.:** Oh, without a doubt. Johnny, just in assets, Johnny's got to be worth about 25 million dollars. Just in assets that we know of.

**FRANK JR.:** Wow!

**FRANK SR.:** Frankie, he has two car dealerships too....He's got that, ah, he owns, I hate to tell you how many buildings he owns on Grand Avenue and in River Grove over there....

**FRANK JR.:** ...Johnny don't do nothing right now, he just..

**FRANK SR.:** Huh?

**FRANK JR.:** Kinda stays to himself now

**FRANK SR.:** Yeah, he stepped down, Frank. ...See Joey's got the spot now.

**FRANK JR.:** Yeah, I remember you saying that

**FRANK SR.:** But there's a lot of friction. You got South Side guys and the friction in the group. Its all one system, but you have friction.

**FRANK JR.:** With the groups?

**FRANK SR.:** You have, you're getting Johnny, Johnny's guys, Joey's not getting along with, ah, not with our Johnny Apes [John Montelone], but with the old man. What the fuck's his name? Al [Alphonse "Al the Pizza Man" Tornebene], Al. I don't think you ever met him. He's from, ah....

**FRANK JR.:** Far south?

**FRANK SR.:** Not far south...he had a pizza joint there for years. He's a sleeper, nobody knew who he was. I knew he was... he used to work in the pizza joint and he's the boss.... [Y]ou see years ago, you got head and legs broken for that. Its gotten looser and looser

**FRANK JR.:** Hmm, real loose, especially around Elmwood Park. Anybody does whatever they want

**FRANK SR.:** I'm gonna tell you something, uh, the best crew you got down there

is still Chinatown. The best crew. I'm
talking about men.

**FRANK JR.:** Yeah, I know

**FRANK SR.:** The, uh, the money makers
though are Elmwood Park

He talked about dirty police officers, his two moles in
the Chicago police department, Anthony "Twan" Doyle
and Michael "Mooney" Ricci, who fed him information
regarding on going law enforcement investigations:

**FRANK JR.:** Oh, I thought it was Twan
[Doyle] who told Mike [Ricci]

**FRANK SR.:** No, Twan is going to find out
when the stuff went missing

**FRANK JR.:** Oh, okay. So all right,
so its Mike, so this way nobody says
anything

**FRANK SR.:** Right, Mike's been doing this
for years now

**FRANK JR.:** So he's going, so, he'll keep
in touch with you?

**FRANK SR.:** Yeah, he's coming again in
April

**FRANK JR.:** 'Cause he's coming like once
every month

**FRANK SR.:** He's coming in April again.
In fact, he's coming with Twan. In the
meantime, if something comes up that's
important, he'll be here before then

He talked about who he thought was being disloyal, his
belief that his former running mate and convicted murderer, James "Jimmy Poker" Di Forti, was talking to the FBI:

**FRANK SR.:** See what happened here, when
Jimmy come out, a week later they pulled
all his stuff from the case...that's when
they gave him bond and he went on home
monitoring....Now, the two g men, Mike
[Ricci] gives 'em a guy. They take the guy
near his office and they call over and
he's not on [home monitoring]. He says,
yeah, I don't understand, he's supposed to
be on home monitoring, why isn't he?

**FRANK JR.:** Mike said this?

**FRANK SR.:** No the g guy

**FRANK JR.:** Oh, okay

**FRANK SR.:** Okay. Now this is, follow this

**FRANK JR.:** I am, I'm listening

**FRANK SR.:** All right, so now the guy
comes back the next day and tells Mike,
listen disregard what I was telling you.
I got my ass eaten out by my supervisor.
And he says, my supervisor told me that,
ah, I shouldn't be sticking my nose in
it because there's something here that
doesn't concern me. I go to Mike, I says,
this is god, god's working with us. He's
showing you what's going on here, that
this Jimmy Di Forti is cooperating....
So, now he tells me, he says, it sounds
to me Frank, as if its one hundred percent that this guy's working with the g.

[Ironically, Jimmy Di Forti was not
cooperating with the government.]

**FRANK JR.:** Mike said this?

**FRANK SR.:** Why wasn't he at, because he
wasn't on the monitoring. His name never
came up and it was supposed to

He talked about the infamous Spilotro brothers' murders:

**FRANK SR.:** Frank, he [Tony Spilotro] was
stealing like crazy. He was doing things

like crazy. He was also involved with
drugs from what I understand....Yeah,
Michael was a good kid. He was good.
Tony ruined him. Tony, he had him believ-
ing that he was the boss....That's the
last spot you ever want to try to say
you want....So, the old man [Joseph "Joey
Doves" Aiuppa] was going away remember?

**FRANK JR.:** Joey?

**FRANK SR.:** Joey Aiuppa was going away.
Ange [Angelo La Pietra] was going away. A
lot of them were going away and he [Tony
Spilotro] knew they were going away and
he wanted the spot....Joey Aiuppa had
a meeting before they all went away to
jail and he told them he wanted him [Tony
Spilotro] knocked down. I don't care how
you do it. Get him. I want him out.

**FRANK JR.:** So, Johnny was the one that
set it all up?

**FRANK SR.:** Johnny went to [Sam "Wings"]
Carlisi to open the door and he says,
he'll bite. To make his brother without
him there it ain't gonna work. So, they
got an old house with Carlisi and you
know who was there? There was almost fifteen guys there.

**FRANK JR.:** Why so many guys?

**FRANK SR.:** Because they thought they were being made when they walked in

**May 21, 1999**

**FRANK SR.:** That was just like Tony Spilotro when he [Joey Aiuppa] found out about that he was fucking that guys wife. That is a no, no. That is a no, no....

**FRANK JR.:** Right

**FRANK SR.:** Now, that's a no, no. That's a friend and that's a commandment. He, right then, a nail went into his coffin. Right then, that was one nail. The first, the thing that opened up the Pandora's box was when he found out that he had made some accusations that fuck those people in Chicago, I'm gonna be the new guy.

He talked about previous murders he played a part in:

**Feb 14, 1999**

**FRANK JR.:** 'Cause, that's when he was trying to tell me how dangerous the tall

guy was. Ya know, he said he was the one
who was with you that time with...

**FRANK SR.:** The farmer [William Dauber]

**FRANK JR.:** Yeah, and his wife.

**FRANK SR.:** Yeah

**FRANK JR.:** And they were trying to make
you look like a bad guy too, because he
was saying the wife was innocent....

**FRANK SR.:** Wait, wait, wait a minute. I
want to show you right there. I want to
show you right there.

**FRANK JR.:** What?

**FRANK SR.:** He knows nothing about that...
its all what he read. He has no idea of
no conception. But you want me to tell
you about an innocent guy. Tell him
about half and half in Cicero. Shooting
the man next to the guy who had nothing
to do with nothing. That he was involved
with...and now you'll say, well wait a
minute. He just said about my father
being, ah, being with the innocent one
over there. And yet this woman, but he

didn't think about what this other guy,
who had nothing to do with this other guy
at all completely. An innocent Polish guy
who worked everyday from eight to five.

## March 13, 1999

**FRANK SR.:** Then he hit him [John Fecoratta]
in the head. That's when he hit him in the
head, the second time. He hit him once
in the body and he's holding his pistol,
'cause the more I thought about this, I
remember that he had to cut his glove off.

**FRANK JR.:** 'Cause of the bullet he did?

**FRANK SR.:** I'm 99 percent sure

**FRANK JR.:** What did he do with them?

**FRANK SR.:** I think we got rid of it

**FRANK JR.:** Really?

**FRANK SR.:** Yeah. Or I think he might of
thrown it into a sewer. If he did, it was
when he threw his jacket away....Okay? And
he's turning, and he's turning and, he's
fighting 'em with that hand. That's what...

**FRANK JR.:** See, I couldn't understand last time you said that. I thought he probably just went like this and then ya know, was holding him

**FRANK SR.:** Instead of him stepping out of the car like he was supposed to, he stepped out of the car as you're stepping of the car...and then turn. He's gonna pull forward, then you shoot, like that.

**FRANK JR.:** Do you think, any chance he mighta taken one of the gloves off on the car anywhere and touched the car?

**FRANK SR.:** No, because there's too much excitement going on.

**May 21, 1999**

**FRANK SR.:** But it was the fall of that year [1970] he [Nick Calabrese] did one of those with me, which was an okayed one.

**FRANK JR.:** Oh

**FRANK SR.:** Okay, he did one with me. But where we put that person, its no longer

there. It's gone. They had dug up there
and made a parking lot.

**FRANK JR.:** Oh, okay.

**FRANK SR.:** Okay, when we did it, a
building was going up there. And the
person went down pretty and we put lime,
lime that eats in there, and it was there
for a long, long, long time....So, there
was no clothes on the person. We stripped
him. So, so that's the one he [Nick
Calabrese] could go back to and say,
it's in that spot.

**FRANK JR.:** ...I mean he claimed he knew
about the Dauber one, but...

**FRANK SR.:** Don't even mention that name

**FRANK JR.:** Dauber?

**FRANK SR.:** Yeah

**FRANK JR.:** I don't, the wife one?

**FRANK SR.:** How could he not?

**FRANK JR.:** I know Dad, but he made it
sound like you told 'em

**FRANK SR.:** Yeah, well he made it sound like I purposely went after the wife

**FRANK JR.:** Yeah, I know

**FRANK SR.:** I mean, Frank, I wasn't even in that vehicle. I was in the look out vehicle.

The FBI had hit pay dirt. They could not have asked for more. Operation Family Secrets was off and running.

Throughout the next few years, numerous more inquiries were made by the FBI of Nick Calabrese, requesting his cooperation in building its case against The Outfit in exchange for not charging him with the John Fecoratta murder. Staying true to the oath of allegiance he had pledged to the mafia almost two decades earlier, he continually refused. After hearing scuttlebutt that Nicky Breeze was being squeezed by the feds and fearing his cooperation would implicate him in the Spilotro brothers murder, Jimmy Marcello began sending Calabrese's wife $4,000 a month as payment for keeping quiet. It was another incentive to stay loyal.

In one last-ditch effort to persuade him to switch sides, sometime in early 2001, the FBI sent a team of agents back up to Pekin to see him and play a portion of the tape recordings made by his nephew of his brother Frank. Specifically, the portions that demonstrated Frank Sr.'s indifference to and potential sanctioning of his murder. It took a while, but a little over twelve months later, Nick Calabrese was singing a different tune. And, as it turned out, it was a tune that was music to the government's ears.

"We'd been trying to flip Nicky for a real long time, I'm talking several months," recalls Bourgeois. "He was a tough nut to crack, but I think common sense finally made him come around. He knew that either we were going to get him, make him stay in jail the rest of his life or put him down for good with the lethal injection needle, or The Outfit was going to have him killed. Once they found out about the investigation we were putting together, he was a goner. And believe me, when you're sitting behind bars, in a lot of ways its a lot easier for the mob to get to you than it is when you're on the street. So, he really didn't have many options at this point. I think the final straw came when we played him the tapes of his brother giving his blessing if he was to ever have a murder contract issued on his life. There was no place left for him to turn. His brother, no matter how much he hated him, had always been his sanctuary, his ultimate protection. Now that was gone. It didn't happen quickly. Nicky had a long time to think about what he was going to do. In my opinion, he probably would have flipped even if his brother wouldn't have been caught on tape saying that stuff. Nonetheless, Nicky told his wife to reach out to us. When she did, the Family Secrets investigation went into overdrive. We went out there to the prison, got him, debriefed him, and the rest was history."

# 17.

## A Little House Cleaning
### Return of the Wack

There have been over eleven hundred gangland slayings in the history of the city of Chicago. Sixteen Outfit murders took place between 1985 and 1990. Between 1990 and 1994 there were only four. Up until late 1999, following the edict issued by the Di Fronzo administration that discouraged violence for the sake of overall syndicate preservation, there had not been one. From that point forward, in a period spanning less than two years, there would be two.

When reports began to surface at the end of the decade that Jimmy Marcello had moved to the top of the The Outfit power base, it coincided with a return to the crime family's old way of doing business. Talk of a developing rift between Di Fronzo and a jailed Marcello didn't help matters. We were entering the twenty-first century, and the Chicago underworld was being ruled by two leaders with two very different philosophies when it came to discipline within the ranks. Whatever the problems in The Outfit hierarchy were, one thing was for certain: forty-eight hours before Christmas Day 1999, the peace that had been echoing throughout the Windy City streets for the past five years was about to be broken.

**THE** Outfit's hit list of the early 1990s was somewhat unimpressive—at least in terms of cache and in comparison to the high-profile gangland slayings of the Spilotro brothers and mega-bookie Hal Smith at the hands of the Rocky Infelice crew for refusing to pay tribute during the late 1980s.

On November 6, 1991, burglar and jewelry fence Edward Pedote was killed inside a Cicero Avenue furniture store, beaten with a wooden table leg and shot in the face. In April 1992, Glen Devos, one of Pedote's partners in an Outfit-backed burglary crew, was charged with the crime. Just over two weeks after the Pedote murder, Wallace Leiberman, an estate liquidator from the posh north suburb of Northbrook and an associate of mob enforcer, Robert "Bobby the Gabeet" Bellavia, was found shot to death in Cicero. A year later in November 1992, Sam Taglia, an auto thief and convicted narcotic trafficker, was found in the trunk of his car, with two bullets in the back of his head and his throat slit. Albert Vena, an alleged Outfit soldier, was charged with Taglia's murder, but was acquitted of the charges. Two years to the day of the Taglia killing, Giuseppe Vicari, a Sicilian mafia gambling lieutenant was murdered in his restaurant on North Harlem Avenue. Since the five slayings had all been of low-level hoodlums or associates and nobody of any significance in Chicago mob circles was put away for them, the murders made little more than minor headlines. (In the late '90s, South Side mob lieutenant James "Jimmy Poker" Di Forti, was put on trial for and eventually convicted of the Outfit-related homicide of indebted associate William "Bill the Pallet Man" Pellham, but the murder itself had taken place in 1988.)

Then, for the next five years, nothing, not a single homicide attributed to The Outfit. The underworld went relatively silent—with the exception of the Bobby Cruz murder in 1997, the Michael Culter murder in 1998, and the Don Schemel murder in early 1999 that were each rumored to be mob related yet never confirmed as such—and street merchants were allowed to cross the Windy City mafia without paying the ultimate price. Recalcitrant wiseguys were now regularly let off the hook with warnings or simply banned from conducting whichever bread-and-butter activities they partook in instead of getting whacked. Whispers around town said The Outfit had gone soft. People began to think the mob in Chicago could be dead or at the very least on its last legs.

For some members of The Outfit, this type of innuendo didn't sit well. They thought the crime family was losing respect and they wanted it back. In their mind, tongue lashings were no longer a sufficient deterrent, they wanted blood. One of those who wasn't pleased with the syndicate's newfound image was Jimmy Marcello, the alleged freshly installed boss of the Chicago mafia, who although imprisoned and serving out the remainder of a federal racketeering conviction was said to have replaced the semiretired John Di Fronzo. It is believed the first thing Marcello did in his new leadership role was to reenact old school enforcement tactics as a means of reinvigorating slouching Outfit morale. Now it was time to find somebody to be made an example as a way of demonstrating the crime family's recently altered perspective. In December 1999, that somebody was found in Ronnie Jarrett.

A man with an array of valuable skills for a criminal, Ronnie Jarrett was a high-end burglar, truck hijacker, jewelry fence, enforcer, and loan-shark who hailed from the South Side. He broke in with The Outfit's Chinatown crew in the early 1960s and eventually amassed a rap sheet that included over sixty arrests and thirteen convictions. His exploits became so notorious that in 1980 when actor James Caan, famous for playing über-gangster Sonny Corleone in the Oscar-winning movie *The Godfather*, was preparing for his role as a professional thief in an upcoming film project of his, he socialized with Jarrett and used him as a model for the character.

As his profile skyrocketed, he became a driver and bodyguard for Chinatown crew boss Angelo La Pietra, who quickly took a liking to the hulking, no-nonsense, yet eagerly ready to please Jarrett. However, the loyalty that so endeared him to La Pietra early on in his career, began to fade when La Pietra and John Di Fronzo decided that John "Johnny Apes" Monteleone, not Jarrett, would be his successor as caporegime of the South Side. Jarrett thought he deserved the leadership position and bristled at the notion of taking orders from Monteleone, someone he used to work with and viewed as an equal.

He kept his insubordinate behavior in check until after his mentor La Pietra died on May 28, 1999, but, in the following months, he let his actions and his mouth dig him a hole that he would never be able to climb out of. Without a tribute envelope being shuffled to Angelo La Pietra every month like it had in the past, Jarrett was instructed to start redirecting the payment to Johnny Apes. Doing what he was told, in the summer of 1999, Jarrett began meeting Monteleone on a monthly basis and handing him over a percentage of his rackets. There was only one problem—the envelopes Johnny Apes was receiving were significantly less thick than the ones La Pietra had been getting. Confronting Jarrett about the suspected indiscretion, Jarrett denied short-changing his new boss. Monteleone didn't believe him.

Adding to his problems, at some point during the fall, rumors began filtering up to The Outfit administration that Jarrett was dealing drugs without kicking up his profits and bad mouthing the syndicate's power structure, specifically John Monteleone, John Di Fronzo and Jimmy Marcello, to anyone that would listen. According to law enforcement reports, he didn't think Marcello should have as much say as he did from prison, that Di Fronzo was too hands off with his leadership methods, and that Monteleone should be demoted. Already skating on thin ice as it was, the reports of his dabbling in narcotics and not sharing and his spewing such hostile remarks targeted at his superiors, proved to be the final straw. Ronnie Jarrett was set to become the first victim of an official mob hit in Chicago since 1994 and the final gangland homicide of the twentieth century.

It was a brisk and cool-winded early winter morning on December 23, 1999, and Ronnie Jarrett, in what would turn out to be an act of severe irony, was on his way to a funeral. Leaving his Bridgeport home at around 10:15 A.M., he said good-bye to his wife and kids and headed off for a nearby Orland Park cemetery where his cousin was being buried. Unfortunately for the entire Jarrett family, he wouldn't make it there.

While walking the short distance from his porch to his car, which was parked on the street bordering his front lawn, he noticed a yellow Ryder rental truck driving toward him up his block. Most likely he didn't pay it much mind, probably dismissing the vehicle as being used by a neighbor to move a piece of furniture. Turning his attention away from oncoming traffic, he put his head down and started to unlock his car door. Before he could make it behind the wheel, the yellow truck stopped a few feet from where he stood. A man wearing a black ski mask emerged from the front passenger seat, pointed a silencer-equipped .32-caliber pistol at Ronnie Jarrett, and unloaded six shots into his body. Three bullets struck him in the head, one in the left shoulder, and two in his right arm. He was bleeding and unconscious before he even hit the ground.

With little worry about being recognized or apprehended, Jarrett's assailant calmly returned to the truck, pulled himself up back into the passenger seat, and motioned for the driver to leave the scene. Moments later, as Ronnie Jarrett lay almost lifeless on the cold concrete of Lowe Street, the truck pulled into a nearby alley. Both shooter and driver exited the vehicle and were met by a dark blue Lincoln waiting for them. The driver went into the Lincoln's backseat, removed a jug of gasoline, and doused the truck with it. Lighting a match, he flicked it into the truck and watched as it went ablaze. As the truck fire grew, the men got into the Lincoln and drove away.

Clinging to life, Jarrett was driven to Cook County Hospital. He underwent extensive surgery and was placed in a room in the hospital's intensive care unit that was supplied with round-the-clock police protection. The FBI hoped that if he survived the hit, he would cooperate with them in trying to take down those in The Outfit that wanted him dead. Those hopes turned futile when on January 25, 2000, Ronnie Jarrett, a suspect in close to a dozen previous homicides himself, was pronounced dead from internal injuries sustained in his shooting. As of today, no charges have been brought in this case.

**LESS** than two years after the Jarrett hit, The Outfit's hit parade continued. The ranks of the Chicago mafia were once again being disturbed. Somebody had to pay the price. Like in the case of Ronnie Jarrett, that price was murder.

In January 2001, John Monteleone died of natural causes. His passing left the post of South Side caporegime, the leadership slot he had held since Angelo La Pietra bequeathed it to him in the mid-1990s and the very same job Ronnie Jarrett felt slighted by being passed over for, up for grabs. Anthony "Tony the Hatchet" Chiaramonti, three years removed from serving a five-year federal prison sentence on a racketeering conviction and one of the most feared mob enforcers to ever walk the Windy City streets, thought he deserved the promotion. The Outfit's administration thought otherwise. Feeling that Chiaramonti lacked enough balance in his personality and was too much of a wild card to hold the highly valued position, the job was bestowed on Frank "Toots" Caruso. Similar to the situation surrounding Jarrett in 1999, Tony the Hatchet was angered by the snub and began acting out against his bosses as a result.

Chiaramonti had been a significant presence in the Chicago underworld for over four decades, making his mark in mob circles throughout the city as a premiere loan shark and debt collector. The very mention of his name elicited terror and anxiety in anyone who had ever crossed his path. With a nickname deriving from his preferred weapon of choice when trying to intimidate those slow to pay what they owed, Tony the Hatchet quickly became known as the person to go to when any Outfit heavyweights needed difficult collections made on their behalf. This skill did wonders for his reputation, and he soon found himself immersed within the inner sanctum of the West Side crew ran by Joe Ferriola and Sam Carlisi. When Ferriola and then Carlisi became boss of the crime family, Chiaramonti figured it was only a matter of time, due to his close relationship with both, before he was elevated to a position in the syndicate hierarchy.

Overseeing all of Carlisi's loan-sharking business, where he was alleged to charge an astounding 250 percent interest on all loans given out, Chiaramonti was indicted in 1992 along with the entire Carlisi crew on a slew of racketeering charges. Convicted and sent to prison in 1993, Tony the Hatchet was the first of those who went down in the highly publicized bust to gain his freedom, and in 1998 he resurfaced as a presence on the streets. Unfortunately for Tony, Carlisi, who people claim always had a soft spot in his heart for the notoriously antagonistic and violence prone Chiaramonti, died in prison in 1997, and his return to active duty in The Outfit was under the supervision of people that were not as partial to his antics.

Upon his release from jail, he was given authority of all loan-sharking operations taking place under the umbrella of the newly formed South Side crew and assigned to report to John Monteleone. He was also said to be given the responsibility of aiding Mickey Marcello in looking after the syndicate's video poker business.

In an interesting shift of events, around April 2001, Tony the Hatchet was removed from Monteleone's supervision and told to begin reporting directly to Anthony "Little Tony" Zizzo, another former Carlisi lieutenant who recently came out from behind bars after serving time. Zizzo was the primary liaison between the still-imprisoned Jimmy Marcello, the one-time number two man to the now-deceased Carlisi and the rest of The Outfit. There were rumors that Marcello and Chiaramonti didn't get along and that Jimmy the Man arranged for Zizzo to supervise Tony in order to keep special tabs on him because he didn't trust him. Whatever the reason, Chiaramonti started to chafe being under the collective thumb of Marcello and Zizzo, and when Monteleone died, he wanted his job. He didn't get it.

Not receiving the bump up to captain status as he had anticipated sent Chiaramonti into a tailspin. His behavior became even more erratic than usual, and his overall demeanor began to increasingly rub his associates and those who worked under him the wrong way. Things got so bad that complaints of his undermining attitude and cantankerous mannerisms were brought to Zizzo and then through him to Marcello. Around this same time, there were also reports that Tony the Hatchet was upset with compensation and started bothering his bosses for a bigger percentage of the joker poker machines he was in charge of.

Things came to a head on the morning of November 15, 2001, at a Cicero pancake house where Chiaramonti took a breakfast meeting with Mickey Marcello and Frank Schweihs. Delivering orders from The Outfit brass to curb his insolent behavior and that he would not be granted his request for more video poker money, Marcello and Schweihs informed Chiaramonti that if he didn't change his ways and begin to fly right, he was going to end up with the same fate as Ronnie Jarrett. He was also made aware that some money had come up missing from his last few joker poker tributes and that if it wasn't repaid, he would be sanctioned by losing a piece of his loan-sharking racket.

Offended by the tone and content of the discussion, Chiaramonti became visibly agitated. An argument between him and his two dining mates ensued. Yelling at each other across the table, tensions escalated to the point where Tony the Hatchet got up and stormed out of the restaurant.

Marcello and Schweihs followed him and the screaming match carried over outside into the parking lot. Garnering the attention of an FBI surveillance team stationed in an adjacent piece of property, Chiaramonti and Marcello got face to face, while Schweihs tried to intercede. Giving Marcello a hard shove that sent him flailing backward into Schweihs, Tony the Hatchet then got behind the wheel of his car, threw out a few more choice curse words, and sped from the scene in a state of fury.

The confrontation spelled the end of the line for Anthony Chiaramonti. It took another five days, but on November 20, just two days before Thanksgiving, all of Tony the Hatchet's histrionics finally caught up with him. He had officially gotten too big for his britches, and The Outfit was ready to put an end to all of the problems they had with him the only way they knew how to—by killing him.

At approximately 6:00 P.M., the sixty-seven-year-old Chiaramonti pulled his black BMW into the parking lot of a Brown's Chicken, a popular Chicagoland area fast food chain, in Lyons, Illinois. He got out of his vehicle and walked into the restaurant to use a pay phone. After finishing, he exited the restaurant and started to walk back to his car. Before he reached his BMW, a hunter green Chrysler minivan drove up and impeded his progress. A thickly built man wearing a Chicago Bears jacket got out of the passenger seat and walked up to Tony the Hatchet, requesting that he get in the van and leave with him. Tony refused, and the pair began to engage in a shouting match. In the middle of the heated exchange, the man tried to grab Chiaramonti and force him into the van against his will. But Tony the Hatchet broke free and ran back toward the entrance to the restaurant with his assailant in hot pursuit. Catching up to his target in the restaurant's vestibule, the hulking man in the Bears jacket pulled out a pistol and unloaded five shots into Chiaramonti's head, chest, and neck and then fled.

Rushed to the emergency room at MacNeal Hospital in Berwyn, Anthony Chiaramonti was pronounced dead at 6:50 P.M. Following a twenty-one-month investigation jointly conducted by the Lyons Police Department and the FBI's organized crime squad, in the summer of 2003, Robert Cooper, a thirty-nine-year-old Outfit thief and strong arm, was charged with the murder. In exchange for information he provided on the slaying, he was sentenced to twenty-two years in prison. During an interrogation in the months leading up to the indictment, Cooper admitted to being the driver in the Chiaramonti hit, while implicating previously fast-rising South Side mob lieutenant Anthony "Tough Tony" Calabrese (no relation to Frank and Nick) as the shooter. Although he has yet to be charged with the Chiaramonti homicide, in 2008 Tony Calabrese was convicted on charges of armed robbery and assault and received a fifty-year prison sentence.

**WHEN** Jimmy Marcello emerged from his decade-long incarceration in the late autumn of 2003, he was well aware of the ongoing FBI probe into his present-day activities as well as murders he and the crime family were suspected of carrying out in years past. Due to the defection of Nick Calabrese to the government in 2002, The Outfit was under siege. Everyone even remotely involved in the mafia in Chicago was on edge, waiting for the other shoe to drop and speculating when the FBI was going to come forth with their indictment. This pervasive climate surrounding the local underworld made Marcello resort to the low-key, bunker-style management techniques employed by Di Fronzo and Lombardo ten years before, instead of the aggressive and bloodthirsty leadership attitude he desired, exemplified by the Jarrett and Chiaramonti hits.

Just as had happened in the mid-1990s, the Chicago mob scene saw no murders from November 2001 until August 2006. Not wanting to make any additional waves for itself while it suspected the FBI was building a juggernaut of a legal assault, The Outfit took a step back from employing its ultimate enforcement tactic. Big-time gangsters and fringe wiseguys alike were once again allowed to go about their work on the street with little worry that mistakes they made would be punished by death. At that point in time, murder was simply bad for business. Even after the wide-spanning Family Secrets indictment was handed down in April 2005, things remained the same. And then, in late summer of 2006, Outfit heavyweight Little Tony Zizzo left his west suburban condominium to attend a meeting and never came back.

Imprisoned in 1993 along with Jimmy Marcello and Tony Chiaramonte in the Carlisi crew bust, the short and stout Zizzo, who in addition to the nickname "Little Tony" also went by the aliases "Tony the Trucker," "Tony the Hat," and "Fat Tony," was released in 2001 and returned to his old haunts on the West Side of Chicago. Back in business and now carrying the added reputation as a stand-up guy because he completed his time behind bars without flipping, Little Tony was thought to be on the rise, a certain fixture in The Outfit's administration of the new millennium. Marcello's release from prison in the fall of 2003 only added to this mind-set, since when running with Carlisi in the early 1990s the pair were practically inseparable. Rumors abounded, although unconfirmed, that Marcello had even tapped the then–sixty-eight-year-old Zizzo as his underboss, and the duo were preparing to take the crime family into its next generation hand in hand, much like John Di Fronzo and Joey Lombardo had done in the years past.

With Marcello back in jail in April 2005, Zizzo's role in the syndicate hierarchy became even more important, and he was said to once again be the main conduit between Jimmy the Man and the street. Throughout this time period, he was often spotted by FBI surveillance teams meeting with Joe Andriacchi and Al Tornebene, the alleged acting *consiglieri* in place of Lombardo. Less than two years later, Zizzo disappeared and was presumed dead.

On the evening of August 31, 2006, Tony Zizzo left home at around 6:30 P.M. for a meeting, alleged by some in law enforcement to be with Joe Andriacchi at a Rush Street eatery. The following afternoon, when he had not returned to his condominium, his wife, Susan, worried and fearing foul play, went to the Westmont Police Station and filed a missing persons report. Soon after the report was filed, Zizzo's Jeep Cherokee Laredo was found in the parking lot of Abruzzo's Italian Restaurant in Melrose Park. No signs of a struggle were apparent in a search of the vehicle and the owner of the restaurant, who claims to have been familiar with Little Tony, says he did not see him on the day of his disappearance. After discovering that he had left his daily kidney medication at home, and his cell phone and I-Pass—a card that allows access to Illinois tollways—in his car, the case went cold.

Theories abound in both law enforcement and mob circles regarding why Zizzo was most likely done away with. One theory has him being ordered to be killed by The Outfit power structure as a punishment to Jimmy Marcello because the pair were so close and they blamed Jimmy the Man for the Family Secrets indictment. Whether this was true or not, at the very least, Marcello's loose lips featured on prison audio surveillance and his inability to keep the Calabrese brothers didn't help matters. Another theory fingers Marcello for sanctioning the hit because he was worried that Zizzo, who knew enough information to put him away for the rest of his life, would be tempted to turn government witness. A final line of thinking attributed the Zizzo disappearance to a falling out between him and Andriacchi and Di Fronzo over either money or rank. The only thing for certain as the Family Secrets trial approached was that any loose ends that Zizzo represented had now been tied up.

# 18.

## The Trial
### A Circus with a Judge

The big top came to Chicago in the summer of 2007 in the form of the Family Secrets trial, a spectacular legal drama over two years in the making. It descended on the Windy City to much media scrutiny and overall fanfare. And following twenty-six months of haggling, from both sides, over tedious pretrial motion after pretrial motion, it didn't disappoint.

Local TV news broadcasts and the city's two major newspapers heralded the trial as the most important government assault against American organized crime in more than two decades. In addition to the slew of racketeering counts charged—juice loans, extortion, and gambling—eighteen murders, some older than twenty-five years in the FBI's cold case file, were finally going to find their way in front of a jury. For some, mostly family members of victims and law enforcement personnel who worked the slayings, it was the inevitable course of things—justice, although much later than expected, was being served.

The press had a field day. And even though the mafia was still very much alive, pundits were rampantly speculating the beginning of the end for the Chicago Outfit. The media wanted an end game, a way to neatly bookend a story they had been tracking since early in the decade when word of a key turncoat inside the local mafia helping the feds make a case against the mob surfaced. You couldn't really blame them, though. It made for great headlines.

However, make no mistake about it, despite the fact that reports of The Outfit's demise were more than premature, the successful prosecution of the much-written about defendants would be a serious setback for the long-standing crime syndicate. As the U.S. attorney's office made its final preparations for trial, and the lawyers for the defense contemplated any last-minute strategy shifts, the city of Chicago held its collective breath for what would be the media event of the year. A real-life soap opera with characters who bore such colorful nicknames like "Bobby the Beak," "Richie the Rat," and "Ernie the Oven" that would play out for the better part of the next three months. The circus was in town and it was setting up shop in the heart of The Loop, specifically, at the corner of Dearborn and Monroe inside Judge James B. Zagel's courtroom on the twenty-fifth floor of the Dirksen Federal Building.

* * *

**BY** late June, the stage was finally set. When the curtain lifted on what was already being dubbed the trial of the century, only five of the original fourteen defendants remained to face to the music. Frank "Goomba" Saladino, The Outfit's alleged man in Rockford and someone reputed to have been involved in several of the eighteen homicides charged, died on the day the arrest warrants were served in the case. When federal agents came to arrest him at the northwest Indiana hotel room he had been living in, they found him dead of a heart attack. Former Chicago Police Department officer Michael Ricci, charged by prosecutors with passing information to and from imprisoned defendant Frank Calabrese, also died before the trial's start date. Frank "Frankie the German" Schweihs, the longtime Outfit enforcer and right-hand man to Joey Lombardo, got severed from the case due to his battle with cancer. Mickey Marcello, Thomas Johnson, Dennis Johnson, and Joe Venezia, each of whom worked for Jimmy Marcello's video poker business, and Nick Ferriola, the son of former Outfit boss Joe Ferriola as well as a liaison for Frank Calabrese to his ongoing rackets on the street, all pled guilty before the trial started. Nick Calabrese, the mob assassin who admitted in his plea deal to playing a role in fourteen of the murders himself, was the government's star witness.

Although more than half of the original defendants were no longer around to stand before the jury, with the exception of Schweihs, all of the biggest fish in the case remained. South Side hit man and loan shark Frank Calabrese was facing thirteen murder charges, implicated in each and every one by his own flesh and blood, his brother Nick. Jimmy Marcello, the alleged street boss of The Outfit until his arrest in the case, was facing three murder charges and one charge of attempted murder. Joey Lombardo, the highly tenured mafia chief and reputed *consiglieri,* and Paul Schiro, The Outfit's representative in Arizona, were each charged with one apiece. Closing out the heavily publicized batch of defendants was Anthony "Twan" Doyle, an Italian man who had an Irish name and was a former Chicago cop accused of giving sensitive police intelligence to and acting as a liaison for Frank Calabrese.

Besides the murders discussed previously—the homicides of Danny Seifert, John Mendell, Vincent Moretti, Donald Renno, Butch Petrocelli, Billy Dauber, Nick D'Andrea, Tony and Michael Spilotro, and John Feccorata— there were plenty more the prosecution threw at the crowded and cramped defense table (actually two defense tables, one in front of the other and placed to the far right end of the courtroom, facing the jury, not Judge Zagel). It was not surprising that most of these slayings were just as heinous as the ones already examined.

- The August 1970 murder of Outfit enforcer, Michael "Hambone" Albergo, who made the mistake of making a juice loan to an undercover police officer and subsequently was subpoenaed to testify in front of a grand jury investigating the local loan-sharking racket. Needless to say, Hambone never made it to the grand jury and was killed by the mob for his dealings with the undercover cop and for fear of him talking.

- The June 1976 murder of thief Paul Haggerty, who had stolen some uncut jewelry that belonged to a member of The Outfit. Haggerty was kidnapped, tortured, strangled, and eventually had his throat slit.

- The March 1977 murder of Henry Cosentino, a local rented wiseguy and friend of Frank Calabrese who was killed by having his throat slit for shooting Frank Saladino in the leg during an argument.

- The June 1981 murder of Michael Cangoni, an area trucking magnate who refused to continue to pay tribute to The Outfit and was blown up in his Mercedes-Benz as he drove on to I 290 in suburban Hinsdale.

- The June 1983 double murder of Richard "Chico" Ortiz and Arthur Morawski, who were both shot to death while sitting in a parked car in suburban Cicero. Ortiz, a local bar owner, was killed because he ran afoul of South Side mob boss Johnny Apes Monteleone for not sharing profits of a loan-sharking operation he was running and for the belief that he was dealing drugs (it was also rumored that Ortiz had committed an unauthorized murder related to his narcotics business). Morawski just happened to be in the wrong place at the wrong time.

- The attempted murder of Nick Sarillo, which took place in April 1982, was also on the trial docket. Sarillo, a local restaurant owner who was running a sports book and refused to pay a street tax to Outfit leader, Joseph "Black Joe" Amato, had his van blown up while he was driving on a street in the north suburb of Wauconda.

Appropriately, the Family Secrets trial started out with a bang—almost literally. On the morning of June 19, the first day of jury selection, Kurt Calabrese, oldest son of Frank Calabrese, found what looked like an explosive device on the back porch of his suburban Kenilworth home. Heading out to his backyard to do some lawn maintenance, he stumbled on a clear plastic bag containing a digital timer tied with black plastic tape to what appeared to be three sticks of dynamite. After evacuating the neighborhood, authorities deemed the device a fake.

The incident was the finale in a long line of the harassment of Kurt Calabrese, who is no longer on speaking terms with his father but who had once worked for a loan-sharking operation he ran in the 1990s, had been experiencing in the weeks and months leading up to the trial. Before the bomb hoax, he had been receiving nasty phone calls, threatening letters, and had a number of dead rats thrown on his property. Since Kurt was not personally involved with the trial in any manner—albeit his brother Frank Jr. and his uncle Nick were the prosecution's two star witnesses—the ongoing harassment left law enforcement looking for answers. Nonetheless they assumed it had something to do with Family Secrets. At the very least it gave the local media outlets, who would normally be hard-pressed to find much excitement during the tedious jury selection process, tantalizing fodder to report.

With a jury consisting of nine men and ten woman— seven of whom were alternates—in place with in a brisk three days, opening arguments began on Thursday, June 21. As Judge Zagel's courtroom filled to capacity in the moments leading up to the prosecution's time in front of the long wood-paneled jury box, there was electricity in the air. The anticipation and excitement were palpable.

Joey Lombardo wore a gray suit and red tie, carried a walking cane, and sat on the far left end of the back defense table, intentionally isolated from Calabrese, Marcello, Schiro, and Doyle. Employing the so-called withdrawal defense, claiming to have left his life in the mob behind after being released from prison in 1992, Lombardo was instructed by his defense team to interact with his co-defendants as little as possible. Jimmy Marcello, at the right end seat of the back defense table, was dressed in a dark brown blazer worn over a black mock turtleneck and Frank Calabrese, at the right end seat of the front defense table, in a powder blue sport jacket, sat closest to the spectators gallery. Finally, Paul Schiro, whose once-tanned and healthy-looking figure had been weathered down to a wrinkled, slumping, and haggard physique from his time already in jail for his part in an Outfit-backed string of jewelry heists, and the hulking and broad-shouldered Anthony Doyle, sat on the left side of the front table closest to the judge and court reporter.

At approximately 9:45 A.M., Judge Zagel brought the court to order with his gavel, motioning with his head for the prosecution to commence their opening argument. Rising from his chair, U.S. Attorney John Scully, with a calm, yet determined look in his eyes, slowly walked the short distance from his seat to the small piece of carpeted floor in front of the jury. A one-time member of the Naval Jag Corps, Scully presented a picture that was the epitome of calm and collected as he readied to begin.

Before an audience that was anxiously waiting, almost salivating, Scully began to unfold the story of Family

Secrets. He spoke in a straightforward, confidant, and measured tone, staying away from theatrics and remaining focused on raw detail and fact. He started out by telling the jury that this was a case based on organized crime, explaining how the mafia makes fortunes on traditional rackets like illegal sports betting, street tax, and loan sharking, preying and profiting off the weak and weary. Then after sternly declaring that four of the five defendants were charged with mafia-style murders, he made certain that the jurors knew the grave severity of the matter at hand. "This is not *The Sopranos,* this is not *The Godfather,*" said Scully. "This case is about real people, real victims. These men are corrupt, violent, and without honor."

Breaking down each individual murder while standing behind whichever defendant had been charged with committing it, he used an overhead projector that displayed each victims' face as a way to augment his verbal re-creation. For most of his opening statement, Scully was in close proximity to Frank Calabrese, the man who was charged with the majority of the case's homicides and who throughout the proceedings wore an ear-to-ear smirk across his face that seemed to scream his indifference to the entire ordeal.

Short, direct, and to the point, Scully concluded in less than an hour, content to rest his opening argument on the shorter end of the norm for most mega trials. Some legal analysts viewed the tactic as a calculated risk, but nonetheless the veteran prosecutor was satisfied that he got his message across. "Longer isn't always better," Scully said just short of a year later. "I think our opening proved that. We drove home our main points of emphasis, which were that this was a case about brutal people doing a lot of brutal things, and we delivered it in a way that was easy to digest for people not familiar with the ways of the mafia. I might have spoke the words to the jury, however, the entire prosecutorial team played a role in our strategy and how we wanted to present our case on the first day. I'm more than happy with the way the opening turned out. In retrospect, I think we all are."

Next up was the famed and flamboyant Joe "The Shark" Lopez, defense attorney for Frank Calabrese. Wearing a black suit with a pink shirt, and tie that matched his socks, Lopez described his client as looking more like a "Wisconsin cheese salesman" than a heartless wiseguy. He claimed that the prosecutors had gotten their hands on the wrong man— that Frank's brother Nick, not Frank was the actual "capo in the mafia." Hammering home the fact that there was no physical evidence linking Calabrese to any of the murders in the case, Lopez said it was Nick that committed the heinous crimes charged and that now, from his role as a star witness, was looking to "do him too," referring to helping take down his brother. Lopez also took aim at Calabrese's son Frank Jr.—also slated to testify against his dad—and referred to him as "ungrateful," "greedy," and "addicted to drugs."

Like Lopez, Jimmy Marcello's attorney, Marc Martin, continually hammered home the fact that there was an absence of any physical evidence tying his client to any murders in his opening. "You can make the charts as big as you want, it won't hide the hole in the case: no physical evidence." Martin made no bones about admitting that Marcello was a mobster, one who had done significant time in prison for racketeering in the past. But he tried to state as many times as possible that that did not make him a murderer. "Just because he was in jail doesn't make him guilty in this case . . . this is not the Salem witch hunts," he said. In addition, Martin claimed that Marcello was being dragged into an internal squabble concerning the Calabrese family that had nothing to do with him. "The evidence will show Mr. Marcello has been caught in the crosshairs of a dysfunctional family."

Schiro's attorney kept it quick, trying to make it clear that the only person saying his client was a killer—he was charged with taking part in the Emil Vaci murder—was Nick Calabrese, a man who admits to having committed multiple homicides himself. In perhaps the most theatric ploy administered in the defense openings, Doyle's attorney, Ralph Mezcek, rolled out a yellow-colored Streets and Sanitation cart, saying that his client used to work for the city department as a street cleaner, and then took the indictment of his client and threw the several page document into the cart for dramatic affect, claiming, "When this trial is over I believe you are going to do the same with this indictment."

The venerable Rick Halperin, Joey Lombardo's lawyer, deferred his opening statement until he was ready to present his case to the jury later on in the trial. When, nearly, two months later, he addressed the jury on his client's behalf, he implored them to "Keep an open mind" and, point blank, "Joey Lombardo did not kill Daniel Seifert," and "Joey Lombardo is not, was not, and has never been a capo or member of the Chicago Outfit." Halperin, who admitted that Lombardo had run a popular neighborhood dice game for many years and chalked up his imprisonment in the 1980s for illegal activity relating to Las Vegas to a poor selection of friends and business associates, told the jury that upon release from prison in 1992 his client went clean. "He decided to withdraw from the life," he said. The new Joey Lombardo was, "older, smarter, wiser."

Opening arguments concluded the following Monday afternoon and the first group of witnesses were ready to be called. The tip of the iceberg had only been lightly nicked. There was an entire avalanche forthcoming and defendants and attorneys alike braced themselves for what would end up being the legal ride of their lives.

**FIRST** up on the witness list was Jim Wagner, former FBI organized crime squad leader and at that time, head of the Chicago Crime Commission. Wagner who was called by prosecutors to kick off their case by outlining the history and structure of the mob in Chicago, so jurors could get a basic understanding of the landscape the trial would be set in. Following Wagner, who was clear and concise with his breakdown of The Outfit, William "Red" Wemette was called to the stand. Starting with Wemette, it appeared that the prosecution was intent on building the first portion of its case against Joey Lombardo, the most high profile of all the defendants.

The owner of an adult bookstore in the Old Town area of the city, Wemette testified to being extorted by the mafia for the fourteen years he had been in business. Having voluntarily worn a wire for a period of time, he explained that to operate in the industry he was forced to get permission from Joey Lombardo and pay 50 percent of his gross profits to Lombardo's collectors. When asked by prosecutor Mitch Mars if he could see the man he knew as Lombardo in the courtroom, before Wemette could point him out for the record, Lombardo stood up and smiled.

To augment its charge of extortion, the prosecution played a tape of a conversation between Wemette and Frank Schweihs in which Schewis informed Wemette to ignore overtures from other mobsters like Michael "Mikey the Fire Bug" Glitta, who were trying to shake him down for protection money and to continue to pay Lombardo, who at the time was in prison.

"Mike (Glitta) has nothing to do with this joint," Schwies told him. "If Mike fucks with you, he's in a world of fucking trouble with me. Serious fucking trouble that he won't overcome. . . . This is a declared fucking joint. He has no business fucking with it and he cannot ever come back and tell us he didn't know. . . . Lumbo [another nickname for Lombardo] said it's real fucking clear to him and he's not to fuck with ya. . . . So what does he think, that things have fucking changed cause Lumbo's sitting in the fucking joint? He knows how things work. . . . This guy is never to come in here no more and he's not to call ya. If he should call you, say listen don't call me, I've made other arrangements, bye. That's all you tell'em. Ok? . . . All right, you're with us, you're with me and there ain't no one gonna fuck with you. Ok? Case closed."

The next afternoon, another audio surveillance excerpt was played—this one involving Lombardo himself. In a conversation with longtime St. Louis–based mob attorney Morris Shenker regarding the lawyer's potential sale of his shares of stock in the Dunes Hotel and Casino in Las Vegas, Lombardo implored him to go along with The Outfit's wishes.

**LOMBARDO:** We're at a point now where its
shit or get off the pot, you know what I
mean. We either get what we got coming to
us or we don't get what we got coming to us.

**SHENKER:** Nobody's telling me what to do.

**LOMBARDO:** Excuse me, I'm just here to
bring back a message. And let me tell you
something, if they make a decision and
they tell me to come back and give you a
message to pay, you can fight the system
if you want, but I'm gonna tell you one
thing: You're 72 now, right.... If you defy
it, I assure you you won't reach 73....
Allen [Allen Dorfman, his contact with
The Outfit before meeting Lombardo] is
meek and harmless. The people behind him
are not.

Alva Johnson Rogers, a one-time Outfit lieutenant
under Lombardo, was brought in to testify. Rogers, a native
of Texas who met Chicago mobster Marshall Caifano in
prison and then followed him back to the Windy City after
his release to work for Lombardo, was a mainstay in The
Outfit for a portion of the 1970s. Nicknamed "Johnny the
Rabbit," he aided Lombardo in the syndicate's takeover
of the area's porn industry and testified to being in The
Clown's presence the morning after the 1974 murder of
Danny Seifert. According to Rogers, while he, Caifano, and

Lombardo were at a local driving range hitting golf balls, Lombardo said, "That son of a bitch won't be testifying against anyone now," referring to Seifert's intent to take the stand against him in the pension fund fraud case he was indicted in.

In one of the most powerful moments to take place during the entire trial, Seifert's widow, Emma, took the stand to conclude the first week of testimony. Describing her husband's slaying, an incident in which she and her son were held at gunpoint in the couple's office, while masked and armed assailants chased him through the parking lot, eventually killing him, she said in an emotional, yet assertive tone, "I screamed, but obviously not loud enough, because Daniel didn't hear me. . . . They killed my husband." Before leaving the witness box, Seifert testified that the physical size and build of one of the masked men, as well as the way he moved on his feet, made her believe it was Lombardo.

The month of July started out with a former electronics store salesman identifying Lombardo as the man he sold a police scanner to around the time of the Seifert murder and an FBI fingerprint expert testifying that a fingerprint from Lombardo's left middle finger was found on an application for a car title for a brown Ford LTD that was used as the getaway vehicle in the Seifert hit. However, following the fingerprint analysis, the prosecution switched the gears in its case. While the opening section of its witness list focused on Joey Lombardo, they now set their sites directly on Frank Calabrese, preparing to pepper the courtroom with the most riveting material available in its arsenal over the next two and a half weeks.

On the Tuesday before the July 4th holiday, which was

going to bring a three-day break from trial proceedings, the government's first star witness, Frank Calabrese Jr., a burly and balding man who bore a stunning resemblance to his father, was called to the stand. Frank Jr., who was now living in Arizona, told the jury the story of his childhood, playing football at Elmwood Park's Holy Cross High School, working at a local pizzeria as a teenager, and becoming a member of his dad's crew, doing collections with his uncle Nick. He spoke of developing a bad cocaine habit and stealing money from his father, which he used on drugs, various exotic vacations, and for opening a restaurant—La Luce, located on the corner of Lake and Ogden—that eventually floundered.

According to Frank Jr., this resulted in physical abuse at the hands of his father. "My father cracked me and started yelling at me," he testified. "He pulled out a gun and stuck it in my face. He said, 'I'd rather have you dead than have you disobey me.' I started crying. I started hugging and kissing him. I said, 'Help me, help me do the right thing.' "

When everyone returned from their holiday the next Monday morning, Frank Jr. continued delivering the lurid details of living under the thumb and in the gargantuan shadow of the man they called The Breeze. He said that by the time he reached his thirties, his dad had begun grooming him to eventually take over his crew.

"One day everything will be mine," Frank Jr. said his father once told to him. As a result, his responsibilities increased to handling most of the bookkeeping for crew finances, the acquiring and stashing of artillery in strategic locations, and looking after day-to-day business of the crew's rackets when his dad or uncle were indisposed.

He was also schooled in the fundamental rules and traditions of life in The Outfit. "You could never leave," Frank Sr. told his son. "Once you're in, you're in for life." While enduring glares and loud scoffs from his father just a few feet away at the defense table, Frank Jr. said that his dad explained to him that, "One of the rules of The Outfit was that your family, your Outfit family came before your blood family . . . and also came before God."

Fed up with his dad's bullying and bravado, Frank Jr., in the midst of serving his almost five-year sentence in federal prison for being a member of his crew, told the jury how he decided to turn against his father—after his promise to go straight was broken—and help the government build a case that would keep the already imprisoned Calabrese Sr. behind bars forever.

To conclude his direct examination, the prosecution played their first trump card of the trial, a virtual smoking gun—the tapes Frank Jr. made of his father basically talking his way into a life jail sentence. He explained that he baited his dad into pouring his heart and mind out to him by feigning interest in becoming more involved in his rackets and by pitting his father, a bitterly jealous and spiteful man, and uncle against each other. The jury was thoroughly enthralled as well as disgusted by some of the many jarring portions of audio surveillance played for them.

Upon cross-examination, Frank Jr. admitted to loving his father, yet at the same time detesting his life in the mafia. "I love him, but not some of his ways," he said to his dad's attorney, Joe Lopez, who did his best to paint his client as a harmless blowhard whose boasts were mostly empty of any substance. Constantly pounding home the fact that Frank Jr. was an admitted thief and drug addict, not to mention a failed professional actor, Lopez tried his best to discredit him to little avail. The fact remained that no matter how many insults he threw the younger Calabrese's way in his effort to undermine his testimony, the tapes and Frank Sr.'s own voice on them didn't lie.

**FRANK** Calabrese Jr. was excused from the witness box on July 13. He was soon followed by Michael Talerico, the fifty-five-year-old reputed Chinatown Outfit heavy, who at one point in the 1980s was suspected by the FBI to be acting as a currier of syndicate skim money from Las Vegas to Chicago. Talerico, Angelo and Jimmy La Pietra's nephew and a former son-in-law of Frankie Schweihs, testified that at the behest of his uncles, he paid street tax to the Calabrese crew and was physically attacked by Ronnie Jarrett in 1997 when he stopped due to Frank's and Nick's incarceration.

Then when the near-twenty jurors might have thought they couldn't hear anything more disturbing than what they heard when Frankie Breeze's own son testified against him, his brother and former collaborator in chaos, Nick, was called to testify on the late afternoon of July 16— enter government star witness number two. Wearing a gray sweatsuit, Nick Calabrese, arguably the most important cooperating witness in the history of Chicago crime, took the stand to the sound of a hushed courtroom. As Calabrese made the approximately ten-foot walk from the door to the witness box, nobody present could take their eyes off him. He was the living, breathing sound of annihilation to the five defendants sitting before him and possibly many more in the future. The silence of anticipation was deafening. The testimony everybody had been waiting for since the day Nicky Breeze switched sides from the bad guys to the good guys nearly five years earlier, was about to begin.

Even though the first day of his testimony lasted a little more than an hour, it definitely lived up to the hype. To start things off, Calabrese admitted that he was in fact a made member of the mafia and described The Outfit's leadership and protocol up until the time he became a witness for the government in 2002. He recounted how he got his start in the local underworld by working for his brother Frank, and then openly copped to each murder in the indictment that he played a part in personally. Explaining how he quickly learned that killing was just another part of the job, he said, "If you got an order to kill someone, you had to do it or you'd get killed yourself." Later on in his testimony, he would talk about his official entry into the mafia through a making ceremony overseen by Joey Aiuppa and Al Tornabene that he, his brother, Jimmy Marcello, Frank Belmonte, "Little Tony" Zizzo, Albert Tocco, and Rocky Infelice went through inside a closed restaurant basement in 1983.

The next morning Calabrese, dressed in a starched, white, button-down shirt and blue jeans, was back on the stand and while being carefully guided by Mitch Mars, began detailing all of the aforementioned murders. Resembling more stockbroker than sociopath, wearing thin spectacles with his gray hair shortly cropped, he first spoke of participating in the August 1970 homicide of Michael "Hambone" Albergo. Calabrese told of being asked by his brother to help him dig a hole to put a body in, thinking it was a joke because he had only been working with his crew for a few months. It wasn't.

Instead, according to Nick, he was taken to a construction site near the old Comiskey Park and once there aided Frank in shoveling a large-size crevice into the earth where a soon-to-be dead gangster would be placed. Continuing the tale of his inaugural slaying, Calabrese recalled how one of his brother's cronies, Ronnie Jarrett, lured Albergo into a stolen four-door Chevrolet and while on the way back to the construction site, he helped Jarrett hold Albergo's arms behind his back while Frank strangled him to death. Albergo was stripped of his clothes and eventually thrown into the hole that Frank and Nick had dug earlier. "At this point, I wet my pants, I was so scared," Nick said of the burial.

Noticeably shaken, he told the story of planting a bomb underneath the car of Michael Cangoni and then watching as his wife drove their children to school, barely missing being blown up themselves by avoiding driving past a plant car housing a detonation device inside it. Shortly thereafter, he watched as Cangoni was blown to pieces as he drove onto the expressway.

He spoke of the 1978 double homicide of Vincent Moretti and Donald Renno in a Cicero bar, where he, his brother, and others (Jimmy La Pietra, Tony Borselino, Butch Petrocelli, Frank Saladino, Joe Ferriola, Ronnie Jarrett, John Fecoratta, and John Monteleone) beat, stomped, and strangled the pair to death in retribution for the break-in at Tony Accardo's house a few months earlier. Moretti was involved in the conspiracy to rip off the Big Tuna, but Renno just happened to be with him when his time was up. "I was pulling one end of the rope and I had my foot against his head," Nick said of helping carry out the savage murder of Vince Moretti. "Then I noticed Goomba [Saladino] got on and started jumping on him . . . three or four times on his chest."

Previously, Calabrese testified about how his brother Frank told him never to speak of the murders they committed together after their completion and to either refer to them in code or by using the term *it*. After the Moretti and Renno hits, the brothers referred to it as "The Strangers in the Night," due to the fact that it was the song playing on the bar's jukebox when the killings took place.

Calabrese talked about the murder of John Mendell, the ringleader of the Accardo break-in, who was beaten and strangled death to death by Nick, Frank Sr., Goomba Saladino, and Ronnie Jarrett in Ronnie Jarrett's mother-in-law's garage and the slayings of Richard "Chico" Ortiz and Arthur Morawski in 1983, where Nick and Jimmy Di Forti blew the pair away with shotguns.

He talked about the Butch Petrocelli murder where the Calabrese brothers, Jimmy La Pietra, and Frank Santucci jumped Petrocelli in a Cicero storefront down the street from a social club frequented by Angelo La Pietra: "It happened so fast," Nick recalled. "He was on the ground. I don't remember if we taped his legs or not, but I do remember holding him down and my brother choking him."

He talked about the Nick D'Andrea murder in which, according to him, D'Andrea was killed when Nick, Jimmy Marcello, Sam Carlisi, Angelo La Pietra, and Tony Chiaramonti accidentally beat him to death while interrogating him for details regarding the botched assassination attempt on Al Pilotto's life: "The bat just bounced off him like I was hitting him with rubber," he said about being instructed by Carlisi to beat D'Andrea with a Louisville Slugger. "So, I dropped the bat and jumped on him . . . I had my arms around his neck and I finally worked my way to having some leverage and he fell on top of me . . . the guy was moaning and Carlisi was hitting him with the back end of a shotgun."

He talked about the Emil Vaci murder where according to Calabrese, with Paul Schiro and Jimmy Di Forti standing lookout, he killed Vaci in a van that was being driven by Joey Hansen: "He says 'oh, no,'" Nick remembered. "He says 'I promise I'm not going to say nothing.' . . . I shot him in the head."

During the most high-profile testimony of the trial, he recounted the Spilotro brothers double homicide. He told of being nervous as he waited in the basement of a suburban residence for the brothers to be brought down under the ruse that they were each receiving a promotion. "At this time I'm wound up," he said. "I'm tense . . . I'm focusing on what I'm going to do."

He remembered greeting Michael Spilotro with a handshake before holding him down as Louie Eboli strangled him and then hearing Tony Spilotro unsuccessfully request a final prayer before being killed.

When he told his brother Frank that he had been assigned to be one of the Spilotros' killers before the murders took place, he recalled his brother being upset that he wasn't included in the bloodletting. "Why didn't they ask me, I want to be there too," he testified that Frank said to him. Nicky Breeze also talked about going out to eat at local Baker's Square with Jimmy La Pietra, Joe Ferriola, and John Fecoratta after the murders and being advised by La Pietra, his captain at that time to "have your brother give you a raise," in return for the good job he had done.

Finally, in concluding his murderous recollections, Nick Calabrese told the tale of the Big John Fecoratta murder, an event that would slowly morph into the catalyst for the entire Family Secrets investigation and trial. Fecoratta, who had upset his superiors with his increasingly erratic behavior and allegedly his mishandling of the Spilotro brothers burial was lured by the Calabrese brothers to a Chicago-area dentist office under the guise that they were going to bomb it.

Nick said that he was the one tagged to do the shooting because it was believed that Fecoratta, already nervous that his bosses in The Outfit were upset with him, would be too suspicious of Frank. "It was decided that I would be the one because he didn't think it would come from me," he told the jury.

Continuing the story, he told how when he went to shoot Fecoratta, Big John "caught the play." The two men began fighting for control of the weapon before it discharged, wounding both—Nicky in the arm and Big John in the chest. Somehow being able to release the gun's cylinder, Fecoratta emptied the bullets from the weapon and bolted out of the car across a busy street. Nick told how he reloaded the gun and chased after Fecoratta with the Ken Eto–attempted murder running through his head the entire time.

"My mind, my adrenaline is going," said a slightly more animated than usual Nick Calabrese. "And he's running and the only thing that I can think of is what happens if I don't do this and he gets away. I'm dead."

Finally catching up with his target, "I shot him in the head," Calabrese said. "I shot him in the back of the head."

Since it was a warm day and he worried he would look funny wearing the pair of gloves he had on, he took them off and tried to put them in his back pocket. "I started pulling my gloves off 'cause its September and I've got black gloves on and it didn't look right," he remembered. "So I took them off. And I thought I had put them in my pocket. I didn't know at that time that I had dropped them."

He wrapped up the story by telling how his universe was turned upside down in May 1999, when FBI agents came to visit him in prison where he was serving a sentence for a mid-1990s racketeering conviction and informed him they had a court order to take a DNA sample and an X-ray of the arm he was shot in during the Fecoratta hit. Calabrese said it was then he realized it was all over and unless he decided to cooperate he would either be killed or spend the rest of his life behind bars.

With four days of direct examination behind him, it was now time for the defense to cross-examine The Outfit's snitch of the ages, Nick Calabrese. Displaying no sympathy for a man who tried at every opportunity to paint himself as a victim of his big brother's strong-arm tactics, the attorneys for each of the co-defendants hammered him hard and with no mercy. Nick told Joe Lopez that he went along with his brother's activities because he feared that he would be killed himself if he didn't participate in the murders they plotted and carried out together. "I was loyal because I was afraid and I was a chicken and a coward because I didn't walk away from it," he said.

Thomas Breen, one of Jimmy Marcello's lawyers, tried to punch holes in Calabrese's testimony by pointing out that when he described the making ceremony he and Marcello underwent nearly twenty-five years earlier, he had said that a prerequisite for initiation into the mob was being of complete Italian or Sicilian descent. When confronting him with the information that his client was half-Irish, Calabrese responded by saying, "Then Jimmy Marcello lied. Sam Carlisi lied. They both lied to the boss." Before finishing Breen scored some points for the defense team by demonstrating that Calabrese couldn't identify a picture of Nick D'Andrea, the man he claimed to have helped beat and torture to death with Marcello in 1981.

On the stand for a total of seven days, Nick Calabrese was excused from his testimony on the afternoon of July 23. He had done more than an adequate job. Even though he was an admitted killer, he came off remorseful and as a result, in many ways, sympathetic. Experts in the local media speculated that he came off extremely credible to the jury and his time in the witness box would go a long way in the prosecution's effort for mass convictions. With the successful testimony from first Frank Calabrese Jr, and then Nicky Breeze, the nails in the proverbial coffin were beginning to accumulate on defense row.

**OVER** the next few days a parade of former gangsters took the stand to detail life in The Outfit. Richard "Richie the Rat" Mara, a former South Side crew member, spoke of accompanying Frank Calabrese's henchmen on collections for his sports betting and loan-sharking operations and watching Frankie Breeze and Ronnie Jarrett deliver a beating with a baseball bat to an underworld associate who was giving out juice loans without the proper permission. Robert

"Bobby the Beak" Siegel, a one-time Outfit thief, recalled delivering payments of bribe money on behalf of the crime syndicate to Chicago policemen and how he had received phone calls from John Mendell and Bernard Ryan, both suspected of taking part in the burglary at Tony Accardo's residence, and told that they had been requested by Jarrett and John Di Fronzo to aid in score opportunities that turned out to be suspected setups before their respective deaths.

Ernest "Ernie the Oven" Severino, who owned a crematory and a gun shop and once paid a street tax to Butchie Petrocelli, testified that he held weapons and money for Petrocelli, and when he was killed he was called to a meeting and told by Gerry Scarpelli that his commitment to The Outfit remained. Richard Cleary, another former Outfit thief, told of visiting Paul Schiro in prison and breaking the news to him that Nick Calabrese had begun cooperating with the FBI. When he asked Schiro if his flipping could end up doing him any harm, he responded, "Yes, he could put me away forever."

Michael Spilotro's widow, Ann, and daughter were each called to the stand on August 1. Ann testified that she met with Joey Lombardo, Tony Spilotro's direct superior in the months he was released from prison in 1992 and was told by him that if he was free man when her husband and brother-in-law were murdered, he would have stopped it. Spilotro's daughter Michelle testified that a man she knew as "Jim" called her house on the day her father was killed and that she was later able to identify that voice as Jimmy Marcello through an FBI audio line-up of different voices speaking the same line of dialogue.

Keeping with a Spilotro family theme, the prosecution

then called Pasquale "Pat" Spilotro, Tony and Michael's brother, to the stand. Speaking about his over two-decade obsession of bringing his brothers' killers to justice, Spilotro talked about keeping up good relations with their suspected murderers in order to help the FBI build a case against them. In fact, he did a lot of their dental work, maintaining a facade of forgiveness and understanding while trying to delicately probe for information at any time possible. He testified to one conversation with Joey Lombardo regarding his brothers' slaying where he was told, "Doc, when you get an order, you follow it or you go too."

Spilotro admitted to turning in Lombardo when the godfather was a fugitive by alerting the FBI to a meeting he had set up with The Clown to treat an abscess in his tooth and helping the feds track down Frank Schweihs when he went on the run by tracing The German's family members' cell phone calls to him in his Kentucky hiding place.

The prosecution wrapped up its case by bringing an IRS agent to the stand to testify that the Marcello brothers' video poker machine business had failed to pay at least half of its income taxes over the previous decade. They then played more audio surveillance tapes of the Marcellos' talking in a prison visiting room and discussing the problems that would arise if Nick Calabrese had indeed turned witness for the government. The Marcello brothers also talked about Calabrese's "baby-sitter," a term the FBI believed referred to a U.S. federal marshall who was passing information to The Outfit regarding Nicky Breeze's whereabouts. On August 8, the prosecution rested, opening the door for the defense to present its case and the trial to reach its crescendo. Soon thereafter, both Joey Lombardo and Frank Calabrese Sr., in almost unprecedented moves for a Chicago mob case, would hit the stand to testify on the their own behalf. With well more than half of the historical trial already completed, the fun was just starting to begin.

**ROLLED** to the front of the witness box in a wheelchair by a federal marshall, Joey Lombardo took the stand with a half-smile across his face and a stack of his trademark clever quips in his back pocket. The Clown, taking the time to flirt with the pretty court reporter as he settled into his chair, seemed genuinely excited to have the chance to address the jury in person and tell his side of the story.

Rick Halperin wasted little time getting to the heart of the matter. "On September 27, 1974 did you murder Daniel Seifert?" he asked. "Positively, no," responded an assured and gravely toned Lombardo. "Have you ever been a capo or member of the Chicago Outfit?" Halperin continued. "Positively, no," answered Lombardo once again. His alibi for the time period in which Seifert was gunned down: He was having breakfast at an area pancake house before realizing he had had his wallet stolen from his car and heading to a police station to fill out a stolen property report.

When you think about it, The Clown's math may be a little off. Lombardo claims to have left the police station between 9:30 and 10:00 A.M. Seifert's murder went down at 8:30 A.M., twenty miles away from the police station. It would have been reasonable to assume that he could have been at the murder scene and still had enough time to travel to and eat breakfast at the pancake house and still make it out of the police station between 9:30 and 10:00.

Reflecting back almost whimsically, Lombardo, sometimes leaning forward to rest his chin on the handle of his cane, told the story of his youth. He told of growing up on the city's West Side and selling newspapers and shining shoes as a young boy to try to make some pocket change. He spoke specifically of shining shoes outside his local police station for a group of officers that were in his own words, "Very cheap people." When instructed by Halperin to not press his luck, he shot back, "You told me to tell the truth and nothing but the truth," to a smattering of laughs from the gallery.

After discussing his early life and business ventures, Lombardo spoke of graduating to running a dice game and running errands for a number of mobsters and several high-level mob associates. In order to run his dice game, he was forced to get the permission of his local alderman. "You can't get anything done without your alderman . . . you want a dice game, you go see your alderman," he said.

Lombardo described meeting Danny Seifert through his relationship with Irwin Weiner, a top-tier mob associate and bail bondsman whom he said he often ran errands for and with whom Seifert was partners in a fiberglass company. It was through his friendship with Weiner, he explained, that he was spotted purchasing the police scanner found in the getaway car used in the Seifert murder. He bought it as a favor to Weiner. "He told me to pick stuff up and I picked it up," he said.

Sometimes, Lombardo seemed to ramble. Talking about his penchant for athletics, he said, "I do a lot of sports. I wrestled in high school. I played basketball for high school.

I took fencing for a year in high school. And I can do other sports too. I can ice skate, roller skate, rollerblade, bowl. I play golf, handball, racquetball."

Closing out Halperin's direct examination, Lombardo explained that the threats he made on the tapes previously played for the jury were simple bravado, trying to act like a gangster, not actually being one. Now it was time for the prosecution to get its chance to face off against The Clown.

The downside of testifying in your own defense is that when you're done relaying your own take on the events at hand, the prosecutor has the opportunity to undermine your story. Mitch Mars was about to have himself a field day. Lombardo's jovial wit and constant clowning around played well in bits, like the times he would throw out slick, humorous remarks from his chair at the defense table in response to some of the daily monotony of the lengthy trial. However, over two full days on the stand, it grew tiresome and came off disingenuous. Like a jaguar stalking its prey, Mars pounced on the opening Lombardo's failing shtick left him.

Responding to the claim that The Clown was only playing the role of a gangster in his recorded threats, Mars challenged him, "That was a good role for you to play, wasn't it Mr. Lombardo?" he said.

"Yeah, like James Cagney or Edward G. Robinson," The Clown retorted.

"And Joe Lombardo, member of The Outfit?" Mars shot back.

"No," said Lombardo

"Capo of the Grand Avenue crew?" the relentless prosecutor continued.

"That's not true, sir," answered a resolute Lombardo.

When Mars tried to press Lombardo on a portion of a recorded statement where he used the term *we* when discussing what to do in retribution against an area business not paying tribute to The Outfit, Lombardo tried to back away from what he said. "Just like the president said, he doesn't always choose the right words."

Often throughout his cross-examination, the ace wise-guy seemed to get rattled, annoyed with having to explain himself.

"Can't you read?" he remarked to Mars at one point bothered by the prosecutor's interpretation of a transcript at issue.

"Sir, are you having trouble understanding me?" he barked another time, to which Mars quipped, "At times, I am, Mr. Lombardo, I must admit."

Stepping down from the stand on the afternoon of August 16, Lombardo's time in the witness box was far from a triumph. Some speculated that it would turn out to be his downfall. Rick Halperin was by far the stand-out star of the defense team. He did an exceptional job of dissecting and poking holes in the testimony of each witness against his client. The government's physical evidence against Lombardo was virtually nonexistent. If Lombardo would have stayed off the stand, all the jury would have would be what the prosecution presented, which in relating to the mafia clown prince, was thin. Instead, Lombardo wanted the spotlight. Maybe it was vanity. Maybe it was him thinking he was smarter than the lawyers attempting to take him down. Trying to portray himself as a deer in the woods, as opposed to a gangster who simply didn't

participate in murder, didn't help matters and eventually
aided him in losing the jury's sympathy. Either way, it
wasn't a success. He crashed and burned. And he had only
himself to blame.

Next up: Frankie Breeze. In the moments directly after
Joey Lombardo left the stand, Frank Calabrese took it.
Sporting a gray-speckled goatee that he had grown over the
course of the trial, the rotund yet still well-built seventy-
year-old man hit the witness box with his trademark indig-
nant grin and a boxful of stories to tell. Some were relevant.
Some weren't. He would drift from one to another with
near-seamless transitions, acting like a mischievous child
thinking he could talk his way out of the heap of trouble
he had carelessly got himself into. While there were certain distinct points throughout his testimony that Joey the
Clown rambled on too long, Frankie Breeze did it over his
entire time on the stand. And the tall tales he was rambling
on about were not remotely believable. He was like that
obnoxious relative at the dinner table who made no sense,
was full of crap, and just wouldn't shut up. In the end, Calabrese testimony made Lombardo's look like the picture of
honesty. There was no longer the veneer of his smooth-
talking lawyer to hide behind. This was Frankie Breeze
raw and uncut. It wasn't a pretty sight.

"Good afternoon, ladies and gentlemen of the jury," he
said enthusiastically as he settled into the witness box,
bubbling with excitement for his chance to reveal his take
on this whole thing.

Besides denying each of the murders he was charged
with during Lopez's initial questioning, Calabrese theorized that he was so busy stacking cash, he would have no

time to participate in the mass killings he was implicated in taking part in. "My earning spoke for itself," he told Lopez, explaining that in the underworld there were hitters and earners and that he was the latter. "I made millions, how would I have the time [to murder]?"

Although Calabrese admitted to at one point during his life running a loan-sharking business alongside former South Side mob capo, Angelo La Pietra, he denied ever being part of La Pietra's crew or ever reporting to him as his boss. "He never controlled me," he said. "Many people feared him, many people couldn't look him in the eye. I never had that problem."

According to Calabrese, the prosecutors had cut a deal with the wrong man. He was quick to finger his brother Nick as the real mafia capo, comparing him to a famous movie character. "My brother was like Alfredo from *The Godfather*," he told the court, misnaming actor John Cazale's famous Fredo Corleone character from the epic film. "If he wasn't running things and screwing things up, he wasn't happy."

Explaining the recordings made of him in prison that heard him copping to murders and telling of his Outfit initiation ceremony to his son, he claimed, "I was just humoring him."

When things were going his way, Frankie Breeze was upbeat, gregarious, and relatively tame. However, when they weren't, when he wasn't able to control the story, things turned bitter, biting, and downright nasty. It didn't play well in court and lent credence to the government's contention that he was a rage-filled, murderous lunatic.

For example, in one instance while was trying to tell

the jury how his son Frank Jr. wanted to keep him behind prison walls as a means to steal his money, he was cut off by a prosecutor's objection and the judge's ruling that he could not testify to things that he couldn't prove as fact. An incensed Calabrese ignored Judge Zagel's instructions and continued speaking. "But they took it from me," he said, his growing aggravation apparent in his facial expression.

Even after Zagel warned that any further testimony regarding anything that wasn't fact would end up with him being held in contempt of court, his temper continued to flair. "Your honor, how I am supposed to defend myself if I can't tell the truth," he asked, his face turning more red by the second. "How am I supposed to prove something to this jury if I keep getting objected. . . . They stole two million dollars from me."

Taken to task for how poorly he treated his two sons by prosecutor John Scully during his cross examination, Calabrese vehemently insisted that it wasn't true, that he pled guilty to loan-sharking charges in 1995 in order to save his sons jail time.

"He's [Frank Jr.] been lying to you people real good," he said. "I would never want to be affiliated with the mob. There's my son! [He pointed to Kurt, seated in the gallery]. Ask him, he'll be glad to tell you."

Challenged on his use of the words *I* and *we* while discussing murder on the prison recordings made by Frank Jr., he got snarky with Scully over semantics. "Who is *we*?" Scully asked

"It's not me," Calabrese replied.

"So we is not you?" Scully said.

"No, it's not," Calabrese shot back.

"So the I is not really I?" a bewildered Scully questioned.

"Correct," Calabrese said.

**THE** final defendant to take the stand in his own defense was Anthony Doyle, the former Chicago cop charged with passing valuable information to Frankie Breeze while he was in prison. Doyle outright denied doing anything illegal during his visits with the jailed mobster, claiming that he was only going to see Calabrese out of loyalty to a boyhood friend. He categorized the visits as boring and difficult to comprehend as Calabrese would often talk in code. At one time assigned to the Chicago Police Department's evidence storage facility, Doyle admitted to divulging the date that the bloody glove from the John Fecoratta murder scene was handed over to authorities from the FBI, yet claimed to not know the specifics of the evidence taken by the feds.

Most of the blame for passing information to and from the imprisoned Calabrese, in his opinion, deserved to be placed on Michael Ricci, his fellow Chicago police officer charged in the Family Secrets case, but who, to Doyle's great convenience, was dead. While being cross-examined by prosecutor Markus Funk, he refuted the implication that a recorded conversation between him and Calabrese, where he responded to Calabrese's comment that his brother Nick should see a psychiatrist by saying he needed "shock treatment," meant that he endorsed physical harm to the mega-informant.

Fearing the jury could be getting restless and numb from

more than two months sitting in the same courtroom, the defense rested on Thursday, August 24, after spending less than two weeks presenting its case. Short and sweet was the name of the game. Attorneys for Lombardo, Schiro, Calabrese, Doyle, and Marcello hoped that that the jurors' deliberations were anything but.

**CLOSING** arguments began on Monday, August 28. The prosecution team, first up to bat, replayed the audiotapes of Frank Calabrese talking about his involvement in the various murder plots charged. Standing behind Frankie Breeze, who was brandishing his trademark smirk, Markus Funk responded to one particular portion of the tapes that heard Calabrese breaking out in a hardy laugh regarding one of his homicide victims. "You can hear that man laughing, laughing about the murders," he said. "There's nothing funny about that is there? It was not laughable. It was outrageous. . . . Frank Calabrese, the man with the smile. There's nothing to smile about in this case."

Funk questioned why, if Calabrese had nothing to hide, was he so outwardly terrified of his brother possibly defecting to the FBI and why, if he was not the murderer he was alleged to be, was he heard constructing an alibi on one of the tapes played. When it was Mitch Mars's time to speak, he told the jury that Joey Lombardo "dummied up" by not acknowledging the extent of his knowledge relating to The Outfit and then outlined seventeen reasons he should be convicted of the Daniel Seifert murder, including his fingerprint on the title application for the rental car used in the hit; testimony by Seifert's brother Ronald, who said that Lombardo called him in the weeks leading up to the hit and told him to straighten his brother out; and the fact that he didn't relay his police station alibi to the FBI agents who came to question him on the evening of the murder.

"I submit to you it's now time to hold accountable four defendants, Joseph Lombardo, James Marcello, Frank Calabrese, and Paul Schiro, who have gotten away with murder for far too long," Mars said.

Joe Lopez, attorney for Frank Calabrese, lived up to his nickname "The Shark" by immediately going into attack mode as soon as he got up to address the jury. He called Frank Calabrese Jr. a lousy son and a compulsive liar who manipulated his dad into telling him stories about murders he only knew from newspaper articles. "He lies and lies and continues to lie because he's nothing but a liar," Lopez said of his client's offspring. He bashed Nick Calabrese, calling him "The Grim Reaper," saying that his murderous ways put a wrench into any possibility of him being able to rebut any of his allegations via trial testimony. "The witnesses I could have called in this case, they're all dead," he said. "Nick killed them all."

Despite admitting that his client probably wasn't being completely truthful on the witness stand—falsely telling prosecutors that he couldn't identify certain mobsters because he was "frightened to death" of the jury. Afraid they weren't going to give him a "fair shake." Rick Halperin, Joey Lombardo's attorney, insisted that Lombardo had never been a made member of the mob and had ceased any mob-related activities a long time ago. "We're not talking about redemption here, we're talking about a decided change in lifestyle," he said, continuing to try to employ the so-called withdrawal defense.

Jimmy Marcello's lawyer, Marc Martin, focused his closing argument on repeatedly trying to undermine the testimony of Nick Calabrese, contending that he said what he said only to save himself from the death penalty. "Do you think he would lie to save himself?" Martin asked. "Do you think he would lie to save his own life?"

Deliberating for four days, the jury finally reached a verdict on Monday, September 10—guilty on all counts for all five defendants. With the guilty verdicts secured, the jurors were sent back to deliberate on finding specific culpability for each individual murder. Before reconvening in the jury room, they were once again addressed by prosecutors, who reminded them of the specifics of the homicides alleged to have been committed by Calabrese, Lombardo, Marcello, and Schiro. As Mitch Mars recounted Calabrese's reputed underworld exploits, he told the jury that Frankie Breeze "has left a trail of bodies, literally."

Upset by the categorization, Calabrese shouted out "Them are lies!" from his seat at the defense table. It would later come out that several jurors saw Calabrese whisper, "You're a fucking dead man," to Markus Funk while he delivered a portion of his closing argument. The ship was going down and in typical, yet pathetic, manner, Calabrese was still trying to bark and bully his way to shore. (Interestingly enough, Funk would go toe-to-toe with another co-defendant just a few months later when at Frankie the German Schweihs's pretrial hearing, Schweihs sneered at him from a wheelchair and barked, "You making eyes at me? . . . Do I look like a fag to you," in the moments leading up to Judge Zagel taking the bench.)

Following an additional eight days of deliberations, the jury came back with guilty verdicts for ten of the eighteen murders in the case and three of the four defendants charged—Calabrese, Lombardo, and Marcello were found liable for the homicides, while jurors deadlocked on Schiro's culpability. Joey Lombardo was found guilty of the Daniel Seifert murder; Jimmy Marcello was found guilty of the murders of both Spilotro brothers; and Frank Calabrese was found guilty of murdering Michael Albergo, William and Charlotte Dauber, Michael Cangoni, Richard Ortiz, Arthur Morawski, and John Fecoratta.

Over a year after the guilty verdicts came down, in December 2008, Judge Zagel began his sentencing of the defendants. In the time since the trial ended, longtime and highly revered U.S. prosecutor and mob nemesis Mitch Mars passed away from lung cancer and Frank Schweihs, one of the original co-conspirators who was still awaiting his day in court after being severed from the first trial due to illness, died of cancer. Surprising no one, Zagel was harsh in handing out punishment—Calabrese, Lombardo, and Marcello were all sentenced to life in prison. Paul Schiro, who the jury was undetermined about in regards to his role in the Emil Vaci murder, got a harsh twenty years. Twan Doyle got twelve years.

"In the end we're judged by our actions, not by our wit or our smiles," Judge Zagel said to Lombardo during his February 2009 sentencing. "In cases like this we're judged by the worst things we have done. And the worst things you have done are terrible."

"The last time I remember seeing my father, I was sitting in the back of a police car," said Joe Seifert at Lombardo's sentencing hearing. "It was sunny out and he was lying twisted in the grass. As I think about that image today, I wonder if I ever said good-bye."

It was a dark day for The Outfit, but far from crippling. The positions held by each of the defendants on the street had long been filled way before the Family Secrets trial had even began. Anyone who believed differently was simply fooling themselves.

"Winning the case was a great victory for us, yet despite our best efforts, the stain on the community that is the Chicago Outfit will never be totally wiped clean," said John Scully, looking back on the prosecution team's outstanding accomplishment and peering forward to combating the mafia in the future. "Family Secrets wounded The Outfit, no doubt about it, but it did so more in shining a light on its activities and making people aware it is still around and kicking, than actually putting a dent into the entity as a whole. There's no question in my mind that The Outfit will and probably already has come back strong from what happened at the trial. It's our job, both as prosecutors and as ordinary citizens, to do everything we can to combat them and what they try to do and make their job as hard as humanly possible. There's no one, singular victory that's going to abolish the mob in Chicago. But it's the little victories, the everyday chinks we can put in the armor of The Outfit, that will slowly undermine the organization and minimize its overall effect."

## 19.

**Now and Forever**
Where Is the Outfit Today and
Where Does It Go from Here?

Judge James B. Zagel issued his final sentence in the case in March of 2009 when Nick Calabrese, the only made member of the Chicago mafia to ever turn government witness, was given twelve years in prison. With credit for time already served, he will be out within four years and then be given a new identity and disappear into the witness protection program. Not counting the inevitable forthcoming appeals, after over a decade in the making, the Family Secrets case—all 125 witnesses and 225 exhibits—was finally over. The good guys won and the bad guys were all locked up. But what amount of damage had The Outfit really endured? Was the legal strike against the crime family a bite-size nick or a staggering blow, as intended?

The answer is probably somewhere in between. By no means has the mob in Chicago been slowed down. The Outfit's assembly-line-type efficiency and multilayered command structure were designed to withstand these kind of government assaults. Yet, at the same time, it's hard to believe that entire ordeal hasn't provided considerable agitation and worry either. At the very least, the information revealed at trial—most shockingly the feds' contention that current don, John Di Fronzo, was an integral participant in the murder of the Spilotro brothers—has informed The Outfit that other major investigations are in the works, information that certainly sent jitters up the syndicate pecking order.

Just like the former political machines that resided and ruled the city of Chicago throughout much of the last century, since its inception the mafia in the Windy City has developed its own machine—a multitiered power base with extreme depth and extraordinary reach that is still pumping today at full capacity. While some crime families across the country have dwindled in power and prestige in the recent past, The Outfit has remained strong. Although it will never regain the monumental influence and strength it once had, for La Cosa Nostra in America, the modern-day Chicago mafia is as good as it gets. The overall stability The Outfit has been able to display through the years is a epic feat and demonstrates the syndicate's resiliency and everlasting durability, a trait that plays well in the mob's always ongoing battle against the federal government.

However, there are still those who have their doubts about how far the current crop of Windy City mobsters can take The Outfit in the midst of the changing times.

"This new group of wiseguys will never be as successful

as their predecessors, there's just too much working against them," said Richard Stilling, "A lot of these guys today plain don't have the work ethic to be great criminals. There are a few that do, but they're getting up in age and are on the way out in the next decade. In terms of quality mob guys, I don't know how many are left. The new breed is get rich quick, bed as many broads as possible, and leave a good-looking corpse. A growing percentage of them are heavy into the drugs. I'm talking both selling and for personal use. They don't have the code embedded in them like the old guys did. The old-school guys were around when the whole thing was built so they took more pride in the sanctity of the Family, living by the rules and stuff like that. Everybody today wants to get as much money as they can in the smallest amount of time and that mentality makes for letting your greed blind you from some traps you might not otherwise fall into. The old-timers knew it was a marathon, not a sprint. I'm not sure if these guys do."

Others see socioeconomic issues as playing a major role in why The Outfit today will never be as powerful as it once was.

"Because of what I call the 'suburbanization' of the area over the last thirty-plus years among a host of other reasons, the mafia in Chicago will struggle to regain its former status," said Robert Lombardo, a former cop and current professor of criminal justice at Loyola University of Chicago. "The core neighborhoods in the city are all gone. Places that have traditionally been fertile mob breeding ground have been virtually abandoned. Families that would have at one time selected to live close to their roots in the city now almost exclusively choose to live in the surrounding suburbs. The result is kids don't grow up around The Outfit like they used to, they aren't exposed to the wiseguy lifestyle that was at one time embedded and woven through all these former neighborhoods and fostered ambition in its young. Now, the wannabe wiseguys learn all they know about the mafia from movies. Its just not the same. The recruiting pool is raided and in turn, the organization loses the ability to grow."

As long as the three pillars of the underworld—gambling, loan-sharking, and extortion—exist, organized crime and the mafia in one form or the other will be around and a force to be reckoned with. The market is bulletproof, a never-ending cycle that will eternally bear fruit. There will always be people who want to place a bet on a game, there will always people who can't go to a bank to get a loan and must instead turn to the street, and there will always be weaker people to exploit and shakedown. The mob's wheelhouse is never vacant. And in traditional mafia hot spots like Chicago, it often works overtime.

On the flip side of the coin, there are a limited amount of endings for those who choose to live there life by the code of the street. A majority of the time it's not pretty or painless. How our story's four main characters—Frank Calabrese, the ringleader; Nick Calabrese, the rat; Tony Spilotro, the rogue; and Joey Lombardo, the relic—concluded their tenures as top-of-the-line crime figures represent the three most likely scenarios. You will either be dead like Tony Spilotro, in jail like Frank Calabrese and Joey Lombardo, or in the witness protection program like Nick Calabrese. Instances of having careers in crime—like Outfit boss Tony Accardo, Jewish godfather Meyer Lansky, or East Coast don Carlo Gambino—never going to jail and dying peacefully—are few and far between.

Taking the hit from the Family Secrets bust and trial in stride, The Outfit has dusted itself off from the fall and moved forward. There are simply too many spokes on the proverbial wheel to have one bust take that much of a toll on the bottom line—which is what everyone in the game knows is the upper-echelons of the crime family making its money. For each crew boss and mob administrator in the city that is taken off the streets, there are dozens more behind him willing and able to take his place. Even in light of the tremendous amount of legal hassles you will be prone to encounter as a mafia skipper, there is simply too much money to be made and power to be had for people not to covet the job

"At some point you have to put the elation of the Family Secrets victory, no matter how satisfying it was and how proud you are of it, behind you and start building more cases and opening new investigations because the fight is always going to be there," said FBI agent Ross Rice in late 2008. "By no means is organized crime in Chicago gone and we certainly know that. Maybe a bit weaker, but not gone. So, you just got to go back to work and fight the good fight. And there's lots of them to fight, and that will probably never change. The Outfit in the new century is growing in a lot of different directions. New scams and shakedowns are being jump-started every day on some street corner, and the old staples are always going to be there for the mob to suck dry. It's an interesting time in The Outfit's history since a big chunk of the post-Accardo bigwigs are getting up in years and a new transition is going to be on the horizon soon. There are some middle-aged guys that have been around long enough to start to know what they're doing and enough veterans on the street right now that can run a tight ship if we let them. It's our job not to let them."

**LIKE** a chameleon, the organization adapts its outer shell to the changing environment, camouflaging its movements to protect from attack. The ability for The Outfit to continually keep the identity of its leadership veiled in mystery is a perfect example. When the need to downsize its street crews emerged in the 1990s, there was no hesitation. That is what the situation called for and that is what was done. The syndicate's hierarchy recognized a need for change due to shifting climate conditions—a growing number of members dying and being incarcerated—and they acted quickly and decisively. The adjustment in infrastructure was an immediate success and the transition from seven crews to just four proved seamless.

Coming into the new millennium, the four-crew system has stayed in place. According to FBI documents and the Chicago Crime Commission, Frank "Toots" Caruso Jr. has authority over the South Side Crew, Peter "Greedy Petey" Di Fronzo looks after the Elmwood Park/North Side Crew, John "Pudgy" Matassa, Jr. is responsible for the Cicero/ Melrose Park Crew, and Joseph "Joe Kong" Cullotta oversees the West Side Crew. Under each captain, there are numerous street bosses and subcrews, a staple of leadership in The Outfit for years and one of the things that sets the crime family apart from its mafia counterparts on the East Coast.

Unlike Families from New York, crews in Chicago don't always have autonomous rule and are oftentimes run in tandem. For example, it's believed by the Chicago Crime Commission that Toots Caruso's brother Bruno and cousin Leo Caruso are "street bosses" for the South Side Crew, while Joey Lombardo's fomer driver, Christopher "Christy the Nose" Spina is said to hold the same position on the West Side. Old Wild Bunch member Jimmy Inendino and Michael "Fat Mikey" Sarno, the crime commission contends, look after the Cicero/Melrose Park Crew on a day-to-day basis on behalf of Pudgy Matassa, and Rudy Fratto and Michael "Good Looking Mike" Magnafichi do the same for Pete Di Fronzo in Elmwood Park.

In terms of No Nose Di Fronzo's current "mob cabinet": longtime ally Marco "The Mover" D'Amico is alleged to have replaced Al Tornabene, who died in May of 2009, as the crime family's new consiglieri and Joe "The Builder" Andriacchi, according to FBI files the Outfit's number two in charge since 2002, remains a slippery target for law enforcement from his reputed post as the Outfit's under-boss and overall street boss.

Occupying The Outfit throne for the last seventeen years, eighty-year-old John Di Fronzo is one of the more tenured mob dons in the entire country. The respect and admiration he garners from his peers in the nation's underworld are second to none. His humble and engaging demeanor is quick to endear those he leads and the loyalty he is afforded by them unquestioned. Much like Joey Lombardo, he has made a conscious effort to stay true to his roots, avoiding moving to a secluded estate in some posh suburb as a means of keeping closer tabs on the pulse of his brigade, and the decision has paid dividends in a more stable organization. If anyone wants to see him they always know they can most likely find him each morning sharing coffee and doughnuts with his brother at either JKS Ventures or D&P Construction, the siblings' Melrose Park–based businesses that officially reside in their wives' names.

Even though he speaks business only with a select few, Di Fronzo, the consummate mob politician, isn't afraid to walk among the commoners and schmooze with his troops whenever he can. On several weekday afternoons he can be seen at one of his favorite neighborhood haunts, The Loon Cafe, a diner and pizzeria in River Forest, sharing meals with his men. During a visit to the restaurant in the winter of 2009, Di Fronzo was met by local TV investigative reporter Chuck Goudie, with camera crew in tow, as he exited a lunch with his two brothers, Fratto and D'Amico, and headed to his car. No Nose was cordial and made small talk with the cameras, denying that he was worried about the prospect of ongoing federal investigations into his activities and then leaving the parking lot in his luxury pickup truck.

Contrary to Di Fronzo's optimistic sentiment regarding the heat he is facing from the government, there are undoubtedly storm clouds on the horizon and with them a good chance that The Outfit's top banana may soon be caught in the middle of a downpour. These clouds spawned their first raindrops on March 26, 2009, when John Di Fronzo, his brother Pete, Fratto, D'Amico, and John Cerone Jr. were hit with a rare civil RICO complaint, alleging an extortion plot stemming from ownership in a Melrose Park medical clinic and the shaking down of one its patients, the son of a former mob-connected labor union boss. Couple the most recent legal action with the swirling rumors about his inclusion in a pending federal investigation and indictment titled, "Family Secrets Part II," and no matter what he says publicly, John Di Fronzo has to be wondering how long it will be until the bottom falls out on his run as mob boss.

For one of No Nose's top lieutenants, Rudy Fratto, the bottom fell out in September of 2009 when he was charged with federal tax evasion for failing to pay taxes on close to two hundred thousand dollars of income from 2001 through 2007. On October 13, 2009, Fratto pled guilty to the charges and will face minor jail time.

Described as a "sleeper" by crook and cop alike, until his death on May 17, 2009, Alphonse "Al the Pizza Man" Tornabene, was a longtime member of Chicago's mafia elite and someone who, without much fanfare, is alleged to have been pivotal in helping John Di Fronzo and Joey Lombardo transition The Outfit successfully onward past the Accardo era.

Acquiring his nickname because of his ownership of a South Side pizza parlor named Villa Nova, Tornabene was raised on the city's West Side and got his start as a bookie under Joe Ferriola. Working directly under Outfit chiefs Sam "Wings" Carlisi—his first cousin—and Joey Aiuppa throughout the 1950s, 60s, and 70s, he gained a reputation as an expert handicapper and mob tactician. Throughout much of his career on the street—a time period which he has no arrest record for—he was somewhat of a mob vagabond, based in Cicero but over the years troubleshooting from crew to crew and reporting directly to The Outfit brass instead of a single caporegime.

When Ernest "Rocky" Infelice and his crew, nicknamed "The Good Ship Lollipop," were convicted of federal racketeering charges in the early 1990s, then don Carlisi is alleged to have named him his underboss. Just a few years later, with Wings himself readying to face a slew of federal charges, he tapped Tornabene to counsel new-don John Di Fronzo on the "ins and outs" of mob leadership.

Hailing from a rich underworld pedigree—his older brother was Outfit soldier Frank "Feech" Tornabene and he is first cousins to Luigi "State Street Louie" Tornabene, a one-time underling of Gus Alex, who ran State Street and most of the prostitution in the downtown Chicago area during the 1950s and 1960s—Tornabene was considered by many as one of the sharpest minds in the entire syndicate, a go-to mediator of any disputes that arose within layers of The Outfit hierarchy.

Stricken with a variety of medical ailments, Al the Pizza Man went into semiretirement in the late 1990s, spending large portions of his time at a vacation property he owned at Lake Geneva in Wisconsin. Upon the Family Secrets bust in 2005, he was called back into active duty, his knowledge and mentorship needed to steady the proverbial ship. In the days and months following the indictment, Tornabene was seen making the rounds around town, being chauffeured by Leo Caruso, a former labor union president and a top lieutenant to his first cousin, South Side captain Frank "Toots" Caruso Jr.

Up until his alleged appointment as a full-time Outfit administrator in the 1990s, Al the Pizza Man had never before held an official leadership position in the crime family. This fact was certainly not due to lack of confidence in his ability as a mob policy maker, because Tornabene had been known to aid in conducting mob initiation ceremonies, like the one he oversaw in 1983 when the Calabrese brothers and Jimmy Marcello were inducted into the ranks of the mafia.

His presence in this recent time of transition for The Outfit was invaluable, everyone around him benefiting from his wisdom and experience. Known to be a key relay man for information from the administration to the street, the FBI observed him holding meetings with Outfit powers Toots Caruso, Pudgy Matassa, Mickey Marcello, and Joe Andriacchi at a number of local eateries like Horwath's and Andrea's, and Cicero Auto Construction in the west suburbs. He was also known to be a frequent dining partner of Little Tony Zizzo's before his disappearance. By the end of his life, Pudgy Matassa, who got his start under Vince Solano on Rush Street, emerged as Tornabene's top proxy to the street and is speculated by law enforcement to be the likely successor to all The Pizza Man's rackets.

"He's was a wild card who knew how to fly under the radar," said Jim Wagner of Tornabene. "It's [the Chicago Crime Commission's and law enforcement's] belief that he was deferred to a great deal in Outfit circles in the days after the indictments in Family Secret were announced. He was seen with different guys from different crews in different parts of the city, and in all these recorded observations he's the one calling the shots and giving the orders. Before the Family Secrets indictment, he was gone from the day to day for a little while. The blow the family took from Family Secrets paved the way for him to be able to assert himself again and take a bigger role in how things are run across the board. I'm not sure he was thrilled about having to do it, but he did it 'cause of the code. He goes back a long way and the Family and its welfare was obviously very important to him. In his mind, it was his duty to come back."

Tornabene's death opened the door for Marco D'Amico, a former capo who was forced to give up his regime when he was imprisoned on racketeering charges in the 1990s, to return to the Outfit's administration. According to the Chicago Crime Commission, in the days after Al the Pizza Man's death in May 2009, Di Fronzo tapped D'Amico to be his new consiglieri. Some in law enforcement say the appointment was a mere formality and contend D'Amico has been acting as Di Fronzo's top advisor since being released from a ten-year federal prison sentence in 2005.

D'Amico was born on January 1, 1936, and as a boy lived in the same neighborhood that spawned No Nose, The Clown, and The Builder. Consequently, the kid they came to nickname "The Mover," as in "Mover and Shaker," due to his fast-living lifestyle, grew up idolizing the triumvirate of neighborhood celebrities and rising mob stars. Di Fronzo and Andriacchi specifically took D'Amico under their wing and their young protégé took his first arrest for running gambling slips for an Outfit-run sports betting operation in June 1958 at the age of 21.

It's interesting to note that through his rise through the syndicate ranks the reputation that D'Amico developed was in stark contrast to that of his mentors. A fan of the local nightlife, D'Amico was flashy and liked to act like a gangster, as opposed to Di Fronzo and Andriacchi's more low-key approach to the wiseguy lifestyle. During the swinging sixties and seventies, The Mover, could be found living up to his nickname almost every night down on Rush Street at his favorite spot, Jilly's, a trendy bar and lounge on the corner of Rush and Oak, the epicenter of high-living in the Windy City.

D'Amico's cowboy status was further cemented with an arrest for street fighting outside of Jilly's in the fall of 1980, one for battery and resisting arrest in 1983, and two arrests for drunk driving, one of which occurred in 1983, and the other 1989. FBI informant reports indicate that D'Amico has been known to partake in recreational cocaine use in the past and is possibly one of the Outfit's top narcotics lieutenants as well.

Despite some of his less than careful behavior, D'Amico is alleged to have been able to wiggle his way into No Nose's inner circle by being a tremendously gifted street-earner—i.e. he knows how to generate money for his boss. In the late 1980s, he was named capo of Elmwood Park. The Mover's crew, which dabbled in the usual mob rackets of gambling, extortion, and loan sharking, had some pretty intimidating figures in it. Street collectors like Frank "Frankie the Gunner" Catapano, Frank "Frankie Franken-stein" Maranto, Robert "Bobby the Hippo" Scutkowski, and Robert "Bobby the Truck Driver" Abbinanti, related to D'Amico via marriage, put fear in all who did business with the group. D'Amico, his right hand man, Anthony "Tony Seymour" Dote, and the rest of his entire crew were indicted in 1994 in a major racketeering indictment and convicted a year later in 1995.

**THE** scene on March 26, 2009 at Nick Calabrese's sentencing hearing was tense. An emotionally charged mix of Nicky Breeze's family and the families of his victims dotted

the packed courtroom making for a heavy-hearted atmo-
sphere. When Judge Zagel delved out a light twelve years
and four months for the admitted murderer of over a dozen
individuals, the reaction was obviously split. Supporters of
Calabrese hailed joyously the soft sentence, claiming, like
the government did in their sentencing recommendation,
that the former hit man's cooperation was so important and
ultimately so influential—he helped identify more than
sixty made members of The Outfit and provided insight on
a staggering thirty-six homicides—that he deserved leni-
ency. Zagel remarked that he felt compelled to keep the
sentence light as a means of encouraging others to step
forward, repent, and turn against The Outfit. Those who
had a loved one killed at his hands were less than sympathetic, extremely hurt by the fact that the judge took it easy
on Calabrese and the prospect that he will be a free man in
less than five years. Paul Haggerty's widow was so upset
by what transpired, she collapsed in the hallway outside
the courtroom and had to be tended to by paramedics.

Having an opportunity to address the court with a statement, Calabrese was introspective. "I let fear control my
life and beneath that fear was a coward who didn't walk
away from that life," he said, wearing a gray sweatshirt
and jeans and led into court by a pair of federal marshals.
"I can't go back and undo what I've done, it's there every
day. It doesn't go away and rightfully so."

In other posttrial news, former U.S. Marshall, John
Ambrose, the son of a once-disgraced Chicago cop, imprisoned for his participation in a major department scandal
involving shaking down drug dealers, was indicted, put
on trial, and eventually in the spring of 2009 convicted of

acting as a mole for the mob. Using a one-time associate of his father's, William Guide—a man who once shared a cell with John Di Fronzo when they were both incarcerated years before—as an intermediary, Ambrose passed sensitive intelligence, primarily concerning where the government was housing star witness Nick Calabrese before his testimony in the Family Secrets trial, to the highest levels of The Outfit's leadership. Shockingly Mickey Marcello, in the midst of serving his eight-year sentence in the Family Secrets case, agreed to cooperate with the FBI and testify against Ambrose regarding his firsthand knowledge of the former U.S. Marshall's divulging top secret government information to the upper echelons of the Chicago mafia. According to Marcello, Ambrose passed intelligence regarding Nick Calabrese's whereabouts from Guide to Pudgy Matassa, who then passed it on to him to deliver to his imprisoned brother.

In 2008, the U.S. Attorney's Office in Chicago, already reeling from the loss of Mitch Mars, was forced to trim its organized crime division—a unit that once housed close to a dozen wiseguy-hungry lawyers—to an all-time low of two attorneys actively pursuing cases against The Outfit. And Chicago is not the only office of federal prosecutors undergoing downsizing and restructuring. Other mob-heavy cities like Detroit, Milwaukee, St. Louis, Kansas City, and Philadelphia, and the state of New Jersey, have all had their offices affected by having their resources against organized crime severely diminished. Moves like this show all too clearly that when times are tight everyone, even the government, feels the pinch,

Midwest mega-don Tony Accardo has been dead for almost twenty years and little has changed in the criminal empire he helped build and maintain for well over a half century. The rackets are pretty much the same, and the money still churns in at a consistent and hardy rate. As always, a decade into the new millennium, gambling, loan sharking, and street tax are the meat and potatoes of the operation. The Outfit's sway in the labor unions has decreased, yet its presence in the local drug, porn, and stolen car market have stayed firm. An ability to access the highest levels of the government remains an asset and continues to provide a decided advantage to the syndicate, as shown by the 2002 conviction of Cicero Mayor Betty Loren-Maltese for conspiring with Outfit member Michael "Big Mike" Spano and others to illegally funnel cash away from the city and into their collective pockets. Unlike the government that is effected by the changing economic fortunes of our country, the mafia is not. Time has shown that crime, in one of its only true virtues, is recession-proof.

Despite the budget cuts and plundering of its resources, the U.S. Attorney's Office remains diligent in its effort to combat the mob in Chicago. Down, but certainly not out, the government's attack against The Outfit scored its first blow of the post-Family Secrets era in August of 2008 when Outfit associates Sam "Sammy the Blaster" Voldepresto and Mark Polchan were indicted on charges of a mafia-related bombing. According to federal prosecutors, Voldepresto, an eighty-three-year-old alleged mob explosives expert, and Polchan, a member of The Outlaws, the leading biker gang in the area, were ordered by Outfit lieutenant Michael "Fat Mikey" Sarno to bomb one of the crime family's competitors in the local video poker machine business.

"We're under no illusions that just because the Family Secrets case was a success that it means the mafia is in any way leaving the city of Chicago," said J.R. Davis, the newly-elected president of the Chicago Crime Commission. "These guys aren't going anywhere and we know that. But it's our job to keep active in the pursuit of chipping away at their infrastructure and exposing their collective activities to the public. The public is affected on a daily basis by these individuals' actions even if they aren't aware of it. The Outfit remains an overwhelming presence in Chicago and on the national mafia landscape. Those who were convicted in Family Secrets have already had their positions replaced and the government is well on its way to building more cases against those who have filled the void as well as those powerful figures behind the scenes who have yet to be caught. It's a neverending struggle, to say the least."

As the Outfit looks forward to the future, at least long term, things look bright. Even if the current administration is swept up in a second indictment resulting from the Family Secrets investigation, there exists a rock-solid new generation of mob players, groomed by John Di Fronzo and company, ready to step in and fill the void. A recent developing trend of intra-marriage between Outfit members' families has boded well for syndicate stability. The Chicago mafia's infrastructure, expertly designed by Tony Accardo, has been built for the long haul, and as of today it looks as if there is no slowing down for this mega freight train of a criminal organization anytime soon. For the Outfit, it is business as usual. Now and forever.